Agile Processes—Agile Teams

Eckhart Hanser

Agile Processes—Agile Teams

Second Edition

Springer

Eckhart Hanser
Studienzentrum IT-Management & Informatik
Duale Hochschule Baden-Württemberg
(DHBW) Lörrach
Lörrach, Germany

ISBN 978-3-662-72725-6 ISBN 978-3-662-72726-3 (eBook)
https://doi.org/10.1007/978-3-662-72726-3

Translation from the German language edition: "Agile Prozesse – Agile Teams" by Eckhart Hanser, © Der/die Herausgeber bzw. der/die Autor(en), exklusiv lizenziert an Springer-Verlag GmbH, DE, ein Teil von Springer Nature 2025. Published by Springer Berlin Heidelberg. All Rights Reserved.

This book is a translation of the original German edition "Agile Prozesse – Agile Teams," 2nd edition, by Eckhart Hanser, published by Springer-Verlag GmbH, DE in 2025. The translation was done with the help of an artificial intelligence machine translation tool. A subsequent human revision was done primarily in terms of content, so that the book will read stylistically differently from a conventional translation. Springer Nature works continuously to further the development of tools for the production of books and on the related technologies to support the authors.

This Springer imprint is published by the registered company Springer-Verlag GmbH, DE, part of Springer Nature.
The registered company address is: Heidelberger Platz 3, 14197 Berlin, Germany

Foreword

For more than a decade now, agile approaches have represented a very popular alternative to the so-called "heavyweight process models." The burdensome nature attributed to the older methodologies such as SADT, SSADM, SA/SD, V-Modell 97, and even the newer models like RUP with UML and V-Modell XT, is justified by developers and users with the high learning effort required, which is presented in the form of several hundred pages of model documentation. Additionally, the strong adherence to a phase sequence or, as in the case of V-Modell XT, to a series of decision points, is criticized as an overly rigid structuring of time. Even though the process can be adapted, and even though backtracking and incremental division are permitted, at the very least a well-founded configuration must be managed. Furthermore, there are extensively defined project products, project activities, and phase states that must be achieved at largely predetermined points in the project lifecycle, which is also perceived as a restriction of flexibility. The configurability of V-Modell XT for a project execution strategy of "Agile Projects" has not changed this perception. Configuration, documentation, phase regulation, product templates, and method prescriptions put the willingness to learn to a severe test, raise legitimate questions about implementability, and therefore face acceptance problems at all organizational levels. This also affects the entire range of involved roles, such as system analysts, developers, line management, project management, and especially the users. In this context, the immediate readiness for use offered by agile methods is a welcome solution for many.

The agile shift became visible with Kent Beck's still hotly debated, extremely condensed approach variant, Extreme Programming, which, as Eckhart Hanser reports, is based on a simple set of principles and practices. The condensation of the approach consists both in the "liberation" from prescribed processes, the omission of method-based specification, and the minimization of the use of methods, templates, and patterns. *Extreme* therefore also refers to the extremely sparse documentation of Extreme Programming. The more agile the methodology, the more questions arose about examples, patterns, and guidance, and thus the lightweight nature was somewhat methodically enriched again in further agile models. The group of agile methods has become more differentiated, has grown, and as a result has lost some convenience and also some clarity.

The current literature market primarily offers monographs on individual agile models, and unfortunately, these works are written in the confident tone of successful projects, and therefore do little to remedy the lack of clarity. The book by Eckhart Hanser makes an important, objective contribution to orientation here.

The proponents of agile methodologies commendably place strong emphasis on people, their efforts toward collaboration, their communication behavior, and the ethical values that guide their actions. This is reflected in some of the principles and in the Agile Manifesto. Nevertheless, it is worth questioning whether premises such as daily morning meetings, pair programming, or equally sized task packages truly correspond to human inclinations and foster more humane collaboration, or whether they remain more of an ideal. It is noticeable that the "agile authors" always rave about their personal positive project experiences, but not about scientifically proven findings. It was high time that these social, agile recommendations were at least examined with the same rigor that even agile developers grant their programs—namely, through testing. For the much more complex act of collaboration, one would expect a social prototype, an organizational form under controlled environmental conditions, in which it can be demonstrated, using social-scientific methods, that the given social premises x and the form of collaboration y are best suited for the task z. Eckhart Hanser has dedicated his work to this gap and has observed the sociological aspects of software development in his "Software Engineering Laboratory." He thus deserves credit as one of the few IT researchers to have incorporated a sociological perspective into software development with his Meta Agile Process Model (MAP), and to have done so using social-scientific methods such as field experiments, participant observation, and group dynamic experiments.

The insights gained in the "organizational laboratory"—here I am conceptually inspired by the work of the Tavistock Institute—are incorporated into suggestions for improving agile approaches. This enables the project manager to replace "agile enthusiasm" with well-founded criteria. And this helps to assess whether a task should be approached in an agile or heavyweight manner. As always, the truth will likely lie somewhere in between: for some types of projects, agile models are more suitable, while for others, comprehensive process models are indispensable. With his book, Eckhart Hanser opens our eyes to an objective assessment of the suitability of agile models for a given project type.

I am pleased that once again an active member of the "Process Models" working group of the "Business Informatics" division of the "German Informatics Society" has succeeded in publishing an interesting book, and I wish the book a positive reception. The fact that the book also coincides with a thematic focus, "Social, cultural, and location-specific aspects," initiated four years ago with Professor Gerhard Chroust by the working group, is especially gratifying for all of us. At this point, I would also like to thank Mr. Heine from Springer Verlag for always having "an ear" for the working group. It is to be hoped that the path of social experimentation started by Eckhart Hanser will be pursued much further, that even more societal measures, social criteria, and their indicators will be observed, and that more computer scientists will incorporate sociology.

Perhaps one day, the activities, methods, and milestones in a project will no longer be reduced to the technical quality of the products, but will be complemented by societal activities, sociological methods, and social milestones. Then software developers will no longer have to face the accusation of developing software without considering the user. Or does anyone really believe that, for example, the world's most widespread process model, the Unified Process with UML, is user-friendly for business professionals?

Spokesperson of the "Process Models" working group of the German Informatics Society 2007–2009, member of the management committee of the working group 2010

Darmstadt, Germany
February 2010

Reinhard Höhn

Preface to the Second Edition

If one considers software development from its beginnings, one observes the tendency to create a single product for even the most complex tasks, which is intended to fulfill all requirements (as far as possible). The model was the industrial assembly line of the automotive industry, where a large number of identical products are manufactured. The automotive industry was a leader in the application and further development of this process philosophy. Of course, enormous financial risks were also at stake if errors occurred in the process execution. In order to achieve trouble-free production, it was therefore necessary to create, in advance, the most precise and complete description possible of the product to be manufactured (in large quantities). One also had to consider and plan for its compatibility and potential sources of error.

Similarly, in the software industry, both the development process and the planned product have been overloaded with increasingly complex alternatives in order to meet all requirements.

The requirements and also the development steps were defined in the so-called 'design'. There, the consistency, correctness, and error-freedom of the design, as well as quality, formal and substantive completeness, were also reviewed.

Basically, however, software development produced and delivered the same product with many alternatives in large quantities for all users. Subsequent changes (unless they had already been anticipated) required restarting the entire planning/development process, resulting in increased costs and/or time overruns.

For certain products such as databases and powerful central software, as well as in medical technology and military systems, this philosophy applies due to today's stringent standards, approval requirements, certifications, and similar factors. Therefore, the requirements and the product to be developed, including any possible additional requirements, must be described as precisely and completely as possible and documented accordingly.

However, in application software, it was overlooked that in the automotive industry, the production of each individual 'copy' requires a great deal of personnel and material. In contrast, the actual 'production' in software is a relatively inexpensive and straightforward process of copying. The real effort is invested in the design. Later changes do require a great deal of technical understanding, but hardly any material.

As a consequence, in contrast to the ‘heavyweight’ processes described above, a different approach was advocated for producing software solutions relatively quickly. About 25 years ago, Ben Kent published the so-called ‘Agile Manifesto’: This approach dispensed with many of the ‘cemented-in’ preparatory steps found in heavyweight approaches in favor of rapid, approximate planning and development, leaving much of the responsibility to the developers. The project emphasized and encouraged the modifiability of existing code with the goal of quickly incorporating new changes as they arose. Detailed documentation was omitted; developers were expected to obtain the necessary information from the existing code. Employee well-being was also emphasized.

The Agile Manifesto provides only very broad guidelines, which were then elaborated and specified in derived process models. A number of different process models emerged, each with different goals and orientations. Initially, among others, Extreme Programming, Crystal, and Crystal Clear were very successful. Nowadays, Scrum and Kanban dominate, and in IT operations, DevOps. All these models are modifiable, change-friendly, and promote the flexible, dynamic development of software or the operation of IT systems.

In Agile development, many variants of the product are actually created in parallel, which are not necessarily compatible. In contrast to heavyweight approaches, where project staff are largely constrained, the Agile approach gives developers relatively more freedom. However, this leads to the problem of integrating the various designs.

This agile world, with its diverse and sometimes ad hoc emerging requirements and development paths, is generally not easily teachable and demands increased responsibility from employees in order to succeed. This also means that the type of skills required from employees often only becomes apparent at short notice during project work and cannot be planned in advance in general. Flexibility is required of employees. This includes a profound knowledge of the various models and practices, which is conveyed in this book concisely for both students and practitioners.

Advocates of agile methodologies particularly emphasize the importance of human behavior with regard to collaboration, communication practices, personal responsibility, self-disciplined accountability, and ethical values. The final part of the book, which I find especially interesting, therefore deals with the social behavior of developers ‘on a small scale.’ With his “Software Engineering Laboratory” in Chap. 8 of the book, Prof. Hanser has created a platform for observation and analysis, in which student projects were observed, recorded, and analyzed. He thus deserves credit as one of the few IT researchers to offer a sociological perspective on software development with his ‘Meta Agile Process Model’ (MAP). Using social science methods, he observes and describes, in field studies, several student project teams and the group dynamics of the project members.

On site, for example, the distribution of tasks and the physical proximity/distance of individual employees are observed, and their personality traits are correlated with their roles. It would be worthwhile to continue these studies, including for software developers who are already working in the profession.

Looking back at the entire evolution of process models up to the present day, from the simple waterfall model to various agile models, one can see in retrospect the changing requirements and necessities of software products and their creation. The increased emphasis on the social and psychological needs of developers is a key perspective, especially for agile development.

Finally, the question must also be asked: What comes next in software engineering? A likely answer is the automatic generation of complex software through the appropriate application of artificial intelligence, in the form of tools such as Gemini Code Assist, chatGPT, and similar generation tools that are already in use.

But how things will actually develop remains to be seen in the future.

Linz, Austria Prof. Dr. Gerhard Chroust
January 2025

Preface to the First Edition

With this book, I pursue two goals: First, to provide an overview of the current world of agile process models. The lightweight software development methodologies *Extreme Programming*, *Crystal*, and *Scrum* are described in detail and their practical suitability is examined using my student software engineering lab at the Baden-Württemberg Cooperative State University Lörrach. Second, I summarize the experiences from six years of experimental software engineering in the student lab in the new agile meta-model *MAP*, which deals with the "ingredients" required for a successful technical project. The basic idea is simple: When assembling a highly qualified project team, it makes no sense to prescribe a process in the form of a flowchart; rather, it is better to bring together the right *characters* or *types* and to correctly assign the project roles identified as necessary in the student lab. A project team that is well "balanced" in this sense has a higher chance of success! This insight is the direct result of my student lab.

For the project roles listed in this book, the masculine form is used. This is solely for the sake of readability. My experience shows that women deliver outstanding performance in project work. In particular, female project managers often excel at motivating their teams to achieve exceptional results (Chap. 9).

Target Audience of This Book

This book is aimed both at practitioners who want to gain an overview of the "market" of agile approaches, and at students preparing for their exams and assessments in the field of agile process models. Practitioners in particular will be interested in which agile practices have proven effective in the student laboratory—and thus under reproducible laboratory conditions—and which have not (Chap. 8). Many assumptions from practical projects have been scientifically substantiated.

Structure of this Book—Agile Manifesto and Agile Process Models

After a brief introduction to the history of software process models (Chap. 1), Chap. 2 explains the Agile Manifesto. This "countermovement" initiated by developers in response to heavyweight process models such as the Unified Process or V-Model forms the basis for the well-known agile process models *Extreme Programming (XP)*, *Crystal* with *Crystal Clear*, and the agile project management method *Scrum*. The agile methodologies listed are systematically presented in Chaps. 3, 4 and 5. The focus is on the process, the proposed practices, as well as the project roles and the resulting artifacts. In the case of Extreme Programming (Chap. 3), particular emphasis is placed on contrasting the traditional XP practices with the "extended" practices.

The Student Software Engineering Laboratory

Chapter 8 presents the student software engineering laboratory at the Baden-Wuerttemberg Cooperative State University Lörrach. For the past six years, this experimental software engineering lab has been investigating agile process models and methods, evaluating their practical suitability. All process models mentioned in the book have been tested in various student projects. After a theoretical introduction as part of the software engineering lecture, student groups were required to work on real projects, acting as project teams and following the respective process model under consideration. The results, particularly regarding the everyday applicability of the chosen agile methods, as well as experience reports from the different projects, can be found in Chap. 8.

Acknowledgments

This book would not have come into being without the help and support of dear people. I thank my family, my wife Susanne and my daughter Stephanie, for often doing without me during the writing of this book. I thank my son Felix for his active participation on the client side in the current student project. I thank my parents for allowing me to study what I always wanted.

I would like to thank the students of the Baden-Württemberg Cooperative State University Lörrach who participated in the student projects for their commitment and enthusiastic involvement. They must have often felt like guinea pigs, especially when they were asked to complete the "hundredth" evaluation. And yet, their feedback was always positive and encouraged me to keep going.

I would like to thank organizational psychologist Mr. Baldegger for the fruitful discussions and valuable comments on MAP, my newly developed "map" of team behaviors.

No project can succeed without real clients. In this context, I would like to extend my sincere thanks to the management of the Vocational Training Center (Berufsförderungswerk) Bad Wildbad, especially Managing Director Mr. Dings and Mr. Birk, for making it possible to carry out the current student project on-site with the client and to publish the results. I would also like to thank Mr. Birk and his colleagues in the IT department for their active participation in the project, which has provided us all with new and interesting insights.

Of course, results from the student laboratory must be verified in industrial practice. This is not so simple, as confidentiality reasons often preclude publication. I therefore thank the management of Evonik Degussa GmbH, Rheinfelden plant, especially Plant Manager Dr. Vierbaum and Mr. Meijlink, for allowing me to use the results of the diploma thesis by Ms. Dipl.-Ing. (BA) Olga Wolf on the application of agile methods in plant IT (Chap. 9). My special thanks go to Ms. Wolf for her excellent work, which I had the pleasure of supervising together with Mr. Sehringer and Ms. Reisch.

I would like to thank the "Process Models" working group of the German Informatics Society for the interesting discussions on the topic of heavyweight and lightweight process models.

I would like to thank Mr. Heine and Ms. Herrmann from Springer-Verlag for their support during the creation and publication of this book. I am especially grateful to Mr. Heine for his encouraging suggestion to "write a smaller book for a change." Without this motivation, the book would not have come into being.

Rheinfelden, Germany
February 2010

Eckhart Hanser

Preface to the Second Edition

Fifteen years have passed since the first edition of my book on agile processes, and it is time to incorporate current developments in teaching and research into this overview of agile software development models. Due to their widespread adoption, *Kanban* and *DevOps* have been newly included—Kanban as an alternative to Scrum and DevOps as a completely new approach that describes the interface between software development and IT operations. For a long time, I considered whether to keep *Crystal* in the book, especially since our own HELENA study indicates that this model family is no longer used in companies. The deciding factor was that Crystal's project classification and concepts such as dense and osmotic communication continue to play a significant role in modern process models. Moreover, the Crystal roles remain current and interesting today. Naturally, my systemic team model *MAP* has also evolved in the meantime. The latest research findings and its integration into the *Viable System Model* have been added.

The expansion to now 6 models has necessitated a change in the book's title. From this edition onward, the title is *Agile Processes—Agile Teams*. This is also intended to emphasize the dynamic interplay between process and team.

The student laboratory for experimental software engineering, already described in the first edition, has since been institutionalized: By decision of the rectorate of the Baden-Württemberg Cooperative State University (DHBW) Lörrach, the *Center for Agile IT Processes* (https://dhbw-loerrach.de/kompetenzzentrumagileprozesse) was established in 2014 at the Study Center for IT Management & Computer Science. The focus of the competence center is research on (mostly student) IT teams and their processes, as well as the measurement and even the *prediction* of their success. For this purpose, the website https://map-model.de has recently become available. Here, interested teams can test their "team psychology" and estimate their performance as a team. My heartfelt thanks go to my "alumni" Jannik Heizmann and Colin Vavra, who developed the "MAP site" as part of their computer science studies at DHBW Lörrach and enriched it with their own ideas. I would be delighted to see this free offering widely used. Of course, the data generated will only be included in my further research in anonymized form!

In this edition as well, I have chosen not to use gender-neutral language. The use of the masculine form is solely for the sake of readability. My experience shows that women in the team deliver outstanding performance and are especially an asset in the fast-paced world of project work!

This second edition, too, would not have come about without the help and support of dear people. I thank my wife Susanne for letting me "get on with it" when I realized that the second edition would require more effort than originally planned. My children Stephanie and Felix may have already "left home," but they have both contributed to my work—especially Felix, who is himself an outstanding computer scientist!

Many thanks also to another "alumnus," Simon Günter, who reviewed the chapter on DevOps and, as a practitioner, was able to dispel some reservations during the discussion. For all ideas that arise in the academic context, it is important that they are tested in a corporate environment. Here, I would especially like to thank Ms. Ramona Bockstaller, who tested MAP in practice as part of her master's thesis. Of course, I would also like to thank all the students of our Computer Science Study Center who have participated in the student projects in the meantime. We have all learned from this experience.

As is well known, the idea for this book originated in our Working Group on Process Models of the German Informatics Society. In this context, our HELENA study on the use of various process models in our dual partner companies was also developed. My thanks also go to my colleagues and the entire team at the Study Center for IT Management & Computer Science at DHBW Lörrach, as well as to the university's rectorate, which has always supported me.

Many thanks also to my editor, Ms. Steinmüller from Springer-Verlag. She was very patient with me!

Rheinfelden, Germany
January 2025

Eckhart Hanser

Contents

About the Author

Prof. Dr. Eckhart Hanser is a Professor of Computer Science at the Baden-Württemberg Cooperative State University Lörrach and heads the Study Center for IT Management & Computer Science as well as the Center for Agile IT Processes.

1 Software Process Models

A software process model is a *model* for the development of a software system. Since modeling always involves abstraction, it is not about representing the course of a *specific* software development project, but rather a whole *class* of projects. As a result, not every process model is suitable for every class of projects. In general, there are heavyweight and lightweight process models, with agile models belonging to the lightweight category.

1.1 A Process Model—What Is It?

A software process model is a *model* for the workflow of developing a software system. Here, it is not about representing the workflow of a *specific* software development project, but rather a whole *class* of projects. For this purpose, the development process is usually divided into *phases*. Typically, one distinguishes between

- planning the process,
- specification of the requirements for the product,
- design of the software product,
- implementation (coding), and
- various tests of the software product.

Within a process model, in addition to the *activities* within these phases, the *roles* and qualifications of the staff who carry out or are responsible for certain activities are also defined. Furthermore, the documents and records, collectively referred to as *artifacts*,[1] are specified, which must be created as part of the development process. Often,

[1] For the term artifact, see (Jacobson et al. 1999).

E. Hanser, *Agile Processes—Agile Teams*, https://doi.org/10.1007/978-3-662-72726-3_1

requirements from authorities must also be observed. There is not *the* one process model for all types of software development models. The decisive factor in choosing a process model is the *project type*.

1.1.1 Classification into Project Types

An early classification into project types was made by Barry Boehm as early as the 1980s (Boehm 1981). He distinguishes between “organic,” “semidetached,” and “embedded” projects:

- *Organic mode* projects have relatively small development teams that develop software in close physical proximity. The team members are usually very experienced, both technically and methodologically. They are generally well informed about the later application area of the software. Often, the code size of the software is quite small.[2]
- *Embedded mode* projects are the opposite of the project type discussed above. They are subject to strict “constraints,” are usually “regulated,” i.e., shaped by official requirements, or are subject to other constraints, such as the uncertainties of hardware-near projects.[3] The developed software must meet high requirements for system reliability, and usually, subsequent software modifications are almost impossible. The development team is usually large. This is also due to the fact that the requirements for the software are described in detail, which often allows for parallelization of development work. The development team consists of both experienced and inexperienced members.[4] Often, the code size of the software is very large.
- *Semidetached mode* projects are *between* the project types described above and form a mixture of organic and embedded mode. The software development teams are usually medium-sized and consist of both experienced and inexperienced programmers. Often, not all aspects of the product are known. The code size is usually large.

1.1.2 Heavyweight and Lightweight Process Models

The classification into project types presented above also enables a corresponding classification of software processes and their process models into “heavyweight” and “lightweight” models[5]:

---

[2] However, this is not a requirement for the organic mode.

[3] The development of software in a military project certainly belongs to this class.

[4] This results simply from the size of the team.

[5] The term “lightweight process” first appeared to the author in (Fowler and Scott 2000).

- *Heavyweight* process models are characterized by a very formal, document-driven approach. Each phase of development is thoroughly documented, the process itself is clearly described in its course, and it can withstand official scrutiny. The use of heavyweight process models makes sense when a malfunction of the software product could pose a danger to life and limb. However, heavyweight process models are also considered inflexible, especially in projects with changing requirements. They are particularly suitable for use in *embedded mode* and usually also in *semidetached mode* projects.
- *Lightweight* process models, on the other hand, are more suitable for software projects in small teams, where the requirements for the product are only incompletely known at the outset. Detailed specifications make little sense here, as the risk of change is too great. At the same time, communication within the team and with the customer is very good due to the small team size. Much information flows informally and does not need to be explicitly documented in writing. The focus is on working software, not its documentation. Lightweight process models are particularly suitable for use in *organic mode* projects, and sometimes also in *semidetached-mode* projects.

The *agile process models* discussed in this book belong to the group of *lightweight* process models.

1.1.3 Process Model vs. Life Cycle Model

In German-speaking regions, instead of the term process model, the word *Vorgehensmodell* (life cycle model) is often used. Basically, these terms can be used synonymously. However, it is noticeable that the life cycle model dominant in Germany, the *V-Modell*, at least in its early version *V-Modell 97*, made no statements about the internals of the actual software development process.[6] Only the document interface between client and developer was extensively defined.

The common back-translation of Vorgehensmodell as "life cycle model" also suggests that there is a distinction from the term process model. Therefore, in this book, the author will distinguish between process model and life cycle model. Whenever the internals of the *software development process* are concerned, the term "process model" will be used. When the focus is more on the *life cycle* and the "external" view of development, the term "life cycle model" will be used.[7]

[6] This was only addressed with the *V-Modell XT*. For this, the reading of (Höhn and Höppner 2008) is recommended. For V-Modell 97, see also (Dröschel and Wiemers 2000).

[7] However, this can certainly be seen differently. Gerhard Chroust, one of the pioneers of the field, especially in the German-speaking world, speaks of "models of software development" and does not distinguish between life cycle models and process models (Chroust 1992, Chap. 3). Ultimately, it is up to the reader!

1.2 The Phase Model

In the 1970s, it was still assumed in software development that the requirements for the software product were defined at the beginning of the project and would not change until completion.[8] For this reason, Royce developed the phase model in 1979 (Royce 1970).[9] In a simplified form (Fairley 1985), it shows the five sequential phases of the software development process[10] (Fig. 1.1).

From Fig. 1.1 it becomes clear why the phase model is also called the "waterfall model." The phases are arranged in the form of cascades of a multi-level waterfall. The backward arrows are *verification arrows*. For example, after coding a module, it is verified whether the module complies with the specifications of the design phase, the architectural details. Thus, verification always takes place against the (temporally) preceding phase. Only during the final acceptance tests is verification performed again against the specifications.

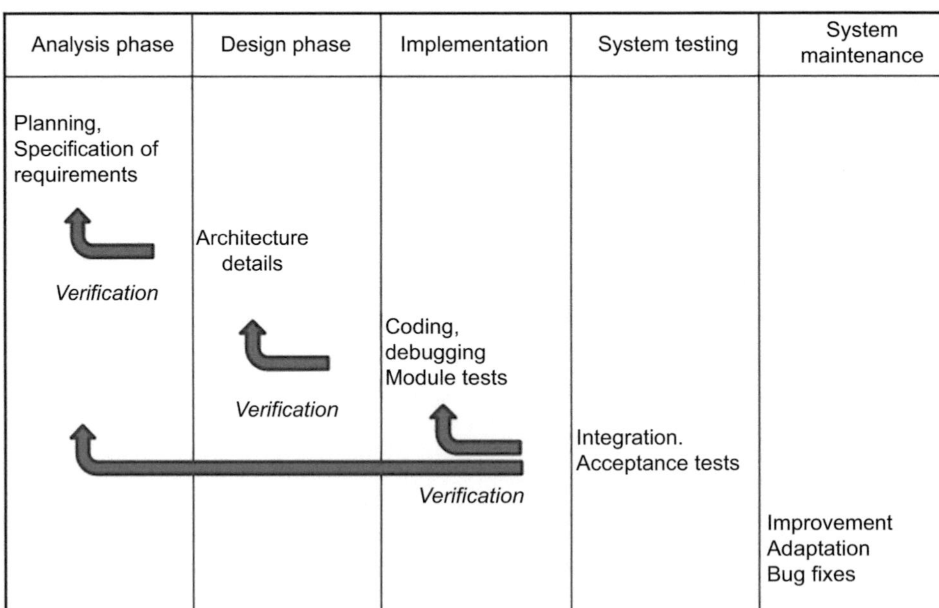

Fig. 1.1 The phase model according to Royce

---

[8] If this did happen, the project would be restarted.

[9] See also (Boehm 1981) or (Fairley 1985).

[10] Boehm identifies eight phases. Essentially, he further details Fig. 1.1 (Boehm 1981).

1.3 The Spiral Model

In the 1980s, it became increasingly urgent to develop process models that allowed software to be developed in successive versions. The phase model was always inadequate when software had to be developed in "pieces," so-called iterations. This was especially the case when the requirements for a software product were not fully clarified at the outset or changed during the course of the project ("moving targets," see Fig. 1.2).[11]

For such cases, Barry Boehm proposed the so-called *spiral model* in the mid-1980s.[12] It describes the so-called *iterative-incremental* software development process.

The development process is divided into time segments in which new functionality of the software is implemented, the so-called *iterations*. For each of these iterations, the phase model with its phases from analysis to system test is applied. The phase model is thus run through *once per iteration*. At the end of each phase stands the increment (unless the iteration was only for correcting errors or misunderstandings), the new functionality of the software. One or more increments result in a new release or version.

Strictly speaking, the spiral model is not a process model, but a "meta model." All modern process models are based on the approach of iterative-incremental software development.

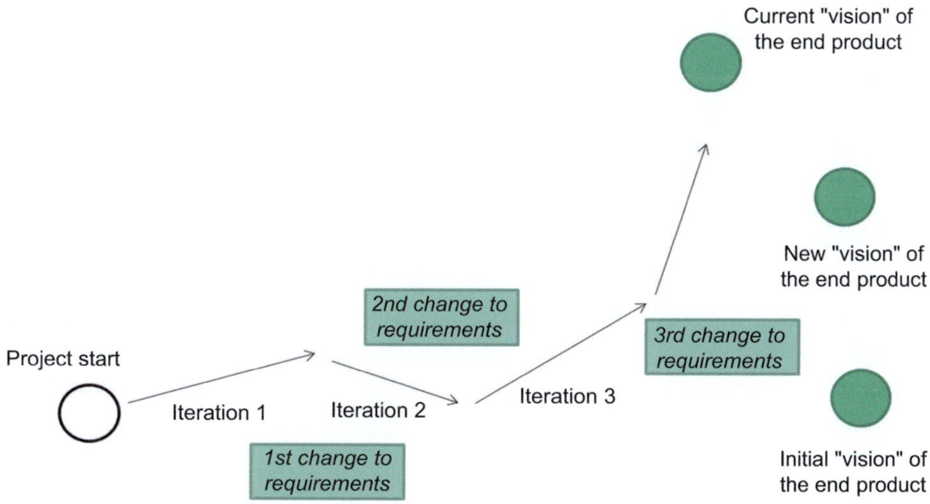

Fig. 1.2 The vision of the end product as a "moving target"

[11] For the development of software for machine control systems, the phase model continued to suffice.

[12] See (Boehm 1986) or (Boehm 1988).

1.4 Modern Iterative-Incremental Process Models

To classify some current process models, the distinction between heavyweight and lightweight process models is used. First, two representatives of the *heavyweight process models* will be mentioned:

1.4.1 V-Model

The V-Model is particularly widespread in Germany and Austria and, in its current version *V-Model XT*, is the official process model of the federal government (Höhn and Höppner 2008). It is very common in "regulated" environments, especially in the pharmaceutical industry, although there it is usually used in its historically oldest version, the V-Model according to Boehm (1979).

Critics point out the model's strong "document-centric" nature, which increases project costs. Especially in the pharmaceutical industry, efforts are therefore being made to apply more cost-effective process models (see also Sect. 9.10).

1.4.2 Unified Software Development Process (UP)

UP is the result of the development of an iterative-incremental process model at the company Rational in the USA[13] (Jacobson et al. 1999). The UP consists of four phases: *Inception*, *Elaboration*, *Construction*, and *Transition Phase* (see Fig. 1.3).

While the Inception phase marks the start of the project, the Elaboration phase is used to create the risk analysis, the specifications in the form of use cases, and the system's base architecture. In addition, the Construction phase is planned, during which the actual system development takes place.

In the Construction phase, the iterations for system development are carried out. Each iteration includes the phases familiar from the phase model: *detailed requirements analysis*, *detailed design*, *coding*, *(module) testing*, and *integration*. The iteration ends with a customer demonstration.

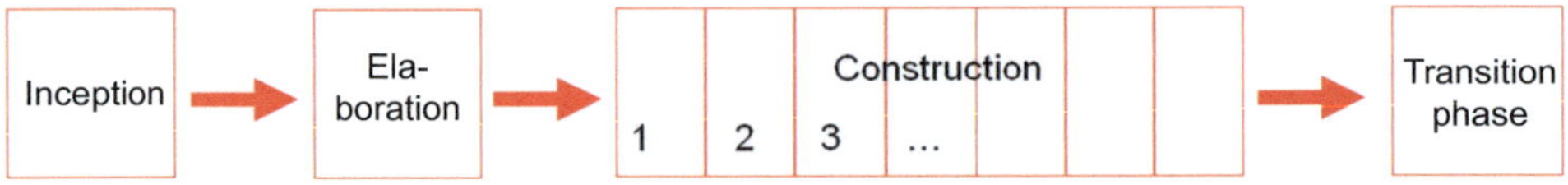

Fig. 1.3 The Unified Process (UP)

[13] Rational was acquired by IBM in 2002.

UP is also considered very document-heavy (and therefore expensive) due to its many prescribed management and engineering artifacts.

1.4.3 Agile Process Models

In contrast to the two process models described so far, agile models are considered *light-weight*. The focus is not on documentation, but on working code. Nevertheless, agile projects are not anarchic. The approach in the project is neither chaotic, nor is documentation forbidden. The weighting is simply different. In principle, only processes that conform to the *Agile Manifesto* may be called *agile*. This will be examined in more detail in Chap. 2.

For current experiences with various approaches or process models in a corporate context, see (Hanser 2024).

1.5 The HELENA Studies

In 2017, during the specialist conference *Project Management and Process Models*[14] of the German Informatics Society (GI) in the working group of the author,[15] the idea arose to conduct a survey on the use of process models, first across Europe and then, in the next step, worldwide. Dual partner companies of the author's university also participated in this survey. The two surveys HELENA[16] (Kuhrmann and Hanser et al. 2017) and HELENA-2 (Kuhrmann et al. 2018) show, at the European and global level respectively, the current dominance of agile models in the number of projects within the surveyed companies (Tables 1.1 and 1.2). However, the figures from HELENA and HELENA-2 are only partially comparable. While the Europe-wide HELENA survey asked about the specific process models used, HELENA-2 aggregated all mentions regarding rare, occasional, regular, and exclusive use of a model. The figures from HELENA-2 are therefore naturally higher.

Although agile models dominate (Table 1.1), Table 1.2 shows that classical models such as the Waterfall model (Sect. 1.2) and the V-Model (Sect. 1.4.1) are still (for now) quite widespread.[17]

The following chapters provide a detailed description of the dominant agile models. Even though Crystal is currently not widely used, it will be included in the list of agile

---

[14] https://pvm-tagung.de.

[15] GI working group *Process Models for Business Application Development* (WI-VM), https://fg-wi-vm.gi.de.

[16] HELENA: *H*ybrid d*E*ve*L*opm*EN*t *A*pproaches in software systems development.

[17] However, this will not be further explored in this book on agile models.

Table 1.1 Use of agile models in the corporate context in Europe (HELENA 2017) and worldwide (HELENA-2 2018)

Agile model:	HELENA (2017) (n = 69)	HELENA-2 (2018) (n = 845)
Scrum	53.6 %	79.8 %
Kanban	23.2 %	61.9 %
DevOps	23.2 %	51.7 %
Extreme Programming (XP)	10.1 %	47.8 %
Crystal family	0.0 %	4.6 %

Table 1.2 Use of classical models in the corporate context in Europe (HELENA 2017) and worldwide (HELENA-2 2018)

Classical model:	HELENA (n = 69)	HELENA-2 (n = 845)
Phase model (Waterfall)	34.8 %	53.6 %
Spiral model	1.4 %	18.5 %
V-Model derivatives	20.3 %	25.9 %
Unified Process (UP)	1.4 %	18.8 %

models considered here for the sake of completeness. The final chapter questions the approach of continually developing new process models and instead places the focus on team structure (Chap. 9).

References

Boehm B (1979) Guidelines for verifying and validating software requirements and design specifications. EURO IFIP 79, pp. 711–719, North Holland 1979.

Boehm B (1981) Software Engineering Economics. Prentice-Hall.

Boehm B (1986) A Spiral Model of Software Development and Enhancement. ACM SIGSOFT Software Engineering Notes, August 1986.

Boehm B (1988) A Spiral Model of Software Development and Enhancement. IEEE Computer, Vol.21, Ausg. 5, Mai 1988, pp 61–72.

Chroust G (1992) Modelle der Software-Entwicklung. Oldenburg.

Dröschel W, Wiemers M (2000) Das V-Modell 97. Oldenbourg.

Fairley R (1985) Software Engineering Concepts. McGraw-Hill.

Fowler M, Scott K (2000) UML konzentriert. Addison-Wesley.

Hanser E (2024) Der VM-Blog – praktische Erfahrungen mit aktuellen Vorgehensmodellen. https://map-model.de/vm-blog.php, Zugriff Oktober 2024.

Höhn R, Höppner S. (2008) Das V-Modell XT. Springer.

Jacobson I, Booch G, Rumbaugh J (1999) The Unified Software Development Process. Addison Wesley.

Kuhrmann M, Hanser E et.al (2017) Hybrid Software and System Development in Practice: Waterfall, Scrum, and Beyond. ICSSP'17, ACM.

Kuhrmann M et al. (2018) Complementing Materials for the HELENA Study (Stage 2). [online] DOI: https://doi.org/10.13140/RG.2.2.11032.65288, published: 2018-11-28.

Royce W (1970) Managing the Development of Large Software Systems, Proceedings of IEEE WESCON, Vol. 26 p. 1–9.

2 The Agile Manifesto

Industries such as military or pharmaceutical software development, which bear responsibility for life and limb, cannot do without comprehensive documentation. This is rightly required by the relevant authorities. However, these are narrowly defined fields. In the majority of software projects, however, the development of working software should be the main focus, as emphasized by critics such as Ward Cunningham, Martin Fowler, Alistair Cockburn, and Kent Beck. This led to the proclamation of the "Manifesto for Agile Software Development," the Agile Manifesto, in 2001.

The Agile Manifesto is a response by developers to the so-called "heavyweight" process models, such as the Unified Process (UP) (Jacobson et al. 1999) from Rational (now IBM) or the V-Model,[1] the process model of the German federal authorities. Although both approaches are very different—UP highlights the iterative-incremental software development process, while the V-Model emphasizes the customer's perspective on the software project—both are considered very "documentation-heavy," which, at least for "beginners," means considerable additional effort. It is important to understand that software developers choose their profession to design and implement software solutions. Excessive documentation is rather a nuisance to them. It usually takes a great deal of persuasion to convince them of the necessity of extensive documentation, as the author knows from personal experience.

The *Agile Manifesto* (Beck et al. 2001) offers a way out of this dilemma. It defines four guiding principles for successful and efficient software development:

- Individuals and interactions over processes and tools.
- Working software over comprehensive documentation.

[1] For the current V-Model XT, see (Höhn and Höppner 2008) or (Friedrich et al. 2009); for the "old" V-Model 97, see (Dröschel and Wiemers 2000).

E. Hanser, *Agile Processes—Agile Teams*, https://doi.org/10.1007/978-3-662-72726-3_2

- Customer collaboration over contract negotiation.
- Responding to change over following a plan.

The agile principles are best read "from right to left":

- Processes and tools are important, but in case of doubt, the people involved in the project and their interactions are more important.
- Documentation (even comprehensive documentation) is important, but if in doubt, delivering working software takes priority.
- Contracts are important, but if in doubt, collaboration with the customer is more important.
- Plans are important, but if necessary, requirements must be changed (i.e. adapted) in the customer's interest.

The interpretation of the second principle is particularly interesting: *Documentation (even comprehensive documentation) is important, but if in doubt, delivering working software takes priority.* This does not mean that documentation is not required in agile projects. It merely states something about the priority of documentation. Agile projects therefore require a special, flexible type of documentation. Static documents do not meet the needs of the situation. The solution is often wikis or commercial document management products that enable versioning and thus easy modification of documents. An electronic signature can also simplify the document approval process. This makes it possible to use agile models even in so-called "regulated environments".[2]

Regarding contracts and plans, it should be noted that when changes and adjustments are made, especially in later phases, the goodwill of both parties—the customer and the developers—is of course required: Developers need to know and be confident that the customer is not simply trying to "annoy" them with a change request, but usually has a vital interest. The customer, for their part, must be aware that both specification and plan changes entail considerable additional effort, which must also be compensated. Especially with fixed-price contracts, it may be necessary to renegotiate or to redefine the scope of functionality as part of iteration planning. It is important in all of this that the quality of the software product never suffers as a result of such changes. This must be ruled out by predefined testing procedures (especially through automated testing).

With its four guiding principles, the Agile Manifesto provides a kind of framework for lightweight software development. However, as practical aids for implementation in a concrete process, they are less suitable. The various process models, such as those discussed below, have the task of putting the agile principles into practice.

[2] A regulated environment refers to project environments controlled by authorities.

References

Beck K et al. (2001) https://agilemanifesto.org/. Zugriff September 2024.
Dröschel W, Wiemers M (2000), Das V-Modell 97, Oldenburg.
Friedrich J, Hammerschall U, Kuhrmann M, Sihling M (2009), Das V-Modell XT, Springer.
Höhn R, Höppner S (2008) Das V-Modell XT, Springer.
Jacobson I, Booch G, Rumbaugh R (1999) Unified Software Development Process. Addison-Wesley Professional.

Extreme Programming (XP) 3

When Kent Beck developed his process model Extreme Programming in 1996 as part of the Chrysler project *C3*, the project was already as good as failed. People were therefore willing to listen to new approaches, giving Beck the opportunity to formulate his initially informal agile practices as a new process model. According to Beck himself, the C3 project was ideal for his new approach because the specifications changed rapidly and because the customer had no definitive idea of the required functionality. In its initial phase, C3 was very successful and went live in 1997. Thus, C3 became the "flagship" for XP.

Kent Beck developed his process model Extreme Programming (XP) (Beck 2000) as part of the Chrysler project *Chrysler Comprehensive Compensation* (*C3*), which aimed to develop payroll software (Beck and Andres 2004). At the time Beck joined, the project was already as good as failed. Unfortunately, this is often the prerequisite for giving new approaches a chance. Beck was thus given the opportunity to formulate his initially informal agile project practices as a new process model and to restart the Smalltalk project. According to Beck himself, the project was ideal for his new approach,

- because the specifications changed rapidly,
- because the customer had no definitive idea of the required functionality,
- because high programmer productivity was required,
- because the project entailed a high (including time-related) risk,
- because the project team, including managers, programmers, and customers, consisted of fewer than twelve people,
- and because the software to be developed allowed for automated testing.

In contrast to other proponents of the Agile Manifesto, such as Alistair Cockburn, the founder of the Crystal process model (Chap. 4), Kent Beck prescribes the procedures in

E. Hanser, *Agile Processes—Agile Teams*, https://doi.org/10.1007/978-3-662-72726-3_3

the project strictly. XP defines "Rules and Practices" for planning, design, coding, and testing, and insists on their adherence. Above all rules stand the five values: *communication, simplicity, feedback, courage*, and *respect*.

3.1 The Five Values

3.1.1 Communication

Communication is crucial for the success of an agile project. We distinguish at least two types: communication with the customer and internal communication within the development team.

Internal communication forms the foundation for a collaborative approach within the project. Only when team members communicate with each other is it ensured that every team member is aware of the team's shared goals. Furthermore, it allows for highly efficient responses to shifting project goals.[1] Internal team communication does not come for free. As will be shown later, a sound psychological process is indispensable. This can only be achieved through the appropriate selection of team members.

Communication with the customer is significantly more challenging than internal team communication. The team often resists "including" the customer in the team, i.e., accepting them as an *on-site* team member, as Beck demands (Beck 2000). It is repeatedly observed that the team fears giving the customer too much insight into internal project processes. One often hears the argument that the customer would not trust the team to deliver professional software development if they knew how things are "cobbled together" internally. In practice, the opposite is usually true. The customer appreciates the internal perspective on the project that is granted to them. They feel taken seriously and are involved in both the successes and failures from the early stages of the project. Their respect for the team's abilities grows, and they develop an understanding for problems that arise during the project.

3.1.2 Simplicity

XP always seeks the simplest solution, at least at the current point in time. This applies not only to software design but also to the process and project planning. Deliberately, one does *not* deal with things that only need to be implemented in later releases. The simplest solution to a problem is always chosen, for example, when implementing an algorithm. The author has personally witnessed a measurement technology project in which a brilliant generic algorithm for the dynamic creation of objects for hardware

[1] So-called *Moving Targets*.

encapsulation became unmaintainable after a few years. The "father" of the algorithm had left the project team, and no other team member had understood the code well enough. Considering that only about five hardware objects were dynamically created with this algorithm in total, the complexity of the generic algorithm was, in retrospect, certainly not justified.

3.1.3 Feedback

Feedback has several facets. On the one hand, it refers to feedback from the system. When test cases are written and successfully executed, the software system provides feedback that the specified functionality has been correctly implemented. The sum of all test cases increasingly replaces the classic functional specification. Changes to the specification no longer necessarily have to be documented in writing. The system's feedback that an adapted test case has been successfully executed is proof that the change in requirements has been successfully implemented.

Feedback is also important in the customer-supplier relationship. In the classical approach, the customer develops a user requirement, the *User Requirements Specification* (URS). However, this requires the customer to have an engineering or comparable background. If the customer does not have this qualification, they must hire a suitable consultant. Since the functional requirement, the *Functional Specification* (FS), is written by the supplier, it often happens that, from the customer's perspective, two parties unfamiliar with the subject matter write both the requirements and the functional specification. At best, the customer is left with the task of signing the resulting documents. If, during the course of software implementation, deviations from the original (but undocumented) expectations of the customer arise in terms of functionality, conflicts occur. Since these usually arise in later project phases, it becomes increasingly difficult to "build in" the customer's wishes into the software. Agile approaches, especially XP, attempt to avoid this problem through feedback. The supplier, i.e., the software development team, commits to presenting the customer with the *current state* of the software as quickly as possible. Ideally, the customer can always see a version that is no older than one iteration step, usually just a few weeks old. On the other hand, the customer must provide *qualified feedback*. This means it must be the *right* customer (This requirement is actually trivial!). They must later be one of the users of the software and must have the competence to make decisions about the scope of functionality, both professionally and responsibly. The development team can therefore expect the customer to have the professional expertise of the software's target group—but not expertise in software engineering! Communication must take place *in the customer's language*. This is best done using the current implementation (release). Only if the customer is a user and can work with the software can they ultimately judge whether it meets their needs. In the author's experience, it is not so crucial whether the software runs error-free. You can explain faulty features to the customer and refer them to the next release. Most of the time, the customer can judge whether the software meets their needs despite some minor errors. It is therefore more important to quickly obtain the customer's feedback on new features than to present them with flawless software. The same applies to project planning. Presenting the customer with an honest schedule enables them to provide honest feedback. Giving the customer such deep insights into the project is generally difficult for the development team, as already described in the section on communication. It takes a good deal of trust and courage!

3.1.4 Courage

Rapidly changing projects inevitably result in second-rate designs. This effect is seen in student lab groups just as much as in corporate projects. Code is often modified to the point where it would be easier to throw everything away and restart. The same applies to design. If the team does not have the final goal in mind at the start of the project, it cannot take it into account in the design. Nevertheless, the willingness to adapt designs and, if necessary, rewrite code is very rare. Often, when test cases fail, a design or piece of code is modified until more test cases fail with each new change than are added successfully. And yet the team shies away from the consequences. The problem is, among other things, justifying this to superiors—and perhaps also to the customer. It becomes apparent that more time is needed for the next iteration. Nevertheless, *refactoring*, i.e., restructuring the design or code, is essential in the long run to reduce the error rate in test cases. Martin Fowler even recommends restructuring 10% of the code per iteration (Fowler and Scott 2000). However, the author considers this figure somewhat high.

XP also demands courage in other areas. As described above, communication and feedback in the customer-supplier relationship require courage from both sides. But adapting the process model as a whole can also require great courage. If certain rules and practices of XP do not work, they too are up for discussion: *Fix XP when it breaks*, as Kent Beck himself writes (Beck 2000). More on this later.

It is important to note that the three values of communication, simplicity, and feedback already implicitly presuppose courage. Only a courageous team and a courageous customer will be able to meet the demands of an agile project.[2]

3.1.5 Respect

Courage goes hand in hand with respect for one another—especially when things go wrong! In contrast to the four values mentioned above (Beck 2000), Beck only added this value later (Beck and Andres 2004). Respect is an important value for how we inter-

[2] And this statement holds true regardless of XP.

act with each other. Both within the development team and in the relationship with the customer, respect is the basis for a trusting collaboration. From the author's perspective, respect is the foundation for a successful project.

3.2 The 14 Principles

XP defines 14 principles derived from the five values. All concrete XP practices must be checked for compliance with these principles:

- Humanity
- Economics
- Mutual Benefit
- Self-Similarity
- Improvement
- Diversity
- Reflection
- Flow
- Opportunity
- Redundancy
- Failure
- Quality
- Baby Steps
- Accepted Responsibility

The following provides a brief explanation of the 14 principles:

3.2.1 Humanity

It is people who develop software. Therefore, working conditions must be humane. Opportunities for personal development for software developers, their integration, and their acceptance within the team must be ensured. Developers must feel comfortable in their project environment.

3.2.2 Economics

Software development must be economical. The mere "beauty" of a technical solution is of no use to anyone (even though engineers sometimes tend toward this). Software developers must also accept that the company ultimately wants and needs to make money with their solution.[3]

3.2.3 Mutual Benefit

Everything done within the team should benefit all involved groups. One should always strive to achieve "win-win" situations. For example, if you document code extensively, you incur an immediate time overhead. In contrast, there is the advantage of easier readability (at a *later* point in time!). Your own disadvantage is thus balanced against a potential future benefit for someone currently unknown. This must be weighed and balanced.[4]

3.2.4 Self-Similarity

Self-similarity in nature exists when a structure is the same at different scales. This is known, for example, from ferromagnetic structures. But it also applies to the structure of a successful solution to a problem. One should not shy away from (but rather make it a principle to) copying such successful solutions into other contexts. Once a successful principle has been discovered, it can work at different (temporal) scales.[5]

3.2.5 Improvement

Continuous improvement is a fundamental principle of software development. Iterative approaches offer the opportunity for constant improvement of the solution. Agile processes are subject to improvement: practices that do not prove effective are eliminated by the agile team and replaced with better ones.

---

[3] It is no coincidence that, nowadays, engineering students at German universities are increasingly engaging with business management topics.

[4] A solution mentioned by Kent Beck would be the introduction of well-documented automated tests (Beck and Andres 2004) instead of (elaborate) code documentation. The advantage of tests is that they benefit both current and future developers. In addition, regular refactoring keeps the design simple. Thus, we have a "win-win" situation between current and future developers. However, the author recommends not *completely* dispensing with code documentation.

[5] In software design, this principle is implemented with design patterns.

3.2.6 Diversity

Teams must consist of a diverse group of members with different characteristics and skills. This brings potential for conflict, but also the opportunity to develop entirely new solutions. Different people, for example, develop different designs, from which the best can then be selected. The composition of the team is crucial to the team's success (Chaps. 8 and 9).

3.2.7 Reflection

A good team reflects on how it works and how it could improve its work. It makes sense for the team to formalize this reflection, i.e., to consciously hold meetings with the goal of improving the process. But informal conversations between team members also serve this purpose. Agile processes are always in motion and on the path of continuous improvement.

3.2.8 Flow

The iterative development of software should result in the most continuous possible flow of delivered releases. Only in this way can the customer be constantly shown a *current* (interim) result of the development. This stands in contrast to the development in a "big bang" of the 1970s and 1980s.[6]

3.2.9 Opportunity

Every problem presents an opportunity for improvement. If a team encounters problems, it must actively address them. It is not enough to merely "survive"; the team must get better. This principle leads to the XP practice of *pair programming* (Sect. 3.3.3.4): If a programmer makes too many mistakes, this problem can be addressed through pair programming.[7]

---

[6] Phase or waterfall model (Chap. 1).

[7] Statement by Kent Beck in (Beck and Andres 2004). Of course, improving training would also be conceivable.

3.2.10 Redundancy

By tackling critical problems multiple times, you can select the best solution from those that arise. Different design approaches can be developed up to the prototype stage, and then the most effective approach can be chosen. Redundancy can also be useful in testing, for example by adding a test phase *after* delivery of the finished release.[8] Working in programmer pairs is also a redundant XP practice.

3.2.11 Failure

Sometimes you have to accept failures in order to find the best way forward. If you are unable to determine the best of several design proposals through discussion, you must try out the design proposals and accept the failure of one or more of them. The important thing is to gain new insight.[9]

3.2.12 Quality

Quality is non-negotiable. A team does not become faster simply by accepting lower quality. In most cases, productivity increases as quality improves. Quality work also strengthens the team's self-confidence. The team is proud of what it has accomplished.

3.2.13 Baby Steps

Iterations should proceed in small steps. Especially in agile projects, it is important to be able to quickly demonstrate progress (even *small* progress) in order to receive feedback. Small, regular steps in software integration reduce the overhead caused by integration. Only when integration is taken for granted will it be performed regularly.

3.2.14 Accepted Responsibility

Responsibility cannot be assigned; it must be accepted. The team must take responsibility for the product that is created in the agile project. If no one takes responsibility, the project will fail.

---

[8] In regulated environments, such as the pharmaceutical industry, also called *Operational Qualification.*

[9] This principle naturally correlates with the principle of redundancy.

3.3 Process Steps and Traditional XP Practices

The set of XP practices proposed by Kent Beck has changed and expanded since the first publications. The "traditional" XP practices mentioned in (Beck 2000), which are also described on Don Wells' website (Wells 2009), differ in part from the practices explained in the more recent book (Beck and Andres 2004).[10] This is attributed to the further development of XP and the growing experience with this agile process model. However, it is usually a difference "at first glance" that appears greater than it actually is.

This chapter will explain the traditional XP practices. The four phases of the waterfall model reappear here, slightly modified, as categories of *Rules and Practices*:

- Planning
- Design
- Coding
- Testing

All XP rules and practices proposed by Kent Beck are assigned to these categories (Wells 2009). However, XP does not prescribe the order of rules and practices. Of course, it is clear that the project team starts with planning and design before implementation can begin. But once the project is underway, there is no clear sequence. Agility also means freedom in the order of process steps.

However, as already known from the spiral model (Sect. 1.3), there are iterations and increments that must be planned or designed. The software is then implemented piece by piece as *increments* in small process steps, the iterations. Each increment can be reviewed and approved by the customer.

It should not go unmentioned that Kent Beck adapted the traditional rules and practices a few years later. Nevertheless, they can still be found on the official XP website (Wells 2009) and thus remain valid. Since they are central and reveal much about the origins of XP, the "traditional" rules and practices will be examined in more detail below.

3.3.1 Planning

In the planning phase, XP recognizes the following traditional rules and practices:

3.3.1.1 User Stories

User stories, like the *use cases* known from the Unified Process (UP) (Fowler and Scott 2000), are a modern specification technique. In contrast to the classic static specification of the functional scope, both approaches describe what is to be *done* within the scope of

---

[10] In this book, they are referred to as "extended" practices.

the software project. The new aspect of this approach is its dynamic nature. While the use case represents a specific type of mini-specification and the sum of the use cases specifies the system, the user story is more of a work package, which is used in particular for risk analysis, effort estimation, and iteration planning (Figs. 3.1 and 3.2). The goal is therefore not to describe a use case as precisely as possible, but merely to outline the topic in two or three short sentences. Details are then worked out later during implementation in collaboration with the customer. In this sense, the customer is the "walking specification."

Working out the user stories particularly requires the two XP values of communication and feedback (Sect. 3.1).

3.3.1.2 Release Planning—The Planning Game

When planning a software release to be delivered, XP distinguishes between two participating parties: the *business side* and *development*. The business side needs the software, while development, that is, the team, develops the software. During planning, conflicts of interest between the involved parties may become openly apparent. Based on the author's experience, developers tend to build "safety" into all their effort estimates, while the business side likes to declare the best possible project outcome as the standard. The role of the customer is somewhat unclear; although they actually belong to the business side, due to their constant proximity to the team, as a team member, over time they will increasingly understand the concerns and needs of the developers. Nevertheless, in case of doubt, the customer will try to represent the interests of their company, which usually means pushing for a rapid delivery.

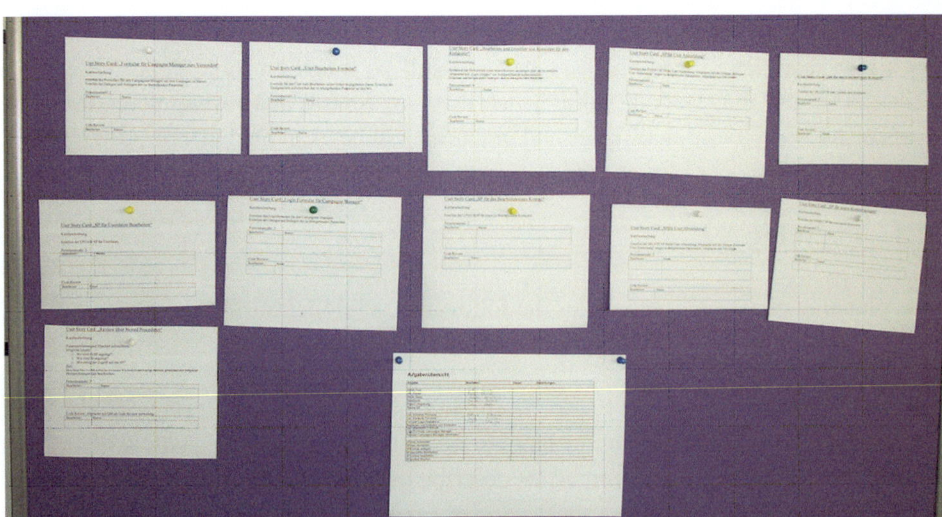

Fig. 3.1 User story card board from the student lab

User Story Card: "Database"

Brief description:

- Check the existing database
- Expanding the database with missing tables
- Recording the database schema on a flipchart sheet

Number of people: 2

Processed by:	Status
Bensch, Konnat	Sussarische Tabelle wurde modifiziert. Bitte neue Spalten beachten und bei Validierung die DB-Regeln beachten!

Code review: (consult with QM to determine whether review is necessary)

Fig. 3.2 Details of a user story card

The XP planning game recognizes four variables: *scope, resources, time, and quality*. From the author's perspective, quality plays a special role. It is not a true variable. The goal must always be to produce software of the highest possible quality, since the effects of poor quality—such as dissatisfied customers, necessary rework, etc.—will always impact the other variables. Thus, three variables remain, of which the business side may influence at most two. The third variable "belongs" to development.

As part of the planning game, the business side drafts user story cards (Fig. 3.2), usually with the assistance of some members of the development team, as will be explained in more detail in Chap. 8. Kent Beck stipulates as a rule that user stories should be defined so that their implementation takes about one to three weeks. A release plan should consist of approximately 80 ± 20 user stories (Wells 2009).

In the actual planning game, the user stories are scheduled, weighing market requirements, risk, and other factors, so that all parties agree with the resulting project schedule (Fig. 3.3 and 3.4).

In addition to the XP values of communication and feedback, courage is especially required to not shy away from the resulting conflicts. Developers in particular are warned not to "adjust" their deadlines downward at the request of the business side without simultaneously reducing the scope of the software. Overly optimistic deadlines will come back to haunt you, especially since the business side usually no longer remembers that it was they who demanded them.

Fig. 3.3 Planning game in a student laboratory

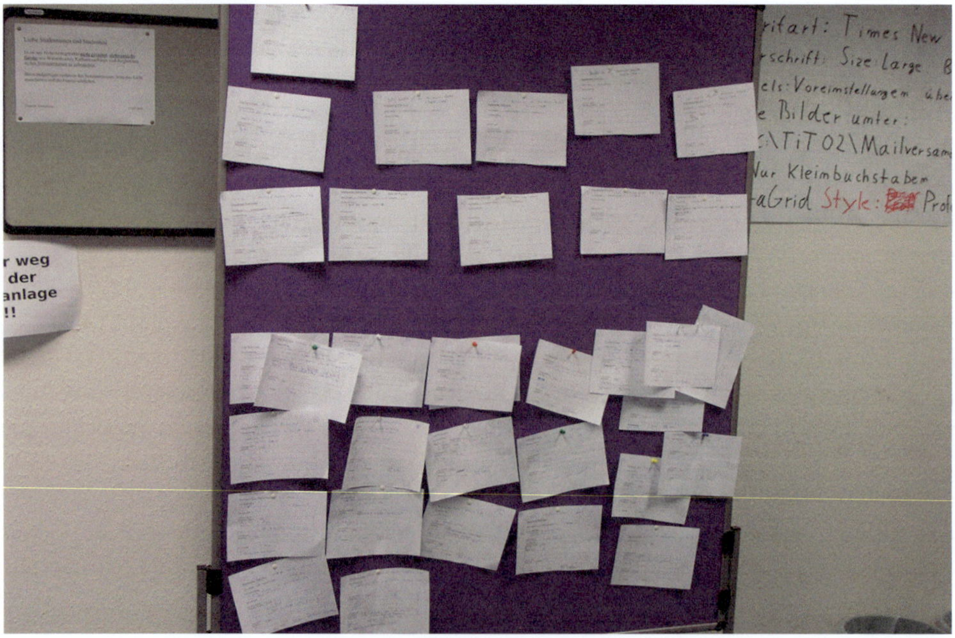

Fig. 3.4 User Story Card Board in the planning game

3.3.1.3 Small Releases

Small releases guarantee rapid feedback. If you plan releases that represent a visible benefit to the customer, such as a new input form, the customer can immediately give their opinion. Since the customer is a team member, there is of course nothing to prevent them from reviewing a completed user story directly at the developer's workstation. However, based on experience in the student laboratory, the author knows it is important that the customer can see the current state of the release with all current user stories on an integration machine. More on this in Chap. 8 and 9.

3.3.1.4 Measuring Project Velocity

If you add up the estimated efforts for the user stories per iteration and compare them with the actual efforts for the tasks derived from the user stories, you get a measure of the project's progress. Essentially, this is a simple planned-versus-actual comparison, as is known from project planning.

Of course, you can also estimate more professionally using *Function Point* (Hürten 1999) or *COCOMO II* (Boehm et al. 2000). The author likes to use such more complex methods. Simplicity of the process does not necessarily imply simplicity of the estimation method. It is always worthwhile to take a look at project management literature.[11]

3.3.1.5 Iterations and Iteration Planning

Beck suggests iteration lengths of one to three weeks. The iteration is planned together with the customer as part of an *Iteration Planning Meeting*. Typically, the customer selects one or more user stories that are important to them for the team to implement. The purpose of the meeting is to reach a mutual agreement on programming tasks that arise from the selected user story or stories.

During iteration planning, programmers select individual tasks to implement. The author has had good experiences with programmers choosing entire user stories, as this means taking responsibility for a part of the software that is important to the customer. This ultimately fosters communication with the customer.

The programmers create a detailed plan for the selected tasks, whose estimated efforts are again included in the measurement of project velocity. Developers also consider suitable test cases for measuring the achievement of the iteration goal right from the start. The test cases are usually derived directly from the user story being worked on (Fig. 3.5).

3.3.1.6 Move People Around

Agile approaches have a major weakness. Due to the rather sparse documentation, much of the knowledge resides in the minds of the developers or the customer. The question arises as to how many team members can leave, or as John Coplien puts it somewhat pointedly, "how many can be run over by a truck" (Williams and Kessler 2002), before

[11] See (Schelle and Linssen 2018) or (Drews and Hillebrand 2007).

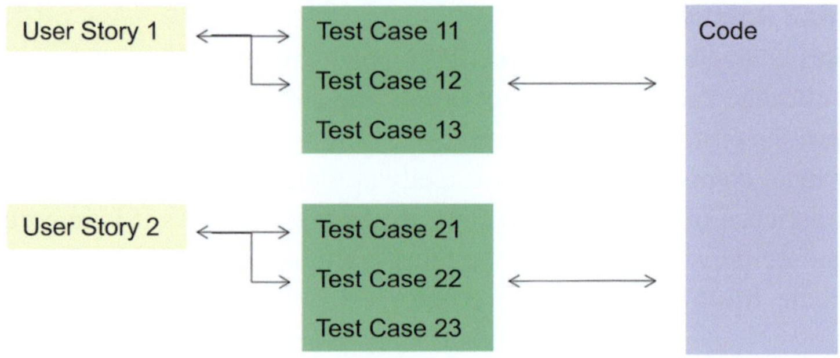

Fig. 3.5 Relationship between user stories, test cases, and code

the project can no longer be continued in a reasonable manner. Beck therefore proposes the so-called *truck factor*, which indicates, from 0 to 100%, the probability of project failure if a particular team member leaves the project.

If all team members participate in every area of the software at least once, this truck factor can be reduced. Thus, an agile project needs generalists as team members. However, the author's experience in the student lab shows that there are programmers who have no interest whatsoever in knowing the *entire* software. Yet these are often important specialists who can handle complex detailed tasks. In XP, it is necessary to persuade such individuals of the importance of knowing the whole software. In general, however, the author has not had good experiences with forcing developers into their "happiness."[12] It certainly takes *courage* here to find the best solution for the team.

3.3.1.7 Stand up Meeting

How often have developers and engineers complained about endless meetings with no significant results. A good friend of the author reported on a meeting at a German car manufacturer that began with hours of travel and ended in hours of boredom. The result was a wasted day! A proven agile technique (and by no means an invention of XP) is the "stand-up meeting" (and not a "sitting" meeting). These daily meetings are often held in front of a coffee machine. The goal is to reflect on the project status as quickly and precisely as possible, to highlight identified problems, or to communicate solutions of general interest. Such meetings often form spontaneously, but in the author's experience, it is better to agree on a fixed time (not too early!).

Another possible variant is that in each meeting, one developer receives a "free pass" that allows them to skip the meeting due to other important tasks. However, it is

[12] See also *Collective Code Ownership* in Sect. 3.3.3.6.

important that this developer only receives their second free pass after all others have also had the opportunity. This ensures that no developer uses the free pass carelessly.

3.3.1.8 Fix XP When it Breaks

In the interest of reasonable process improvement, it must be possible to abandon rules and practices that do not prove effective in practice. XP also allows for this possibility of correction. However, it is important that process improvement is not a gradual, creeping process. At any given time, it must be clear which rules and practices are in effect and which are no longer valid. In the student lab, the team tended to speak of "implicit process improvement." Of course, this is nonsense and rather shows the team's laziness in making changes to the process public and thus also communicating them to the customer.

It takes courage to implement and publish changes to the process. The question to ask is, after how many changes does the process being followed cease to be XP? The author will go on to show that a higher-level perspective on the process is promising here (Chap. 9).

3.3.2 Software Design

For modeling software, XP offers the following traditional rules and practices. Here, too, it is evident that the proposed practices are not new. Rather, it is the combination of rules and practices that defines XP.

3.3.2.1 Simplicity of Design—Implement Functionality Only When Needed

Simplicity is especially important in agile design. Since, for fundamental reasons, it is not possible to know at the start of an agile project what the final design will look like, it makes no sense to design classes or interfaces that will not be implemented in the same iteration. This leads to the problem that the overall architecture of the system only becomes visible shortly before the end of the project. What is not yet known cannot be designed. An XP design always reflects the team's current state of knowledge. For example, if a PC-based measurement system is to support, in addition to a TCP/IP bus, a modern laboratory bus in a later iteration, this should not appear in the initial design. There is a real possibility that the laboratory bus will be deemed unnecessary as the project progresses.[13] Do not implement functionality before it is needed!

[13] This is, at any rate, the author's experience.

3.3.2.2 System Metaphor

According to Kent Beck, a system metaphor is a "story that everyone—customer, programmer, manager—can use to illustrate how the system works" (Beck 2000). In the original Chrysler C3 project, which aimed to develop payroll software and was the first documented XP project, the system metaphor was an image from automobile manufacturing. The software was compared to an automobile production line, since it was assumed that all Chrysler employees were familiar with this conceptual world.

Finding a suitable metaphor is generally difficult, so the author has dispensed with this practice in the student lab. In the context of the lab, the "classic" approach of *system architecture* has always been followed—that is, the idea of representing the key relationships in the software system and neglecting the details of the software, which corresponds to the concept of a model as used, for example, by Balzert (Balzert 2001 and 1998). Of course, even with this approach, a metaphor is used by comparing software modeling to the modeling of a house—this is already implied in the use of the term *architecture*!

3.3.2.3 CRC Cards

Class, Responsibilities and Collaboration (CRC) Cards are an extremely practical design tool. In a very simple format, each class is described in no more than four short phrases, stating what the class should accomplish and with which other class it must interact to do so.[14] In this way, per iteration a set of corresponding classes can be created and managed in the form of index cards. If these cards are arranged on a pinboard and connected by associations, an initial UML diagram emerges.[15] It should also be mentioned that UML classes in the non-object-oriented world can certainly represent database tables or, more generally, software modules (Fig. 3.6).

3.3.2.4 Risk Minimization Through "Spike Solutions"

A *spike solution* is best described as a prototype implementation of the solution to an emerging (technical) problem.[16] This "vertical slice" demonstrates that the problem can be solved. However, this prototype is usually not suitable as a component of the final software. It is generally better to discard the "quick and dirty" code. It does, however, take courage to abandon working code solely because of poor design. Experience shows, though, that continuing to use poorly designed code is a mistake that comes back to haunt you.

---

[14] For example, by calling an appropriate method.

[15] Unified Modeling Language; a very good book on this is (Fowler and Scott 2000).

[16] The author also refers to this as a "proof of concept."

class ***MailVersand***	
Responsibility	Relationship to class
Organize mail campaign	Campaign
Assign newsletter	Newsletter
Assign subscribers	User
Send email	

Fig. 3.6 CRC card from an email delivery software

3.3.2.5 Refactoring

Refactoring is best translated as *restructuring* the design or code (Fowler and Scott 2000). Behind this lies the problem of *software entropy*: if you develop long enough, even the best design will eventually become a bad design. Let's stick with the example of the measurement system: after a TCP/IP interface has been implemented, a laboratory bus is added independently (at a later point in time).[17] Suppose these different interfaces are each represented by a class; it will soon become clear that an optimal design should include an *interface* from which the aforementioned classes are derived. The (wildly) grown system of two independent interface classes is replaced by the clean design *interface inherited by classes*. This approach has another advantage: if, in a later user story, the implementation of another bus interface, such as Profibus, becomes necessary, the developer can derive the corresponding class from the interface.

Refactoring improves the design and thus reduces the error rate in test cases over time. Martin Fowler even recommends restructuring 10% of the code per iteration (Fowler and Scott 2000). Comparing this to the practice in the student lab, the author finds this value somewhat too high. However, over the years, it can certainly happen in a student project that more than half of the code is revised.

Unfortunately, refactoring does not work properly without the appropriate tool support. With a good *Model Driven Development* (MDD) tool, the author has found that a design change can be reduced to just a few mouse clicks. Therefore, refactoring in an agile project almost inevitably requires the use of *Computer Aided Software Engineering*

[17] For example, IEEE-488/IEC-625.

(CASE). Otherwise, even a system-wide variable name change becomes an almost hopeless undertaking.[18]

Refactoring takes courage! Courage to rewrite working software for "aesthetic reasons." This starts with variable names and ends with the aforementioned design adjustments. However, a clear design ultimately improves the results of software tests (Fowler and Scott 2000).

3.3.3 Coding

The traditional rules and practices that XP provides in the coding phase were in part new and are at least partially controversial.

3.3.3.1 The Customer is Always Available

XP requires the permanent membership of the *customer in the team*. This is intended to enable a rapid response to changing customer requirements, even in the later phases of a project. Specification details can be discussed "face to face" with the customer. The required constant presence of the customer in the project is, of course, a practical problem, since experienced customers are rarely available to a software project on a full-time basis. However, practice shows a middle ground: The author has had good experiences with a "red phone" that connects the customer with the team. This can be, for example, a separate mobile phone whose number is ideally known only to the development team. When this phone rings, a two-stage mechanism is triggered: The customer answers the call as directly as possible, at the latest within an hour. Within one working day, the customer provides the final answer. These time frames are usually sufficient for both the developers and the customer. Developers can generally bridge a day of response time, and the customer can usually provide a qualified answer within a day.

Another objection to the constant presence of the customer is that in this way, the customer might learn too much about the project's internal workings (including mistakes that have been made). Wouldn't this reduce their confidence in the quality of the development team? And does this really improve project communication, especially with the customer? In practice, it turns out that the customer generally appreciates being integrated and involved in decision-making processes. Their trust in the team grows! However, communication between the team and the customer does not happen automatically. The author, who always takes on the role of the customer in the student lab, has repeatedly had to make himself heard or actively prompt the team to communicate with him (Fig. 3.7).

---

[18] Just imagine if the variable were called *i*.

Fig. 3.7 Customer strives for communication in the student lab

3.3.3.2 Coding Standards

Coding guidelines are now indispensable in modern software development. There is *no* reason to do without them. They standardize the code and enable team members to easily understand each other's code. In the student lab, such guidelines "survive" on the wall for years (Fig. 3.8). Of three successor teams, none felt the need to change or adapt the guidelines of the previous teams. Coding standards are the foundation for successful refactoring.

3.3.3.3 Code Unit Tests First

"Test first!" is an important principle of XP (Beck and Andres 2004). If you write *unit tests* at the beginning of an iteration, you can use them to clarify the user story in question. As a reminder: User stories usually consist of no more than three short clauses and do not even come close to the information content of a classic specification. Together with the customer, a mini-specification is created during the implementation of the user story, but this is never written down in detail. In the student lab, you will find in the wiki[19] only

[19] A wiki (Wiki Web) is a collection of pages available on the World Wide Web that users can not only read but also edit online. Wikis are therefore similar to easy-to-use content management systems, see https://de.wikipedia.org/wiki/Wiki.

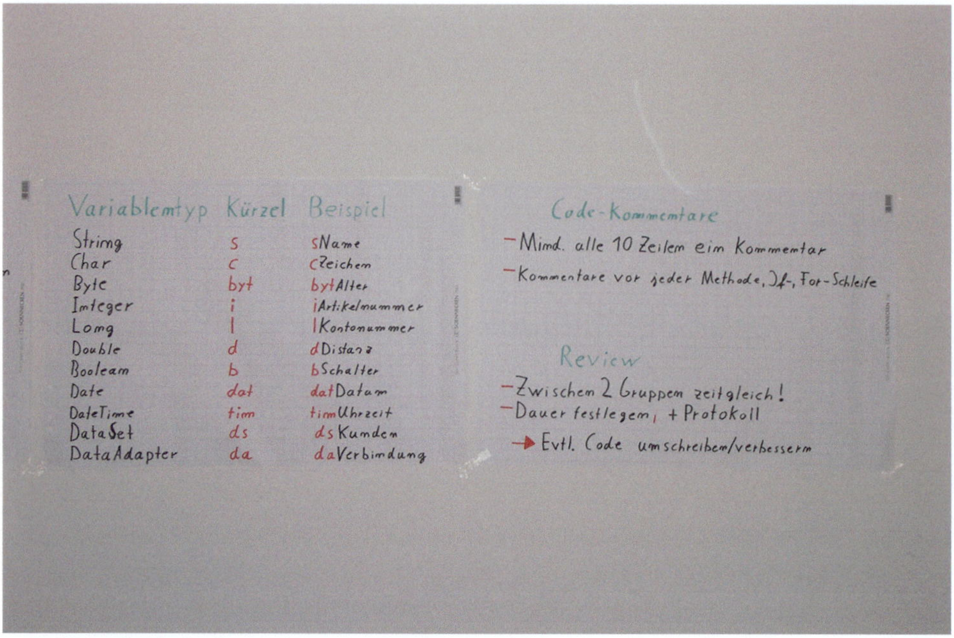

Fig. 3.8 Coding guidelines in the student lab

excerpts of the detailed specification and the fine design. It is noticeably easier to motivate developers to generate test cases in parallel with the (not written down) mini-specification, which are intended to document the achievement of the specified goal. These can also be easily coordinated with the customer and thus replace the written detailed specification (Fig. 3.9). Naturally, these test cases are at the level of the software module (i.e., at the level of software units). Higher-level system tests, in which the environment of the software can also be tested,[20] are excluded here, or postponed on the timeline (Sect. 3.3.4).

3.3.3.4 Pair Programming

The idea of programming in pairs states that all code in the software project should be written by groups—the author also calls these groups *mini-teams*—consisting of two developers. The two developers *share* a single computer (Fig. 3.10). They periodically pass the keyboard back and forth. One thinks tactically, for example, implementing a method of a class, while the other sits beside them and thinks strategically: Do we need this class at all, or should it be changed?

---

[20] Performance tests, stress tests, etc.

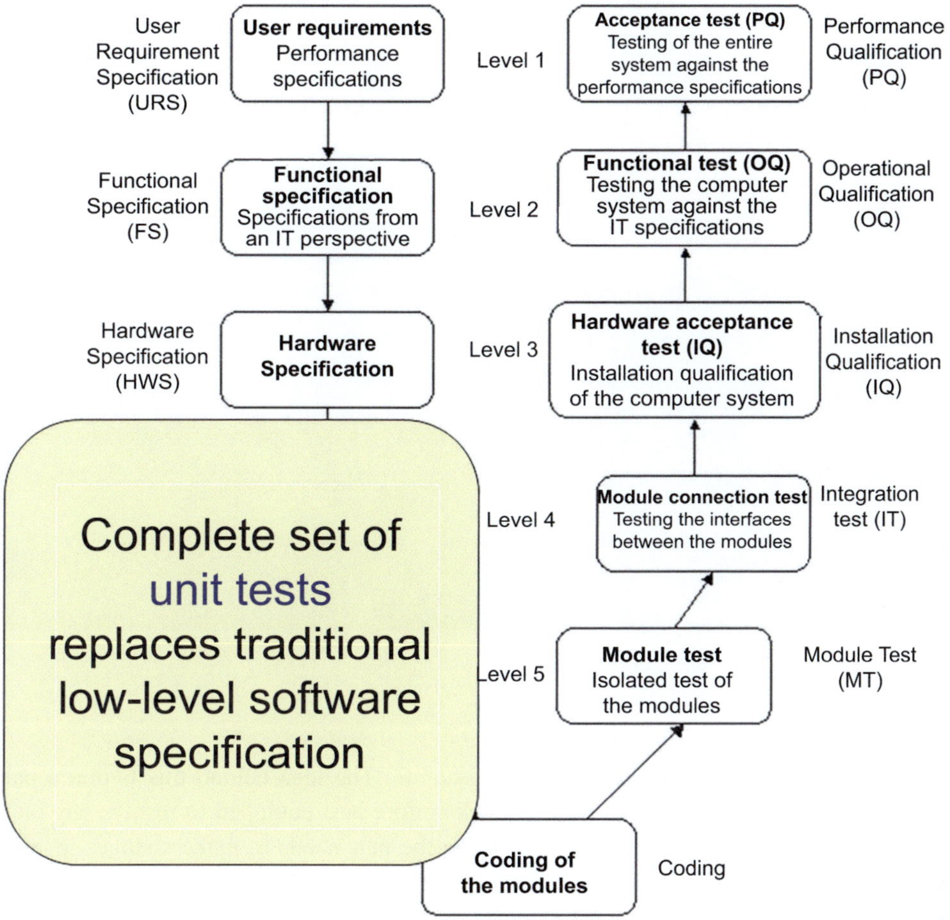

Fig. 3.9 Detailed specifications of the V-model are replaced by unit tests

Beck claims that pair programming increases the quality of the code produced, which certainly benefits the project. Interestingly, he also claims (without any proof known to the author) that the pair develops just as quickly as two independent developers at two different computers. This does not match the author's experience in the student lab. In low-level implementations at the detail level, it is more often the case that the specialist does the programming while the partner watches. However, when it comes to design decisions, working in mini-teams makes sense. In Sect. 8.5.3 the question is addressed as to whether these mini-teams really need to consist of two members.

3.3.3.5 Code Integration by Pairs—Integrate Often!

XP requires that pairs integrate their own code. However, this may only be done by *one* pair at a time. This pair holds a *token*, which enables only them to integrate. This token

Fig. 3.10 An XP pair in the student lab

can, for example, be a free integration workstation. The idea behind this is that a pair knows its newly developed code best and is therefore best equipped to resolve any integration issues that arise. Problems occur when the pair needs to make changes to code written by other pairs in order to integrate their own code. Due to the following rule of *Collective Code Ownership*, XP assumes that at least a basic understanding of other pairs' code exists. And with the available test cases, it is easy to determine whether a change to "foreign" code introduces errors or not.

This practice of *sequential integration* by pairs prevents absent or unavailable team members from becoming bottlenecks for project progress. Kent Beck explicitly rejects the use of integrators or integration teams. This would also reduce project velocity (Wells 2009). This in no way matches the author's experience in student labs or in practice! The truth is that all mini-teams, including pairs, try to "avoid" integration. No mini-team of developers is eager to make changes in "foreign" code. As a customer of the student lab team, the author experienced that each mini-team proudly demonstrated its implemented user story, but always only on its *own* machine.[21]

[21] This issue will be examined in more detail in Chap. 8.

Beck calls for continuous code integration (*Continuous Code Integration*). "Integrate often!" is his motto. He aims for integration cycles of less than a day. This ambitious goal can never be achieved without automated tests.[22]

3.3.3.6 Collective Code Ownership

The code belongs to the team as a whole! In XP, this means the team is also the chief architect. All team members can thus contribute to a good software architecture. Certainly, the team as a whole knows more than a single architect. Good ideas are no longer lost. No one becomes a bottleneck for fast and efficient software development.

This rule can only work if the *unit tests* are developed before the architecture. After the pairs have selected "their" user stories for each release, they must write unit tests that prove the correct functionality of the user story. This allows any pair to make changes to code written by other pairs without running the risk of unintentionally introducing errors. If the original unit test of the other pair still passes, the change is considered successful.

Applying this rule takes courage! As previously mentioned, practice in the student lab shows that developers usually show little interest in modifying "foreign code." One often encounters outright disinterest. Out of a team of about 20 people, never more than a third were interested in the overall codebase. This rule will also be questioned in Chap. 8.

3.3.3.7 Optimize Only at the End

This is not a specific XP rule. Optimization also takes place only in the *transition phase* in the *Unified Process* (Jacobsen et al. 1999). During optimization, debug code is eliminated, which during development provides valuable clues to programming errors. Furthermore, it is only at the very end that it becomes clear where performance bottlenecks arise in the system. These should then be addressed specifically. Mere suspicion of a possible bottleneck is not enough.

3.3.3.8 No Overtime

As the author knows from personal experience, sustained overtime destroys team motivation. If you work ten hours a day and sacrifice weekends for several weeks, after a maximum of one month "the air is out." The team no longer wants to continue, and productivity drops. As you learn in project management lectures, you can hardly work productively on the project for more than 6.5 hours a day. The rest of the time is needed for other things.[23]

---

[22] See also Chap. 7 DevOps.

[23] Checking emails, administrative tasks, etc.

3.3.4 Testing the Software

As already becomes clear in Sect. 3.3.3, software testing permeates the entire development process. Through the principle of *Test first!*, writing unit tests is even placed at the beginning of implementing a user story. Nevertheless, there are tests that, by their nature, occur at the end of the implementation of a release: the acceptance tests.

3.3.4.1 Unit Tests for All Code! If a Bug Is Found, a Test Must Be Generated! All Unit Tests Must Pass Before Release!

These rules once again explicitly emphasize the importance of unit tests. As already described in Sect. 3.3.3, unit tests written at the start of an iteration can help clarify the user stories under consideration. Test cases can easily be coordinated with the customer and thus replace "classic" written detailed specifications (Fig. 3.9). Unit tests are at the level of the software module (i.e. software *unit*). However, if bugs are found during testing or in live operation, a test must be generated for the bug. One can assume that this test did not previously pass, otherwise the bug would have been discovered.[24] All unit tests must be successfully executed *before* a release.

3.3.4.2 Acceptance Tests

In all considerations of software testing, it has so far been ignored that certain errors, e.g., regarding performance, internet connectivity, or general system load, cannot be found in unit tests. The delivered system ultimately consists of software *and* hardware. And this complete system must also be tested.[25] Acceptance tests also result from the user stories. The difference from unit tests is that acceptance tests can no longer (and should not) be clearly assigned to a software module. With the help of acceptance tests, the customer can test "their" user stories; they replace the (usually not properly documented) high-level specifications of the system (Fig. 3.11). Acceptance tests are *black box tests*. The code does not need to be available to conduct them. This is where *quality assurance* comes in, which otherwise does not explicitly appear in XP, but which, in the author's experience, is indispensable even in an agile project.

Acceptance tests should also be automated as much as possible in XP (Wells 2009). However, in practice, this is much more difficult than automating unit tests. In the student lab, teams have not yet succeeded in doing this.

It makes sense to introduce a *score* for these tests, so that the development team (and anyone else) can see the status of the tests at any time. The author also considers a system of *traffic lights* useful, which visually (red and green) display the success of the most important tests, e.g. on an intranet page.

---

[24] At least for unit tests, this is correct.

[25] See also Chap. 7, which deals with this issue in detail.

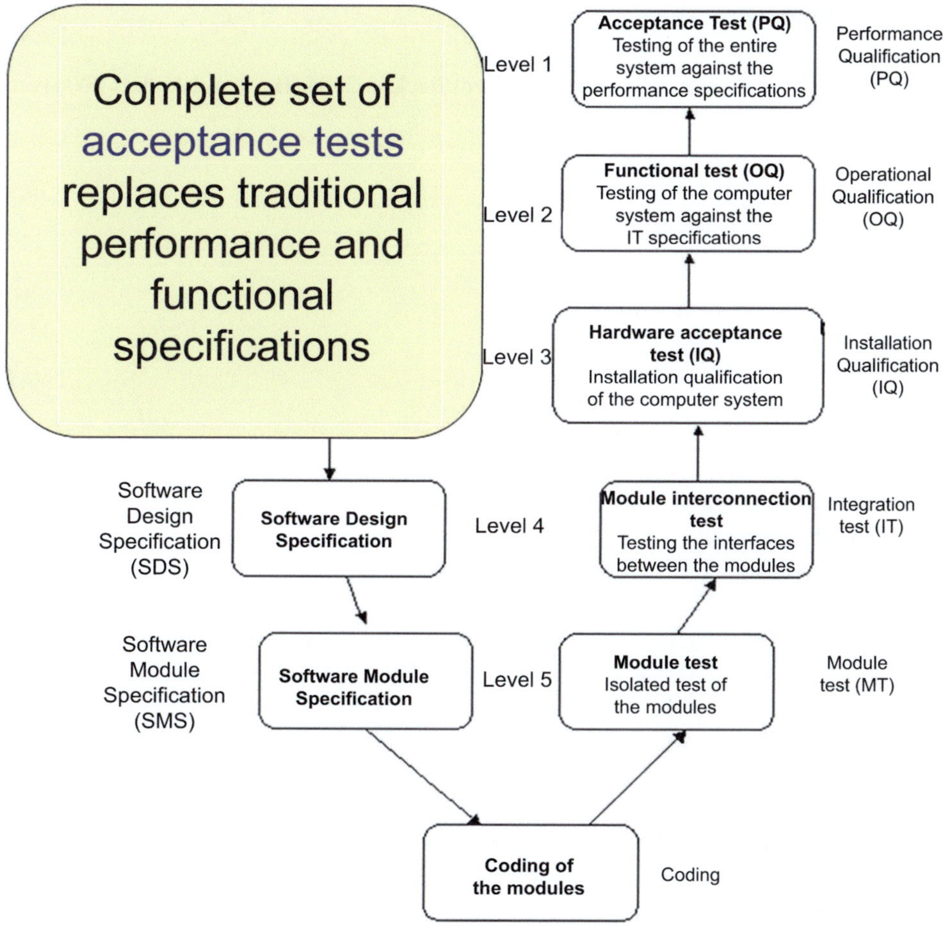

Fig. 3.11 High-level specifications of the V-model are replaced by acceptance tests

3.4 Extended XP Practices

The "traditional" XP practices described so far were already proposed by Kent Beck in 2000 (Beck 2000) and are still valid today. They continue to be maintained and applied in projects (Wells 2009). Nevertheless, Kent Beck replaced the traditional XP practices in his more recent book (Beck and Andres 2004) with a new set of 13 primary practices and 11 corollary practices. This is justified by the further development of XP and the growing experience with this agile process model. However, the difference between the traditional and the "extended" XP practices described in this chapter is not as great as it may seem at first glance. XP remains true to itself!

3.4.1 Primary Practices

The 13 primary practices newly defined by Kent Beck in 2004 (Beck and Andres 2004) are:

- Sit together
- Whole team
- Informative workspace
- Energized work
- Pair programming
- Stories
- Weekly cycle
- Quarterly cycle
- Slack
- Ten-minute build
- Continuous integration
- Test-first programming
- Incremental design

Some of the primary practices are already known as traditional practices and do not need to be described again. These are *User Stories* (Sect. 3.3.1.1) and *Incremental Design* (Sect. 3.3.2.1) as well as *Pair Programming* (Sect. 3.3.3.4), *Continuous Code Integration* (Sect. 3.3.3.5), and *Test-First Development* (Sect. 3.3.4.1). The "new" XP practices are of particular interest:

3.4.1.1 Team Sits Together in one Location

This primary practice is not really new. The requirement for pairwise work (with changing partners) already demands physical proximity of the team. What is new is that XP explicitly requires this agile self-evidence.

3.4.1.2 Whole Team

The team must combine all the skills necessary to accomplish the given task. This important aspect will be discussed in detail in Chap. 9.

3.4.1.3 Informative Workspace, Energized Work, Slack

The workspace should be tailored to the needs of the team, but also reflect the current status of the project. For example, it makes sense to arrange the user story cards on pinboards in such a way that it is immediately clear how many have been completed and how many are still open (Fig. 3.12). Within a few seconds, any visitor can get an overview of the project's status.[26]

[26] Of course, this can also be solved "digitally" with large screens on the walls.

Fig. 3.12 The arrangement of user story cards shows the current status of the project (2009)

A good and well-adapted workspace "inspires" the team and enables it to do "energized work," that is, to work with commitment and energy. Only in this way can the team achieve extraordinary results.

Equally important is the *slack* for individual team members. They should be able to pursue their own activities, that is, spend a (limited) part of their time on things that interest them (which, as a rule, are related to their project topic). The team benefits from the new ideas gained.

3.4.1.4 Ten-Minute Build

What is new is Kent Beck's clear statement on time scales in the project. He points out that a build of the software system, including all automated tests, should not take longer than ten minutes. This is a reasonable size, because waiting longer leads to fewer builds. The author worked on a project in the 1980s where a build took over an hour. The result was builds only every few days, with the risk of interface problems between separately implemented user stories. Thanks to the falling prices of powerful hardware, this problem can nowadays (usually) be easily managed.

3.4.1.5 Weekly Cycle

The second time scale specified by XP refers to the length of iterations. In contrast to the traditional practices (Sect. 3.3), Kent Beck proposes a shorter time scale. While he initially spoke of two to three weeks, he now prefers one week, as this allows everything to focus on Friday. Friday marks the end of a work segment. It therefore makes sense to plan iterations on a weekly basis.[27] The week begins with planning, followed by writing automated tests, and the rest of the week is spent implementing the code so that the previously written tests are satisfied.

3.4.1.6 Quarterly Cycle

The next larger specified time unit is the quarter. Analogous to the (natural) length of a season, larger units of software can be implemented. It is advisable to plan and carry out quarterly releases.[28]

Retrospective meetings in XP also take place once a quarter. It is important not only to identify problems, but also to initiate solutions, that is, not to lose sight of the "big picture" of the project.[29]

To make it absolutely clear: The statement on time scales is *new* and cannot be found in this clarity in the early approaches to XP.[30]

3.4.2 Secondary Practices

XP recognizes 11 secondary practices, which should only be applied once the team has mastered the primary practices:

- Real customer involvement
- Incremental deployment
- Team continuity
- Shrinking teams
- Root-cause analysis
- Shared code
- Single codebase
- Daily deployment
- Negotiated scope contract
- Pay-per-use

[27] Although Beck does not explicitly require this in the relevant chapter (Beck and Andres 2004).

[28] Although Beck does not explicitly require this either (Beck and Andres 2004).

[29] Scrum requires significantly shorter intervals (Chap. 5)!

[30] See also (Beck 2000) and (Beck and Andres 2004).

Some of the secondary practices are already known as traditional practices. *Customer involvement* in the team[31] was a requirement of Kent Beck from the very beginning. Equally important has always been *incremental delivery* of small releases.[32] *Shared code* corresponds to the traditional practice of *Collective Code Ownership* (Sect. 3.3.3.6). What is new is the explicit mention of the following secondary practices:

3.4.2.1 Team Continuity

Effective teams should, as far as possible, be kept together, because a team is more than the sum of its individual members. A good "climate" within a team ensures that individual members feel comfortable and can therefore perform at their best. The problem of teams being broken up occurs mainly in large development organizations.

3.4.2.2 Shrinking teams

Over time, the skills of a project team grow, and with them the speed at which defined user stories are completed. In such cases, it makes more sense to keep the workload constant and reduce the team size.[33]

3.4.2.3 Root-Cause Analysis

If a bug has been undetected through development, the root causes must be investigated. First, a (preferably automated) system-level test should be developed that exposes the bug. Then, at the module level, the corresponding test case should be implemented.[34] Once the bug is fixed, the next step is to investigate why it was not detected. Was the person who could have found the bug not a member of the team? These and similar causes must then be clarified.

3.4.2.4 Single Codebase, Daily Deployment

The team and the project always have a current codebase. Of course, each XP pair will first implement a user story locally. But at the latest after a few hours, the code should be synchronized with the others. Otherwise, the effort required for code integration becomes too great.[35] For the same reason, it is advisable to generate a new *build* of the software every night. Only constant synchronization of a programmer's work with the "production code" can prevent integration risks.

---

[31] "The customer is always available" (Sect. 3.3.3.1).

[32] "Small releases" (Sect. 3.3.1.3) and "Integrate often!" (Sect. 3.3.3.5).

[33] Within the context of student projects, however, the author does not have this option. The team size is determined by the course size.

[34] However, this will only be possible for functional errors. Performance issues are generally difficult to identify at the module level.

[35] See also Sect. 8.4.

3.4.2.5 Negotiated scope contract

In software development contracts, time, cost, and quality should be defined. However, the exact scope of functionality should be continuously adjustable. The contract should allow for this flexibility. It is in line with the agile philosophy that specifications in the form of user stories are developed over time. This practice is therefore a direct consequence of the agile approach. Nevertheless, clients often struggle to accept such flexibility in contracts.

3.4.2.6 Pay-per-use

Pay-per-use means that the customer only pays when they use the software. Thus, each use of the software incurs appropriate fees. The usage rate of the software ultimately provides an indication of customer satisfaction. This can be taken into account by the development team during further development. The closer the product is to the customer's needs, the higher the usage and thus the fees the customer is willing to pay.[36]

However, this approach is problematic for custom developments for specific clients. Here, the client rightly expects cost certainty, while the development team wants to see its costs covered. (Perhaps pay-per-use should only be understood in a figurative sense!)

3.4.3 Differences Between Extended and Traditional XP Practices

Since his first book (Beck 2000), Kent Beck has removed some of the traditional *Rules and Practices* from the list of XP practices. These are mainly practices that are not specific to XP, such as

- measuring project velocity
- stand-up meetings
- the use of CRC cards
- implementing prototypes (spike solutions)
- refactoring software
- optimizing at the end
- no overtime

These practices are now considered "good engineering" and are no longer seen by most developers as specific to XP.

[36] This approach is also known as *Application Service Providing* (ASP).

Other traditional practices have (usually only slightly) changed or are no longer explicitly mentioned:

- The planning game (Sect. 3.3.1.2) is replaced by the contract with negotiable scope.
- Iteration planning with small releases (Sect. 3.3.1.3) is specified as a weekly cycle. Beck reduces the original two- to three-week iterations to *one week* to focus the team on Friday as the delivery day.
- *Move People around* (Sect. 3.3.1.6) no longer needs to be mentioned separately. This practice serves to spread knowledge of the code within the team. Pair programming and team continuity ultimately achieve the same goal.
- The rule *Fix XP when it breaks* is no longer found among the extended XP practices. The tricky part of this rule is determining at what point the process is *no longer* XP.[37]
- It is interesting to note the disappearance of the requirement for a *system metaphor* (Sect. 3.3.2.2). It is known from student labs that finding a metaphor generally proves difficult. For this reason, this practice is omitted there. It can be assumed that this general difficulty led Kent Beck to abandon this practice.

3.5 Famous XP Practices

As already mentioned, many of the XP rules and practices are not new. Rather, it is their combination and strict adherence that defines XP. The XP practices can certainly be divided into two categories: rules that any modern project manager would immediately accept and most likely already uses, and rules that provoke opposition:

No experienced and up-to-date project manager doubts the importance of sensible version and release planning, small releases, an iterative-incremental approach, and simple design with naming conventions. Likewise, comprehensive and automated testing "from day one," even at the module level, is now part of modern software project techniques.

The other group of XP rules and practices gives more cause for discussion, as the author knows from personal experience and was able to verify in the student lab. These rules and practices, which have made XP famous, are examined for their practical suitability in the student lab (see Chap. 8).

3.5.1 Creating User Stories

Requirements should not be documented in the form of documents, but rather as short, three-sentence mini-specifications written by the customer in their own "language." The

[37] See also Chaps. 8 and 9.

effort required to implement the corresponding software module should not exceed three weeks. Can the customer do that? How can they estimate three weeks of effort? Does such a fine-grained temporal breakdown even make sense? Do they need support? (And if so, from whom?)

3.5.2 Pair Programming

Two programmers work together at *one* computer. Beck promises an increase in software quality with the same efficiency as a team of two programmers at two computers. In the pair, one programmer is supposed to think tactically, focusing on the functionality of a current class method, while the other thinks strategically, considering whether the above class method even belongs in this class. The programmers regularly switch, possibly every few hours, between these roles. This requirement is probably met in very few projects. The question of the sense of this XP rule will be examined further below.

3.5.3 Collective Code Ownership, Shared Code

Every team member should take responsibility for the entire code and understand it accordingly. Anyone who needs to make a change to code written by another pair can do so independently, since automated testing with appropriate version control makes it possible to restore the "original state" of the software before the change. This point is delicate! Anyone who has ever worked with such tools knows that you need a deep understanding of the software to be changed, or at least the willingness to acquire this understanding. This rule will also be examined.

3.5.4 Continuous Code Integration, A Single Codebase

Integration at short intervals, ideally continuously, serves the purpose of always having an up-to-date codebase. Code integration is performed by the XP pairs, who independently link the project modules into a runnable release one after another on an integration machine. Here, the question must be clarified as to whether all pairs have sufficient motivation and know-how to successfully carry out what is usually a complex integration.

3.5.5 Customer in the Team, Customer Involvement

Beck calls for the permanent membership of the *customer in the team* (at least in the traditional practices and in the extended practices/follow-up practices). This is intended to enable a quick response to changing customer requirements, even in late project phases.

Specification details can be discussed "face to face" with the customer. The required constant presence of the customer in the project is naturally a problem in practice, since experienced customers are rarely fully available to a software project. Another objection is that the customer might learn too many internal details of the project in this way. And does this really improve project communication, especially with the customer? An indication of the problematic nature of this practice is that Kent Beck classifies it as a follow-up practice for experienced teams in his extended practices.

The XP practices discussed here were intensively examined in the student lab and are discussed in detail in Chap. 8.

References

Balzert H (2001 u. 1998) Lehrbuch der Software-Technik. Band 1 und 2. Elsevier-Verlag.

Beck K (2000) Extreme Programming. Addison Wesley.

Beck K, Andres C. (2004) Extreme Programming Explained—Embrace Change, 2nd Ed. Addison-Wesley.

Boehm B, Abts C, Brown W, Chulani S, Clark B (2000) Software Cost Estimation With Cocomo II. Prentice Hall.

Drews G, Hillebrand N (2007) Lexikon der Projektmanagement-Methoden. Haufe.

Fowler M, Scott K (2000) UML konzentriert, 2. Auflage. Addison-Wesley.

Jacobsen I, Booch G, Rumaugh J (1999) The Unified Software Development Process. Addison Wesley.

Hürten R (1999) Function-Point Analysis—Theorie und Praxis. expert-Verlag.

Schelle H, Linssen O (2018) Projekte zum Erfolg führen, 8. Auflage. DTV.

Wells D. (2009) www.extremeprogramming.org. Zugriff September 2024.

Williams L, Kessler R (2002) Pair Programming Illuminated. Addison Wesley.

4 Crystal and Crystal Clear

Crystal is a family of agile process models developed by Alistair Cockburn. Drawing on the analogy of the *crystal*, Cockburn classifies the process models in his family by color and criticality. The color corresponds to the team size. The criticality corresponds to the severity of the damage the software can cause. In particular, Crystal Clear will be considered here, which was developed for relatively non-critical projects in small teams.

The Crystal family of agile process models was developed in the 1990s by Alistair Cockburn.[1] Cockburn classifies the process models of the Crystal family by *color* and *criticality* (or "*degree of hardness").* The color corresponds to the team size—the darker the color, the larger the team. The criticality corresponds to the severity of the damage that faulty software can cause.[2] This classification makes sense, since larger projects entail increased communication effort, while higher criticality requires more effort in quality assurance.[3] Nevertheless, the focus of the approach is *not* on a specific, defined procedure in the project. Instead, general principles are postulated and project properties to be achieved are defined.

---

[1] The personal website of the founder of this family of methods (Cockburn 1996) is interesting and informative; incidentally, his name is pronounced *Co-burn*.

[2] Crystal was examined in more detail in 2007 as part of a student project at the Berufsakademie Lörrach (Baden-Württemberg Cooperative State University) (Hättich 2007, see also Sect. 8.5.5).

[3] Especially for testing the correctness of the code.

E. Hanser, *Agile Processes—Agile Teams*, https://doi.org/10.1007/978-3-662-72726-3_4

4.1 Team Size and Risk—The Crystal Family

Crystal classifies software development projects according to the number of team members as follows:

- Crystal Clear: 1 to 6 team members
- Crystal Yellow: up to 20 team members
- Crystal Orange: up to 40 team members
- Crystal Red: up to 100 team members
- Crystal Maroon: up to 200 team members
- Crystal Blue: up to 500 team members
- Crystal Violet: up to 1000 team members

The process model selected according to the number of team members is then *hardened* according to the criticality of the project. Four risk categories are provided for this purpose:

- C: *Loss of comfort*, e.g., limitations in user convenience
- D: *Loss of discretionary money*, loss of available (usually non-critical) funds
- E: *Loss of essential money*, loss of essential funds (usually loss of the company)
- L: *Loss of life*, loss of human life

A project with 15 team members and the risk of loss of human life in the event of a software error thus belongs to class *L20* in the process model *Crystal Yellow* (Fig. 4.1).

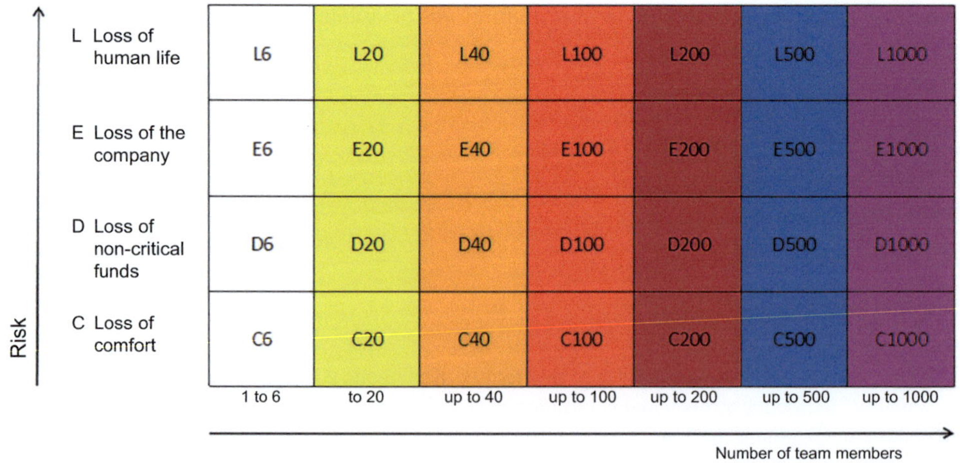

Fig. 4.1 The Crystal family of agile process models

4.2 The Seven Crystal Properties

Based on surveys of team members (Cockburn 2005), the following project properties are identified as important and are therefore required for Crystal projects:

- Frequent Delivery
- Reflection Improvement
- Osmotic Communication
- Personal Safety
- Focus
- Easy Access to Expert Users
- Agile Technical Environment

Among these, regular delivery, reflected improvement, and osmotic communication are considered the most important properties. The following sections will examine the listed project properties in more detail.

4.2.1 Frequent Delivery

The tested code should be delivered to the customer on a regular basis. This allows the customer to provide feedback on the current state of the software project at regular intervals. Deviations from the requirements can thus be quickly identified. For the customer, it is easier to check the implementation of their requirements on the "running system" than to assess the correctness of comprehensive specification documents. In addition, the customer's approval motivates the development team.

4.2.2 Reflection Improvement

In reflection meetings, the team lists what is working well in the project and what is not. The team discusses possible improvements and discontinues practices that have not proven effective. The results of the team meetings are incorporated into the next development phase. Such a team meeting should take place at least every three months or as needed. It can last from half an hour to half a day.[4]

---

[4]The author's experience shows that the team will also resist if, in their opinion, these meetings are held too frequently.

Fig. 4.2 Osmotic communication in the Crystal team

4.2.3 Osmotic Communication

A team has *condensed* communication when short and productive communication channels are available. The most cost-effective form of communication arises in small teams working in *one* room. This is also referred to as *osmotic* communication. Information flows simply due to the physical proximity of team members. When a mini-team of developers discusses a topic, the other team members become aware of it (Fig. 4.2). Provided the conversation is not too loud, they can filter it out—unless the topic also concerns them. In that case, they can join in and actively participate in the mini-team's discussion.[5]

Osmotic communication keeps communication costs low, but can only take place if all participants are in the same room (as is the case in the student lab).[6] Thus, it is particularly suitable for *Crystal Clear* projects with one to six team members. In larger projects, where the team can no longer all fit in one room due to the number of participants, osmotic communication can only occur in correspondingly small subteams. However, communication *between* the subteams should at least be *condensed*. This does not

[5] The author has often personally benefited from the advantages of this type of informal communication.

[6] See also Sect. 8.5.5.

happen automatically, but only through appropriate communication-promoting measures (e.g., through regular and detailed video or telephone conferences). Nevertheless, there is already a reduction of information between the subteams, which must be carefully monitored.[7]

4.2.4 Personal Safety

A team member must be able to tell the truth at any time without fear of reprisals. This is especially true if one does not consider the project manager's schedule to be realistic. But personal failures or shortcomings (which occur in every project and are always visible in student projects) must also be admitted within the team without losing face. This way, one can accept support to successfully solve the problem at hand. Only then can the project move forward successfully!

Personal safety arises from trust: trust in the project manager, but also in the supervisor, that personal weaknesses will not lead to negative consequences, but to help and support. But even a successful team needs trust, especially that of the customer.

4.2.5 Focus

Establishing focus areas means that management sets priorities for the project, but also for the company, and communicates them to all team members. Each team member should take responsibility for two focus areas and make these their personal main priorities. Ideally, this will develop personal strengths. To accomplish these tasks, the team member should have at least two consecutive days with two uninterrupted hours each day available.

The background to this requirement is the widespread bad habit of assigning developers to too many different projects. Since all these projects often appear equally important to the developer, it is difficult for them to focus. However, if their main focus areas are defined, they can prioritize the demands placed on them and give precedence to their main focus areas.

4.2.6 Easy Access to Expert Users

As already required in XP (Chap. 3), easy access to expert users (i.e., the customers who use the software system) should ensure that they get the functionality they want and need

[7] The student lab demonstrates that communication, especially over physical distance, must be actively maintained (e.g., through web-based conferencing tools).

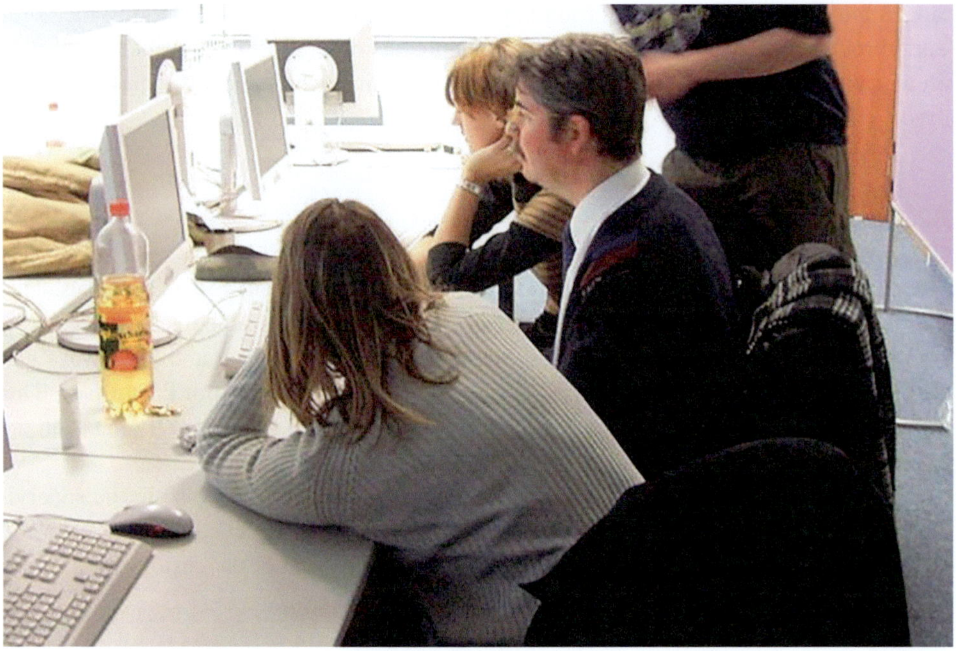

Fig. 4.3 Direct customer feedback in the agile team

(e.g., via a "red phone," Sect. 3.3.3.1). Rapid feedback from the end user through regular deliveries avoids misunderstandings and enables the development team to respond to changing customer requirements (Fig. 4.3).

It is interesting when the customer's representative and the end user(s) differ. In this case, it is especially important that misunderstandings between these groups can be resolved based on the functionality of the freshly delivered release.

4.2.7 Agile Technical Environment with Automated Tests, Configuration Management, and Regular Integrations

This requirement should actually be a matter of course and a "Good Engineering Practice." Automated tests have the advantage of being repeatable at any time. Good, tool-supported configuration management is the key to reliably integrating new functionality or rolling it back. With the support of such tools, at least two weekly system integrations should be possible, which correspondingly increases the number of regular deliveries to the customer.[8]

[8] This will be an important topic in DevOps. See also Chap. 7.

4.3 Crystal Clear

The following will take a closer look at *Crystal Clear*, the process model for smaller project teams. Crystal Clear is an iterative-incremental process model.[9] It is suitable for projects with one to six[10] team members and is mainly used in risk categories C and D (Sect. 4.1). Crystal Clear is *not* suitable for the development of fault-tolerant or life-critical systems.[11]

4.3.1 Characteristics and Practices

According to Alistair Cockburn, Crystal Clear is intended to be a "simple and tolerant set of rules that brings the project into safe waters" (Cockburn 2005). The focus is on good communication and a high tolerance for varying work styles. This "high degree of tolerance" in the process model leaves room for the individual requirements of different projects, because Crystal Clear only requires the first three Crystal project properties (Sect. 4.2):

- Frequent Delivery
- Reflection Improvement
- Osmotic Communication

The required project properties are the result of surveys of successful teams. It should be noted that communication in Crystal Clear takes place as *osmotic* communication. The small project team and the physical proximity of the team members make this possible. The process flow is usually "individualized." The typically *experienced* teams[12] use both well-known and individually developed, project-specific methods. Crystal Clear deliberately allows for this tolerance; no specific tools or project methods are prescribed. The emphasis is rather on communication and *reflection improvement* of the process. The team regularly takes time to question and, if necessary, improve the process flows. The software development process is viewed as an evolving conversation or as a cooperative "game."

[9] See also Sect. 1.3.

[10] possibly up to ten team members! This is supported by experience from the student lab (Sect. 8.5.5) and other literature, such as (Wolf and Roock 2008).

[11] The necessary validation activities there, such as regulatory reviews of the design or tests against pre-formulated and regulator-approved specifications, are not provided for in Crystal Clear.

[12] At least the team leader should "rise above it all," that is, bring a lot of experience with Crystal Clear (Cockburn 2005).

Despite the particularly confusingly few properties required for a Crystal Clear project,[13] Alistair Cockburn describes in great detail what a Crystal Clear project must look like (Cockburn 2005). The following requirements must be *strictly* met:

- Communication channels must be short and productive. Ideally, the team sits in one room (*osmotic communication*).
- Increment cycles typically last one to two months, but never longer than a quarter.[14] Otherwise, one can no longer speak of *frequent delivery*.
- An end user is involved in the project. This can also be only part-time if necessary. It is important that the user interface is developed together with this end user. In addition, their feedback is important. This close interaction with the end user also contributes to *osmotic communication*.
- The project assignment is defined. This can be high-level in the form of business requirements, or low-level in the form of user stories. There must also be high-level statements about the system design.[15]
- The responsibilities for the team's work results must be clearly defined. For each class, module, or procedure, it is defined who is allowed to make changes. These can be individuals or entire sub-teams, but never the whole team.[16]

A team that uses the *following* practices is still in alignment with Crystal Clear:

- The team is small, but sits in adjacent rooms and visits each other frequently. The *personal* conversation (not over the phone) is important![17]
- Borrowing methods from other process models is allowed. For example, the Scrum backlog technique (Sect. 5.3.1) for prioritizing project requirements fits well with Crystal Clear and can also be used here.
- For each code delivery, there is *only one* iteration. However, many demonstrations are conducted for the end user. In this way, their comments can be incorporated into the development process.[18]

---

[13] Compare with Extreme Programming (XP, Chap. 3).

[14] Nowadays, 2 to 4 weeks are more advisable.

[15] If necessary, as rudimentary UML diagrams.

[16] This requirement may, under certain circumstances, be somewhat at odds with *Collective Code Ownership* in XP (Sect. 3.5.3). There, it is required that the *entire* team can make changes to the code.

[17] However, experience in student labs shows that even with adjacent team rooms, communication suffers unless active countermeasures are taken, e.g., through regular team meetings at short intervals (at least daily).

[18] However, the author of this book advises against developing code deliveries in only one iteration each. The longer integration is delayed, the more difficult it becomes. Unexpected problems usually arise at the end of the iteration. The end user also benefits if they not only see the software but can occasionally work with an (interim) release.

- Not all completed increments and partial functionalities are delivered immediately to the end user, who would be overwhelmed by this; instead, for example, they are "collected" by an integrator on a separate notebook or server and made available to the end user at suitable intervals.[19]
- For design documents, custom formats are used instead of standards. However, it is important that the representations are clear in their meaning and understood by all participants.[20]

To provide a distinction, practices should be mentioned whose use does *not* correspond to Crystal Clear, even though they may work in practice:

- The team works in different buildings or at different locations. Communication takes place via telephone, email, or occasional visits.
- Iterations last more than *four* months.
- No review by the user takes place before delivery. As a result, there is a high risk that the user will not get what they actually want (and need).
- The team cannot communicate with an end user, but instead receives the necessary information, for example, from marketing.[21]

Finally, it is also interesting to examine the seventh Crystal property: the establishment of an agile technical environment with automated tests and configuration management. A Crystal Clear project is not strictly required to have this, but it is extremely beneficial and should by now be considered part of "Good Engineering." There should be no way around configuration management these days, but automated regression tests are ultimately not *strictly* necessary for project success.[22] Thus, they remain an important option for a successful project (which the author strongly recommends!).

4.3.2 Roles in the Project Team

Crystal Clear defines eight named roles, of which four must be filled by different people (Cockburn 2005). The four most important project roles are:

---

[19] The author also assigns the task of integration to a special project role, the *integration engineer* (Sects. 8.4 and 9.5.3).

[20] The author advises against this! UML has become so widespread in the meantime that it should be used as the standard for design documents.

[21] The author's experience shows that this usually does not work well! This issue also arises with the Scrum Product Owner and is addressed there as well (Sects. 5.1.1 and 8.5.6).

[22] Even though they massively increase the speed and safety of redesigns.

- Executive Sponsor
- Experienced User
- Lead Designer
- Designer/Programmer

These roles will be briefly introduced below:

4.3.2.1 Executive Sponsor

The sponsor is often also referred to as the *customer*, because they finance the project and thus maintain the contractual relationship with the development team. They represent the project externally and must make economic decisions, especially if the business value of the project changes during its course.[23] They also decide on a possible termination of the project.

4.3.2.2 Experienced User

The importance of this project role has already been highlighted several times in this chapter. The experienced user is familiar with the tasks that are to be performed with the software system to be developed. As a rule, they know how the predecessor system works and are aware of its shortcomings, which usually led to the commissioning of the successor project. They are the point of contact when it comes to designing the user interface of the software system. The experienced user must be available to the team often enough.[24]

4.3.2.3 Lead Designer

The lead designer is the technical leader of the project. They have experience in software development and software design and are responsible for system design. They possess the highest Crystal competency level, *Level 3*. Crystal defines *Level 1* as imitating Crystal practices, *Level 2* as moving beyond these practices, and *Level 3* as the ability to mix practices or invent new ones.

Since there is no explicit project manager in Crystal Clear, the lead designer is also responsible for managing the project. This requires both technical and methodological skills, especially since the lead designer also codes themselves. With the lead designer, a Crystal Clear team thus has at least one team member at Crystal experience level 3. In general, the rule is that small teams without standardized process workflows should mainly consist of experienced members at levels 3 and 2.[25]

---

[23] This is necessary, even if very unpleasant for the project team, as the author knows from personal experience.

[24] This was already discussed in Sect. 4.3.1.

[25] Boehm (1981) provides a comprehensive discussion of the dependency between the experience of team members and the success of the project.

4.3.2.4 Designer/Programmer

This combined role designation demonstrates the close connection between the two activities. A Crystal Clear programmer must *both* design *and* program. If these two activities are split between different team members, misunderstandings arise that are unacceptable in a Crystal Clear project.

In addition to the four main project roles described, there are four further "combined roles" in the project, which can either be assigned to one of the four main roles or temporarily taken on by one of the team members:

4.3.2.5 Coordinator

The coordinator coordinates the project. They record project planning and project status and inform all team members of their findings. They communicate the structure and status of the project, including the release plan, to the sponsor. This task is usually taken on by the lead designer or another qualified team member.[26]

4.3.2.6 Business Expert

The business expert knows the business processes and thus the business context of the project. They provide the developers with the business background and can also assess which elements of the business processes (and thus the business foundations of the software product) might change in the future. Ideally, this additional role can be filled by the experienced user, if they also have the necessary business background for the project. As already mentioned, it is crucial for the project that both the experienced user and the domain expert are available to the team often enough and can answer the team's questions comprehensively and competently.

4.3.2.7 Tester

The general rule is that you cannot test what you have developed yourself (Who likes to find their own mistakes?). Therefore, in a small team, it is advisable for developers to test each other's modules. Even better is if the team can engage external testers for a certain period.[27]

4.3.2.8 Author/Writer

The authors are responsible for creating the documentation, especially user documents such as user manuals or acceptance tests. Often, these tasks are shared among team members, but sometimes a team member or external staff member specializes in this role (Fig. 4.4).

---

[26] Cockburn also suggests that this role could be rotated among different team members (Cockburn 2005). The author advises against this, as the project should always present the same "face" to the sponsor, especially externally.

[27] Automated tests and detailed test plans are also helpful here.

Fig. 4.4 The author of the new CMS informs the student team about the progress (Content Management System for managing project documentation)

In Sect. 8.5.5 the "functioning" of Crystal Clear in the student lab is examined. The interaction of a Crystal Clear team is analyzed in more detail, and the problems that arise, especially in the area of reflection improvement, are discussed.

References

Boehm B (1981) Software Engineering Economics. Prentice-Hall.

Cockburn A. (1996) https://alistair.cockburn.us. Zugriff September 2024.

Cockburn A (2005) Crystal Clear: A human powered Methodology for small Teams. Pearson. Dt. Übersetzung: Crystal Clear: Agile Software-Entwicklung für kleine Teams. mitp-Verlag.

Hättich N (2007) Das agile Prozessmodell Crystal, Studienarbeit, DHBW/BA Lörrach, Studiengang Informationstechnik.

Wolf H, Roock A (2008) Agile Softwareentwicklung—ein Überblick. dpunkt Verlag.

Scrum

5

In contrast to the agile process models discussed so far, Scrum is an agile project *management* method. The focus is not on team collaboration, but on the *course of the project*. Notable are the project roles defined in Scrum: Product Owner, Team, and Scrum Master, especially the absence of a "classic" role, that of the project manager. In addition to the responsibilities of the project roles, Scrum regulates the project workflow in the form of *Sprints*, i.e., development cycles of a few weeks.

Scrum differs from the agile process models discussed so far, as it is an agile project *management* method, summarized in the *Scrum Guide* (Schwaber and Sutherland 2020). Questions of collaboration and team structure are not the focus, but rather the course of the project. Nevertheless, it is a very interesting agile method with widespread adoption. Scrum follows the idea of *Lean Management*, "lean" management, as particularly practiced at Toyota[1] (Gloger 2009).

Scrum was developed in the early 1990s by Ken Schwaber and Jeff Sutherland, with the basic concepts laid out in (Schwaber 2004). The project roles defined in Scrum are notable

- Product Owner
- Team
- ScrumMaster

and thus, in particular, the absence of a "classic" role, that of the project manager. In addition to the responsibilities of the project roles, Scrum regulates the project workflow in the form of *Sprints*—development cycles of a few weeks.

[1] Even though Ken Schwaber repeatedly emphasizes that Scrum did *not* originate from Lean Production.

E. Hanser, *Agile Processes—Agile Teams*, https://doi.org/10.1007/978-3-662-72726-3_5

5.1 Scrum—The Project Roles

The following section will take a closer look at the project roles that are mandatory in Scrum.

5.1.1 Product Owner

The *Product Owner* adopts the perspective of the end customer. They steer software development and work closely with the development team. Similar to the customer in XP (Sect. 3.3.3.1), they are constantly available to the development team. Unlike the XP customer, the Product Owner alone determines "where the journey is headed"[2] (Pichler 2008).

The role of the Product Owner is twofold. They must not assume the "innocence" of the customer and simply wish for new features, but must also immediately consider the feasibility of implementation. This creates the risk that great ideas are not realized because the Product Owner does not believe in their feasibility.

Specifically, the Product Owner has the following responsibilities:

5.1.1.1 Requirements Management

The Product Owner captures the customer's requirements for the software and describes them in the form of a product concept[3] and the *Product Backlog.* A traditional Scrum Product Backlog contains all types of requirements or activities that need to be completed in connection with the project.[4] The goal is always to create added value for the customer. The Product Owner prioritizes and estimates the requirements as the basis for the team's work. The Product Backlog is "alive." It is constantly updated and expanded throughout the agile process.

5.1.1.2 Release Management

The Product Owner is responsible for the success of the project. They alone decide on functionality, costs, and deadlines. Thus, they are also responsible for the delivery of the various releases.[5] They therefore create a release plan and adjust it if necessary. The Product Owner is well advised to do this in consultation with the team. The effort estimates from the team form the basis for their planning.

---

[2] And thus becomes the "single wringable neck," as this role is called at Yahoo! (Pichler 2008).

[3] Answering questions such as: What do we as a company want to achieve with the product? What is the purpose of the product?

[4] For the Product Owner, it is easiest to first focus on requirements that create added value for the customer. These requirements are known from (Sect. 3.3.1.1) as *User Stories* (XP), see also (Wirdemann 2009).

[5] Versions.

5.1.1.3 Communication

The Product Owner must constantly communicate with the team and with all involved stakeholders, especially the end customer. Since the Product Owner must work closely with the team, one can speak of internal and external impact from the team's perspective. Internally, the Product Owner should ideally be available to the team for a certain amount of time each day (at least one hour), while being easily reachable for the rest of the day.[6] Externally, the Product Owner communicates especially with end customer groups to obtain the earliest possible feedback on new software functionality.

It is important to equip the Product Owner with sufficient authority and time to fulfill the above-mentioned tasks. Product Owner is a full-time job![7] Only then can the success of the project be ensured.

5.1.2 Team

The team develops ("delivers") the product, i.e., the software. Its composition is crucial for the success of the project. This is not only about professional qualifications, but also about team psychology, that is, how well the team members "fit" together. This will be examined in more detail in Chaps. 8 and 9. It is important to give potential team members the opportunity to apply for interesting projects. This at least ensures that there is genuine interest.[8]

Scrum does not further specify the distribution of roles within the team. As already mentioned, Scrum is a management method. However, it is clear that all roles, or more precisely, all *skills* necessary for successful project development must be present. Here, too, reference is made to Chaps. 8 and 9.

A team must have the following characteristics:

5.1.2.1 Self-organized and small

Within a sprint (i.e., an iteration), the team organizes itself. Only the team members decide which tasks need to be completed to achieve a sprint goal, and who is responsible for each task.[9] The team has no team leader, and thus no traditional project manager. This is partly due to the size of the team: An ideal Scrum team has seven ± two members (Schwaber 2004). On the other hand, according to Scrum, a team leader can be omitted because the team conducts its daily work within a "framework" of reports and meetings, thus providing

[6] Based on the author's experience, it is advisable to ensure availability via a "red phone," a mobile phone possibly with a secret number known only to the team (see also Sect. 3.3.3.1).

[7] If this is not possible, they must at least be allocated 50% of their time for the project (Pichler 2008).

[8] Google encourages developers to apply for projects!

[9] The team is *empowered* (authorized).

Fig 5.1 Team in a shared office

"guardrails" for project execution.[10] A prerequisite for this way of working is that members are full-time on the team. Agile techniques require a team that sees itself as a unit. This team spirit cannot develop if some team members "hop" from project to project.

The team's workspace must also meet the requirements: An agile team must communicate *osmotically* (Cockburn 2005). This requires physical proximity. The team *must* have a shared office[11] (Fig. 5.1).

Osmotic communication typically occurs in such a physical setting as follows:

- A team member gets a coffee, leaves their workstation, and strolls past others. Automatically and without any effort ("osmotically"), they pick up snippets of conversation from others. Either these are uninteresting, or they relate to the team member's work. The team member joins the discussion.

[10] These are: Sprint Backlog, Sprint Burndown Chart, and the Daily Scrum meeting (see also Sect. 5.2).

[11] In the author's experience, this requirement is hardly negotiable and can only be partially replaced by videoconferencing and online collaboration tools (even though this is done in some projects). The resulting loss of osmotic communication is significant and must at least be compensated for by regular team events.

- Due to the physical proximity, you overhear snippets of conversation from developers sitting nearby without intending to. If the topic concerns you, you join the discussion.

Osmotic communication always happens "in passing." You would be surprised how many important things you learn this way!

A note on open-plan offices: The team area should be separated by partitions. It is advisable not to skimp on space. After the partitions, the first desk should not immediately follow; there should be enough "breathing room" around the team area. Otherwise, the team will be constantly disturbed by passersby talking *over* the walls.

5.1.2.2 Multidisciplinary and autonomous

Team members must cover all the skills required to achieve the project goals. Software architects must be present, as well as database specialists, programmers, quality assurance engineers, testers, documenters, etc. It is important that these specialists do not insist on their traditional project roles. In principle, every team member must be able to take on any task in the project (and be able to do so), and thus also share their knowledge with others.

The Scrum team must be independent ("empowered"). Once a sprint goal has been defined, the team must be able to achieve the goal without external dependencies or outside help. If this is not ensured, the composition of the team must be improved by bringing in external expertise.

5.1.3 ScrumMaster

The ScrumMaster (*Change Agent*) is responsible for the process. He is the *friend* of the team. He coaches the team regarding adherence to the process. Especially with teams inexperienced in Scrum, he helps to establish the process. If he does his job well, he ideally makes himself redundant! However, experience shows that this rarely happens, as teams tend to modify the chosen process (sometimes beyond recognition) (which the author does not fundamentally consider alarming, see Chaps. 8 and 9). Therefore, the ScrumMaster must repeatedly intervene and check the correctness of the process. With experienced teams, however, he can gradually reduce the time he spends with the team. Ideally, the relationship between ScrumMaster and team is a one-to-one relationship.[12] The ScrumMaster works with the team.

The tasks of the ScrumMaster are:

5.1.3.1 Introducing Scrum and Supporting Product Owner and Team

The ScrumMaster establishes the process within the team. He identifies obstacles such as entrenched mindsets or "outdated" working methods. He helps the team get to know

[12] In the author's practice, at most one-to-three!

Scrum and gain experience with it. He explains the process flows to the team and supports them in this. He answers any questions that arise about the process. It is also important to protect the team from outside influences. Under no circumstances should members be pulled away by supervisors for other tasks (not even temporarily). The goal is to let the team work undisturbed.

The ScrumMaster also supports the Product Owner. Usually, the Product Owner is also inexperienced at first and needs help. It is important to prevent the Product Owner from falling into the role of project manager. (This risk also exists for the ScrumMaster!) Although the Product Owner must work closely with the team, once he initiates a Scrum Sprint, he must not disturb the team further. The ScrumMaster must ensure this.

5.1.3.2 Removing Impediments

The ScrumMaster must address deviations from the target process, known as *Impediments* (Gloger 2009). Impediments prevent the team from being efficient. These blockages must be resolved. The ScrumMaster records all deviations in a separate list, the *Scrum Impediment Backlog*. He must work through this list step by step. Usually, more complex blockages cannot be resolved in a short time.

Impediments can be problems in team psychology (for example, if team members do not get along), but can also arise from misunderstandings of Scrum roles, such as a Product Owner trying to act as project manager. A missing or unsuitable Product Owner can also quickly become an essential problem. Here, the ScrumMaster's sensitivity is required to defuse the situation and find a suitable Product Owner.[13]

5.1.3.3 Serving the Team

The ScrumMaster leads the team. Every coach knows that, simply by virtue of his greater knowledge, he has a leadership function. However, this must not be abused. The ScrumMaster should maintain a collegial leadership style. His task is to remove obstacles for the team, not to assign or distribute tasks within the team. This is the sole responsibility of the team itself.

5.1.4 Other Scrum Roles

In the literature, one sometimes finds additional Scrum project roles,[14] which are useful for understanding the process, but also appear in "classic" process models:

---

[13] If that is within his power.

[14] See, for example, (Gloger 2009). However, these roles are not mentioned in (Schwaber 2004).

5.1.4.1 The Customer

The customer commissions the product development. He is responsible for the budget, both for internal and external project assignments. He corresponds to the role of the customer as we know it from other agile methods, but does not assume project responsibility.

5.1.4.2 The User

The user is the eventual user of the software. Typically, he already has experience with the predecessor software (if such exists) and can provide the team with valuable tips regarding *usability*. Team and Product Owner would do well to heed such tips and incorporate them into sprint planning, as this greatly increases the acceptance of the software.[15] After the sprint, the user will check whether his suggestions have been implemented.

Separating the roles of customer and user is not unproblematic. In classic, non-agile projects, it reflects reality, while other agile methods[16] instead try to find a customer who can also adequately fulfill the role of user. This way, he can immediately assess the feasibility of a request and thus becomes more reliable for the team.

5.1.4.3 Management

Management provides the framework within which a project is carried out. It usually resolves the problems identified by the ScrumMaster in the project environment.

5.1.5 Risk of Role Misuse

Since Scrum lacks the classic role of *project manager*, there is a particular risk in inexperienced Scrum teams that the Product Owner or ScrumMaster will assume this role, causing the "lived" process to deviate from Scrum. The problem is that, with the introduction of Scrum, former project managers often take on the role of ScrumMaster. This naturally increases the risk of "relapsing" into old patterns of thinking. With inexperienced Product Owners, there is a risk that they will violate the team's autonomy.

Therefore, when introducing Scrum, care must be taken to ensure that Product Owner or ScrumMaster do not misuse their roles. It is advisable to have Product Owner, ScrumMaster, and team repeatedly coached by external Scrum experts over the course of the project.

---

[15] However, the author's experience shows that not all user requests can usually be accommodated. Sometimes requests conflict, and often they cannot be realized within the available budget. This conflict arises from the separation of the roles of customer and user.

[16] For example, XP (Chap. 3) and MAP (Chap. 9).

5.2 Scrum—the Process

The following will examine the interaction of Scrum roles: What does the workflow of a Scrum project look like?

5.2.1 Scrum Flow—Overview

The Scrum process flow is kept simple (Fig. 5.2). At the beginning stands the *vision* of the Product Owner, with a brief description of the product, an estimate of the effort involved, and possible milestones.[17] Ultimately, the question must be clarified as to whether it makes sense to pursue the project before entering the actual Scrum process. Once this business decision has been made, the *Product Backlog* is filled by the Product Owner.[18] Here, all requirements for the software are recorded and prioritized.

The software is developed by the team in iteration cycles, the so-called *Sprints*. All Sprints are of equal length; typically, a maximum of 30 days is chosen for a Sprint.[19] The chosen Sprint length must be adhered to! At the beginning of the Sprint, a *Sprint Planning Meeting* takes place, in which the team creates the *Sprint Backlog*. If necessary, the team must first work with the Product Owner to refine the work packages ("items") to be addressed in the Sprint. This is done in the (optional) *Sprint Backlog Refinement*.

The Sprint Backlog defines which requirements are to be completed for the next increment of the software and which activities are necessary to achieve this. Sprint planning is carried out according to the specifications in the Product Backlog. The Sprint then begins, i.e., the actual implementation of the next increment of the software. Here, the team develops the new software increment with the features specified in the Sprint Backlog, without external interference.

Every day, at the same place and at the same time, a team meeting is held, called the *Daily Scrum*. It is important that this meeting is kept short. In addition to the team, the ScrumMaster *must* be present. The Product Owner, on the other hand, *should* be present. Relevant guests are allowed, but do not have the right to speak. The team has the opportunity to coordinate work and address problems, either solving them immediately or at least passing them on to the ScrumMaster or Product Owner.

At the end of the Sprint is the *Sprint Review*. Here, the resulting software increment is reviewed and accepted by the Product Owner. Only complete and error-free work results are accepted. The Sprint concludes with the *Sprint Retrospective*, which gives the team

---

[17] Naturally, these are not reliable estimates, but rather *goals* one would like to achieve. They must later be substantiated by the team through effort estimations (or not, as the case may be).

[18] At this stage, the Product Owner can already be supported by the team. However, responsibility remains with the Product Owner.

[19] Currently, most companies have found 14 days to be effective.

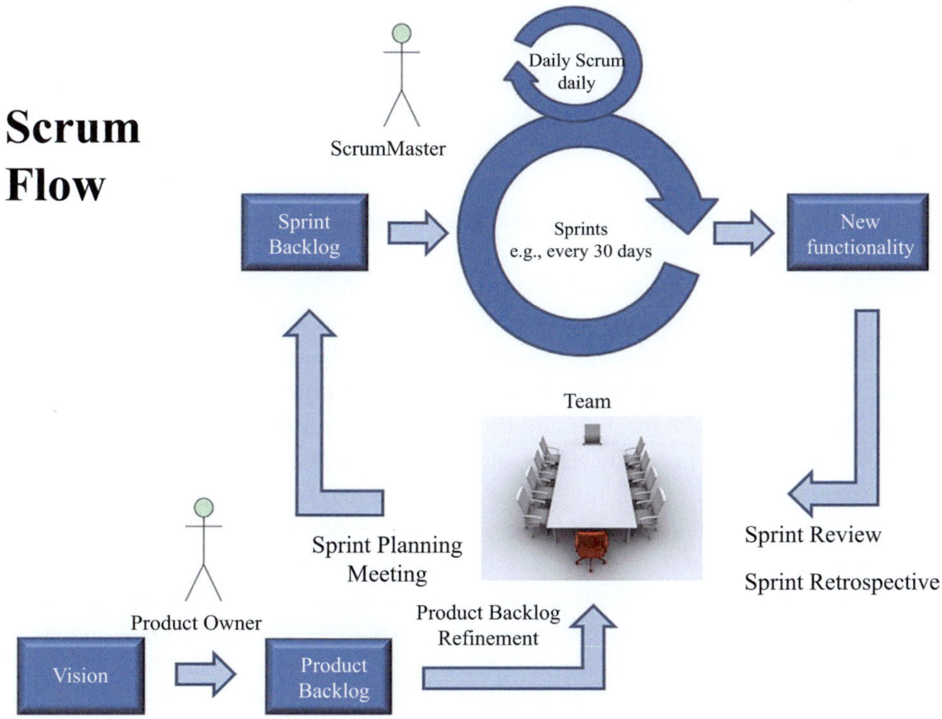

Fig 5.2 Scrum Flow

the opportunity to reflect on the course of the Sprint, especially on team collaboration and possible improvements. These form the basis for the next Sprint.

5.2.2 Sprint—Details

5.2.2.1 Sprint Length

Typically, in iterative process models, the features of the software to be included in the next increment are defined. The effort required for their implementation is estimated by the team at the latest at this point, and features may be postponed if necessary to prevent the iteration from lasting too long. In larger projects, iteration lengths of two to three months are not uncommon. The duration of each iteration varies from one to the next, as the focus is placed on implementing the specific features of the software, and ultimately (from a developer's perspective) there is no advantage in having a constant iteration length.

This is different in Scrum: Scrum Sprints have *fixed* iteration lengths. Ken Schwaber describes the introduction of fixed Sprint lengths as a reduction of project complexity for the team: the team only needs to focus on a fixed period to reach the next goal. Step by step, it manages the increasing complexity of the project (Schwaber 2004). While initially a Sprint length of up to 30 days was favored, most projects have now adopted a fixed Sprint length of 14 days (*Timeboxing*). The team agrees on an end date with the Product Owner according to the Sprint length. This end date (usually a Friday) *must* be met. However, the team must also not be disturbed on the way to the end date.

5.2.2.2 Start of the Sprint—the Sprint Planning Meeting and Product Backlog Refinement

At the beginning of the Sprint, the Sprint Planning Meeting takes place. The Product Owner must define a *Sprint Goal*. It must be a step towards the project goal and provide value to the project. The Product Owner must define the Sprint Goal so that it is clearly recognizable to the team. The team commits to implementing the goal and the associated software features. After the meeting, the Product Owner can no longer make changes to the goal for the current Sprint. Therefore, the goal must be chosen carefully.

For complex requirements, it may make sense to refine the work packages ("items") from the Product Backlog that are to be addressed in the Sprint. This is done in the (optional) *Sprint Backlog Refinement*. For this, the team meets with the Product Owner *before*[20] the Sprint Planning Meeting and has the relevant items explained. Questions from the team help refine the understanding of the tasks. The goal is a smooth process in the subsequent planning meeting.

It is the Product Owner's task, according to the Product Backlog and the previously created release plan,[21] to define the requirements for the product that are to be implemented in the current Sprint. The prioritization of a requirement in the Product Backlog naturally plays a major role. It is also important that it has been clarified in advance whether the requirements to be implemented in the Sprint can be fulfilled without problems.[22] This can be done by the Product Owner and selected team members. This also includes a reasonable estimation of the effort required to implement a requirement (Sect. 5.2.2.3).

In the Sprint Planning Meeting, the team creates the Sprint planning document, the *Sprint Backlog*, according to the Sprint Goal and the requirements selected by the Product Owner. Here, all features of the next software increment to be implemented in the Sprint are identified, the so-called *Sprint Backlog Items*. All activities necessary to realize the increment are also identified. An iterative approach is recommended here as well—a step-by-step refinement of the activities to be performed and the estimation of

[20] Often in the middle of the preceding Sprint.

[21] The release plan provides information on when which feature of the software can be expected (Sect. 5.3.3).

[22] If there are technical doubts, a technical prototype may need to be created in advance. (Caution: creating a prototype must be entered as an additional requirement in the Product Backlog).

the required effort, while simultaneously specifying the new features of the software "ordered" by the Product Owner.[23]

Both the Product Owner, the team, and the ScrumMaster must be present throughout the planning meeting: the Product Owner to be available for questions from the team, the ScrumMaster to monitor the team's self-organization. The planning meeting ends when the allotted time (for 14-day Sprints, usually no more than half a day) has elapsed. The result of the Sprint Planning Meeting must be a realistic Sprint Backlog. The requirements the team has committed to implementing must be defined and estimated, along with the associated activities.

5.2.2.3 Effort Estimation and Planning Poker

In principle, the effort for a Sprint Backlog Item (i.e. a User Story) can be estimated by the team in person-hours. It should not exceed four to 16 hours (Schwaber 2004). For this, a "classic" estimation method such as the Delphi method can be used (see, e.g., Vorgrimmler and Wübben 2003).

However, *Planning Poker* is popular among agile teams. Typically, a card deck is used for this, with card values based on the *Fibonacci sequence* and indicating the complexity of the task to be estimated in *Story Points*. The card values are typically 0, 1, 2, 3, 5, 8, 13, 20, 40, 100, ∞. When estimating the effort for a backlog item, each team member draws (initially face down) one of these cards: 0 means the task can be solved in one's sleep, 1 means the task is "baby easy." 2 can be done "on the side," 3 is "not rocket science." 5 is already "challenging," 8 raises the team member's temperature, while at 13 you might get your fingers burned. At 20 you have to "take the bull by the horns," 40 is a mammoth task, 100 is an iceberg, where you have to fear that most of the task "lies beneath the surface." ∞ is the proverbial "jack of all trades." Sometimes there is also a "?" card, if (even after refinement) it is completely unclear how the backlog task should be solved.[24] All cards are revealed simultaneously, so that the team can then discuss, for example starting from the highest and lowest estimates, and agree together on a "difficulty level" for the task.

It is important to note that the Fibonacci numbers do not correspond to effort in hours, but rather represent the complexity of the task. After a few sprints, the team knows from experience how many backlog items of various difficulty levels it can handle in a sprint.[25]

---

[23] Based on the author's experience, the use of User Story Cards (known from XP) is recommended here. See also Sect. 5.3.2 and Chap. 3.

[24] The author finds, for example, the cards in the "Agile Starter Box" from Ulassa to be very well designed.

[25] There are repeated attempts to convert story points into hours. This is at best possible with a certain "statistical" approach (see Cohn 2024).

5.2.2.4 Definition of Done

To estimate effort correctly, it is important to have a shared understanding of when a task is considered complete. The Definition of Done specifies the criteria that must be met to properly complete a backlog item (Schwaber and Sutherland 2020). In particular, the required functionality must be clearly defined, and the required quality criteria must be met. This must be demonstrated through appropriate tests.

5.2.2.5 Daily Scrum

Every day, at the same place and at the same time, a team meeting called the *Daily Scrum* takes place. It must last only *15 min* (Schwaber 2004),[26] the team and its ScrumMaster *must* be present. The presence of the Product Owner is not strictly required. However, if time permits, they should attend. This way, they can learn firsthand what is on the team's mind. However, these meetings are not intended for the Product Owner to try to influence the course of the sprint. Guests are allowed at the Daily Scrum, especially all project stakeholders, but they do not have the right to speak.

The goal of the Daily Scrum is to coordinate the team's work (self-organization!) and to address emerging problems. For this, the Sprint Backlog must be up to date. The team must be informed about the current status of the project during the Daily Scrum! Given the brevity of the Daily Scrum, each team member should only answer the following three questions (Schwaber 2004):

- What have I done for the project since the last Daily Scrum?
- What do I plan to do for the project before the next Daily Scrum?
- What is preventing me from working as effectively as possible?

The ScrumMaster is responsible for ensuring that these questions are answered by every team member, without the team falling into (endless) discussions. Some psychological skill is needed to recognize where personal sensitivities are at play and where there are real problems that typically also hinder other team members. Minor issues can often be resolved by the team immediately after the Daily Scrum. More complex problems must be identified and passed on to the ScrumMaster or Product Owner. It is important that these individuals take the reported problems *seriously* and understand that unresolved issues generally reduce the team's performance.

5.2.2.6 Sprint Process

Scrum is purely a management method and therefore does not prescribe any development practices to the team. However, it makes sense to apply practices known from other agile methods, such as XP (see Chap. 3).

---

[26] The author has had good experiences with *standup meetings*, i.e., meetings held standing up (often at the coffee machine). Such meetings usually remain brief!

It is important that the team can develop during the sprint *without external interruptions*. During the sprint, requirements are frozen. They may not be changed. Only in this way does the team have a chance to meet the targeted end date. At the end date, the sprint is *finished*, and the results must be presented to the Product Owner.

5.2.2.7 End of the Sprint—Sprint Review

At the end of the sprint is the Sprint Review. The Product Owner is given the opportunity to review and accept the resulting software increment. According to Schwaber, the Sprint Review meeting is limited to a maximum of four hours (timeboxing, Schwaber 2004); for 14-day sprints, two hours are usually sufficient. It is important that the Product Owner only accepts complete and error-free deliverables. Even nearly finished or faulty results are not accepted; incomplete results are considered not done. Such results are, for example, recorded in the Product Backlog and become the subject of the next sprint. The goal is to fix them as quickly as possible (in the next sprint) to complete the current software increment.

The increment of the software developed by the team must be presented as a live demo on a central integration machine. The Product Owner should be able to perform tests on the software themselves and verify (from their perspective) the correct functioning of the software. *Only the Product Owner* decides whether the result is accepted or not! Under no circumstances should the Product Owner accept individual results on local machines. The author has found that integrating such results on a machine is not trivial (see Sect. 8.4) and usually requires considerable effort. Therefore, integration is clearly part of the sprint and must be successfully completed at the end.

In addition to the Product Owner and the team, the ScrumMaster must also attend the Sprint Review. Their task is to moderate the meeting. It is also interesting to have end users of the software present. They can provide valuable tips and ideas for further development of the software. Acceptance of the software increases significantly if an end user can regularly observe the software's progress.

5.2.2.8 Sprint Retrospective

The Sprint Retrospective takes place immediately after the Sprint Review. This meeting is also time-boxed. Ken Schwaber requires a maximum duration of three hours (Schwaber 2004), but in the author's experience, two hours are sufficient for 14-day sprints. The Sprint Retrospective gives the team an opportunity to reflect on the course of the sprint, particularly on team collaboration and necessary improvement measures. These form the basis for the next sprint.[27] Often, it is about introducing, abolishing, or modifying agile practices that the team considers useful or no longer useful (Chap. 8).

---

[27] Of course, this is not an invention of Scrum; in Crystal, this meeting is called a *Reflection Workshop* (Chap. 4).

Participants in the Sprint Retrospective are necessarily the team and the ScrumMaster. The Product Owner's participation is optional. However, experience shows that the Product Owner's understanding of the team grows when they attend the Sprint Retrospective. The ScrumMaster's task is to collect and record the changes proposed by the team. It is not their job to present solutions to the team. Thus, they take on the role of a moderator! The team prioritizes the proposed changes and discusses them in this order. Changes that are jointly agreed upon are implemented in the next sprint. The goal of the Sprint Retrospective is to optimize the process. Problems that are raised but do not lead to any changes are frustrating and undermine the acceptance of the Sprint Retrospective. After all, why should one spend time in an improvement meeting if no improvement comes out of it!

5.3 Scrum Artifacts

The most important Scrum artifacts are the Product Backlog, the Sprint Backlog, and the Release Plan with Burndown Chart. The backlogs are planning tools, while the release plan serves to inform when which feature of the software can be expected. The Burndown Chart is used to monitor project progress.

5.3.1 Product Backlog

The Product Backlog is the central document for capturing and managing requirements. The Product Backlog manages *items*—the functionalities to be delivered. A typical Product Backlog is shown in Fig. 5.3.

After the functionalities have been collected in the Product Backlog,[28] they are prioritized and the implementation effort is estimated. This is done by the Product Owner (ideally with the help of the team).

In practice, an electronic representation of the Product Backlog has also proven effective. This can be done using a common bug tracking tool (Fig. 5.4) or a commercial tool such as *Jira*.[29] It is important that the Product Backlog is clearly visible to all team members, the Product Owner, and the ScrumMaster, e.g., displayed on a large LCD screen in the team office. If this is not the case, it is not possible to quickly glance at the overall project status "in passing."[30] When stored electronically, the items can easily be transferred to the Sprint Backlog during the sprint.

---

[28] A functionality is usually a row in the Product Backlog!

[29] https://www.atlassian.com/de/software/jira.

[30] This has proven to be a clear disadvantage in the author's student lab. The team then tends to assess the project situation too positively if *all* participants do not constantly have the current overall status in view.

Priority	Topic	Description	Acceptance criteria	Estimated effort [in person-days]
3	Input mask for subscribers	The input mask must be expanded to include the "Campaign" field.	Only valid campaigns may be entered.	1
1	Mailing system	Sending must be made interruptible	Interrupted sending must be resumed at this point.	5
2	Create new campaign	New "Campaign" screen with assignment to newsletters (list box for selection)	Campaign must be visible after creation	3

Fig 5.3 Typical Product Backlog for a newsletter distribution system

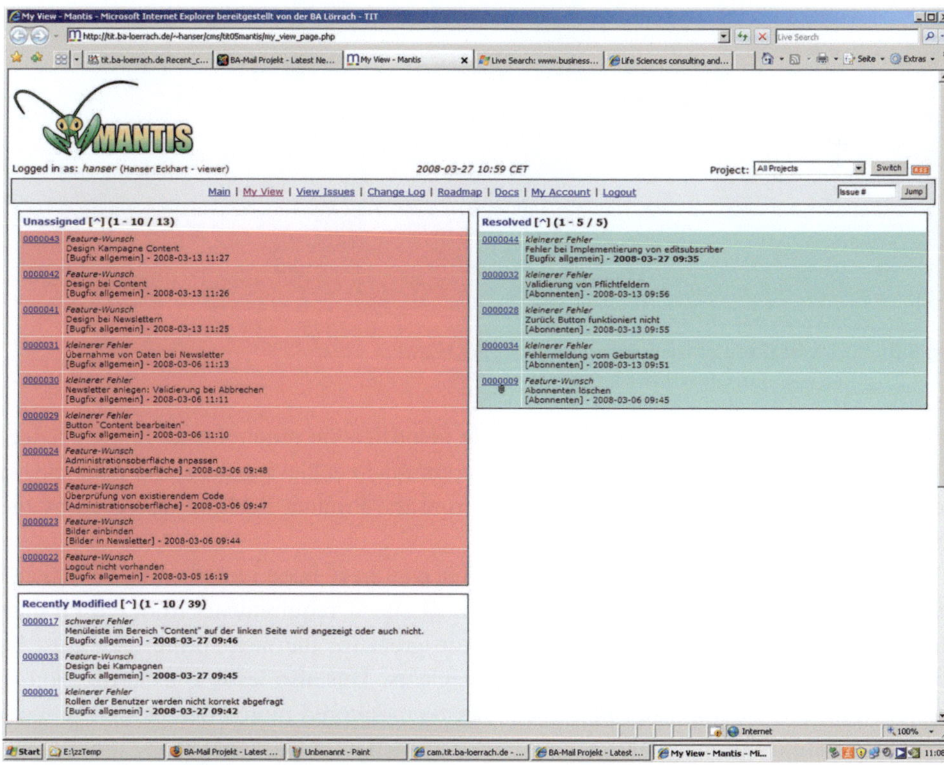

Fig 5.4 Product Backlog in electronic form

5.3.2 Sprint Backlog

The Sprint Backlog is a list of activities that the team must complete within a Scrum sprint. It serves the team for organizing the sprint. The Sprint Backlog is the result of the sprint planning meeting (Sect. 5.2.2.2). In the planning meeting, the Product Owner

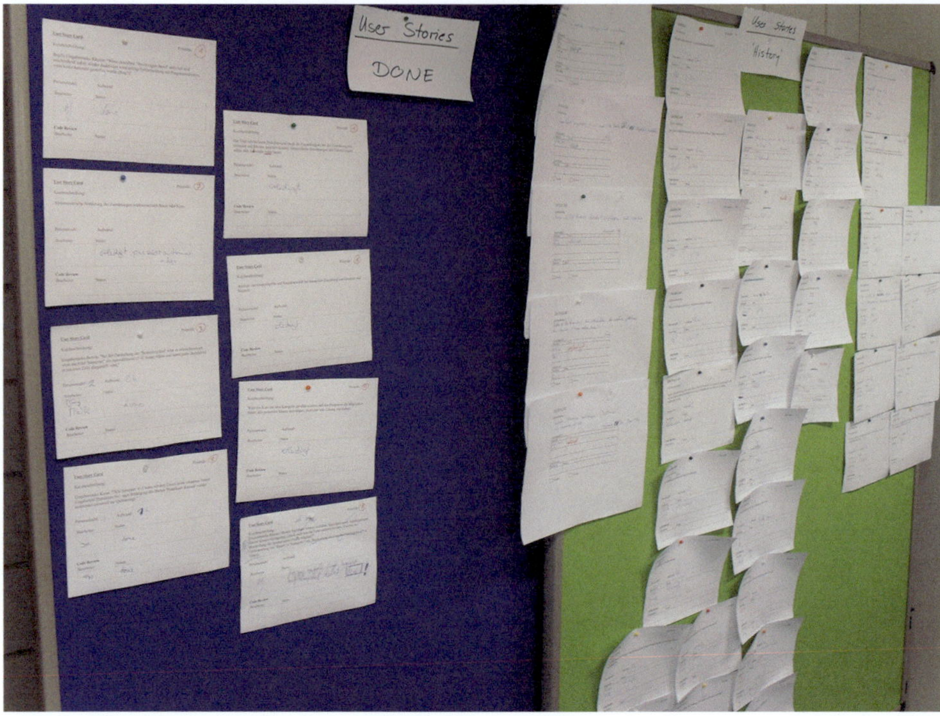

Fig 5.5 Sprint Backlog as user stories on a display board

communicates the sprint goal to the team. He identifies the requirements in the Product Backlog that the team must fulfill. The team commits to achieving the sprint goal and, in doing so, to implementing the requirements from the Product Backlog identified by the Product Owner.

Once the requirements assigned to the sprint goal have been identified and estimated (Sect. 5.2.2.3), they are added to the Sprint Backlog. If requirements from the Product Backlog have been adopted whose effort is too great for the next sprint, they must be broken down into several smaller (sub-)requirements. This also leads to a clarification of the requirements. Small "work packages" can be monitored more effectively. The team knows the status of each Sprint Backlog item (i.e. each work package) at any time.

It makes sense to represent the Sprint Backlog items as *User Stories*.[31] As in XP (Sect. 3.3.1.1), these can then be hung as individual cards (e.g., A5 landscape) on a pin-board. The Sprint Backlog in list form then contains only a brief summary of the items to maintain an overview (Fig. 5.5).

---

[31] See also (Wirdemann 2009).

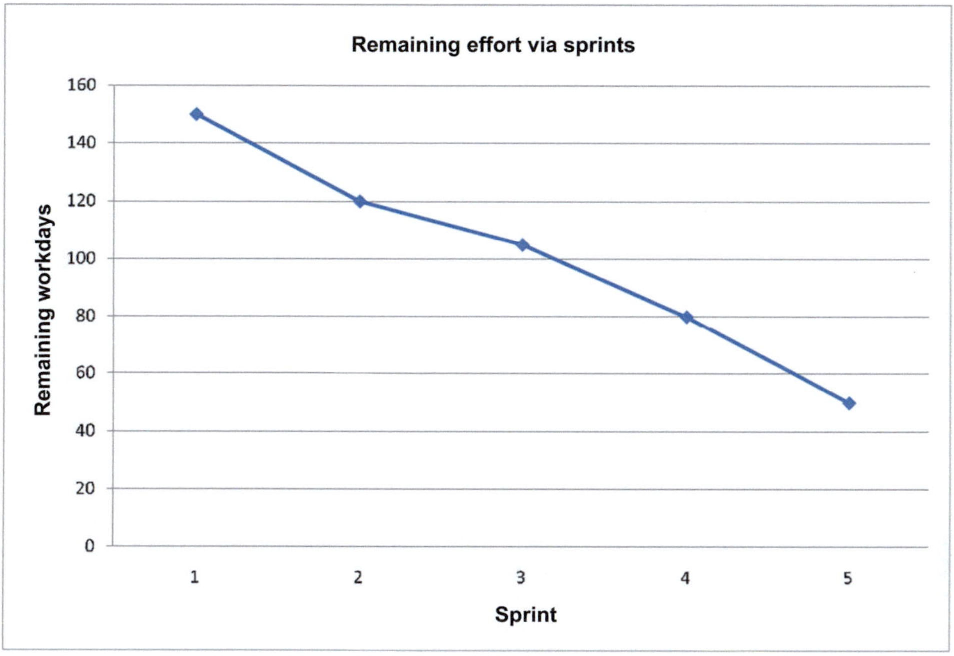

Fig 5.6 Release Burndown Chart

The Sprint Backlog is a "living" document. It is updated daily, ideally before the Daily Scrum, and thus always reflects the current status of the sprint. If the Sprint Backlog is implemented as user stories on a display board, the daily update can be carried out particularly easily. Unfinished user stories should be placed on the left and completed ones on the right of the board. Even better is to use two display boards in different colors.

5.3.3 Release Plan and Burndown Chart

For larger projects, it is advisable to create a Release Plan. This is the responsibility of the Product Owner. The release plan schedules the sequence of sprints, i.e., the iterations of the project. Increment by increment, the software product approaches the final solution. The release plan shows how many sprints are needed or within what timeframe the project is expected to take place.

Monitoring the release planning with the help of the *Release Burndown Chart* is particularly interesting. Here, the total remaining effort in the project is shown for each sprint (Fig. 5.6).

Release planning is not without controversy in agile projects. How does this overall planning fit with an agile approach, which is specifically designed to accommodate changing requirements, so-called "moving targets" (Chap. 3)? The answer lies in Scrum itself: While a sprint must not be interrupted, i.e., the requirements of the sprint cannot be changed (Sect. 5.2), this can certainly happen between sprints. Changed requirements inevitably lead to an adjustment of the release plan. However, this is only taken into account at the next sprint (and not in the current sprint!).

References

Cockburn A (2005) Crystal Clear – Agile Software-Entwicklung für kleine Teams. mitp-Verlag
Cohn M (2024) How Many Hours is a Story Point Worth? ScrumAlliance, https://resources.scrumalliance.org/Article/hours-story-point-worth, Zugriff Oktober 2024
Gloger B (2009) Scrum – Produkte zuverlässig und schnell entwickeln. Hanser
Pichler R (2008) Scrum – Agiles Projektmanagement erfolgreich einsetzen. dpunkt Verlag
Schwaber K (2004) Agile Project Management with Scrum. Microsoft Press
Schwaber K und Sutherland J (2020) The Scrum Guide. https://scrumguides.org/docs/scrumguide/v2020/2020-Scrum-Guide-US.pdf, Zugriff Oktober 2024
Vorgrimmler D und Wübben D. (2003) Die Delphi-Methode und ihre Eignung als Prognoseinstrument. Statistisches Bundesamt, https://www.destatis.de/DE/Methoden/WISTA-Wirtschaft-und-Statistik/2003/08/delphi-methode-082003.pdf, Zugriff Oktober 2024
Wirdemann R (2009) Scrum mit User Stories. Hanser

6 Kanban

In contrast to Scrum, the agile process model Kanban allows significantly more freedom regarding the execution of the process and the definition of project roles. Existing roles can be retained when switching to Kanban; the goal of the development cycle is a steady "flow" of project results.

The Japanese word "Kanban" can be translated as "card" or "signal card." The term "ticket" has also become common. Originally, a "Kanban card" is a way to limit the inflow into a system. A famous example is the admission control to the Imperial Gardens in Tokyo[1] using Kanban tickets (Anderson 2011): A limited quota of Kanban cards is distributed among visitors. Only visitors with such a "ticket" are allowed entry. People who leave the gardens return their ticket. Thus, the Imperial Gardens themselves are the (capacity-limited) system. Visiting the gardens represents an unfinished task, which transitions to the "completed" state when the ticket is returned. The number of "open" tickets held by visitors is also referred to as "Work in Progress" (WIP).

Kanban gained great significance through its use in the "Toyota Production System."[2] However, here we will focus exclusively on the application of Kanban in software projects.

6.1 Software Kanban

Kanban can be easily applied in software development. Work packages and tasks are represented as Kanban tickets and displayed on a "Kanban board." The tickets individually pass through a phase model (see Sect. 1.2) until they reach the "done" state. If necessary,

[1] See, for example, https://www.gotokyo.org/de/story/guide/a-noble-look-at-tokyos-imperial-palace-a-guide-to-the-royal-residence/index.html.

[2] See also https://mag.toyota.co.uk/kanban-toyota-production-system/.

E. Hanser, *Agile Processes—Agile Teams*, https://doi.org/10.1007/978-3-662-72726-3_6

the phase model may need to be traversed multiple times until the result meets the specification. The "Work in Progress" (WIP) is the total number of all started and not yet completed tickets. Their number is limited, i.e. only a limited, predefined number of work packages can be processed simultaneously. The goals of Kanban remain unchanged in software development:

- Faster, more predictable, and continuous workflow, and
- Process optimization through systematic reduction of Work in Progress (WIP).

Kanban does not prescribe any specific development methods or required project roles.[3] Like other agile process models, Software Kanban[4] follows the Agile Manifesto (Chap. 2).[5]

6.2 The Kanban Board

The use of Kanban is often equated with the creation of a Kanban board. This is far too simplistic. Kanban is a model for a software development process, whereas the Kanban board is merely a tool. Nevertheless, the board is central! Fig. 6.1 shows a (very) simple Kanban board.

Three Kanban cards (tickets) are shown. They represent different tasks[6] and move from phase to phase. The phases are represented as columns on the Kanban board. There is a certain temporal sequence from left to right, but this is not mandatory. For example, if the ticket (the task) "Make coffee" were interrupted because the coffee machine "decides" to start its cleaning program, the ticket would have to be moved back to the "Input" column. However, the normal case is that the ticket moves from left to right over time.

Fig. 6.2 shows a somewhat "more sophisticated" Kanban board from software development. Here, the development of an app with database connectivity via web interface is depicted in simplified form. You can see that the use cases have already been developed and are currently being tested.[7] The backend database is already in development, while

[3] In direct contrast to Scrum (Chap. 5).

[4] For simplicity, "Software Kanban" will hereafter be referred to simply as "Kanban."

[5] Software Kanban was first published by David J. Anderson in 2010, with the German translation following in 2011 (Anderson 2011). A good summary can also be found in (Rook 2013).

[6] Since the original Kanban cards in the Imperial Gardens are signal cards, but in Software Kanban represent tasks, Anderson also refers to the software Kanban board as a "virtual Kanban board" (Anderson 2011).

[7] Yes, dear students, you also have to test use cases 😉.

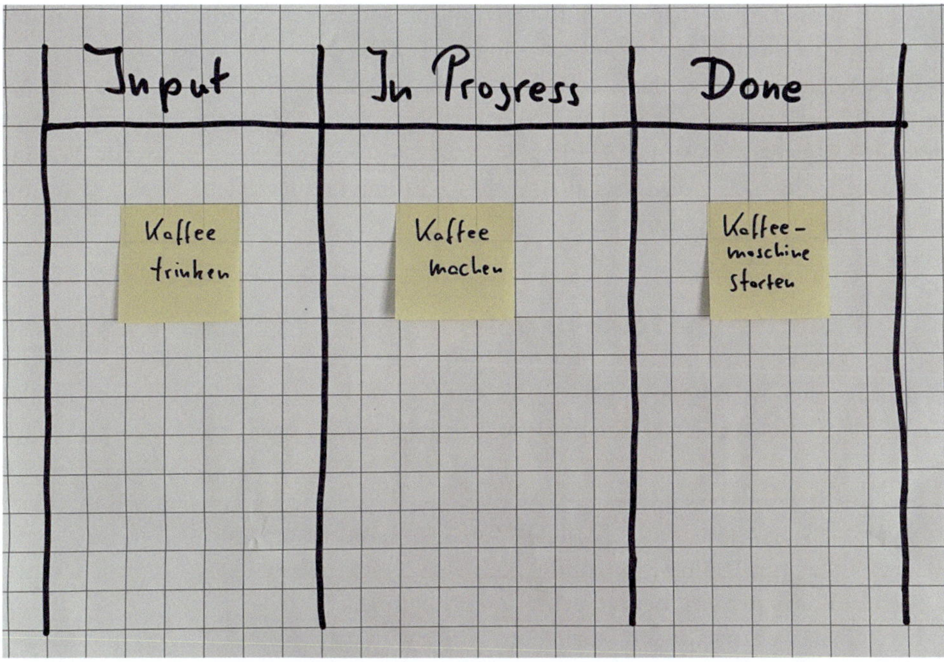

Fig. 6.1 A simple Kanban board with "coffee tickets"

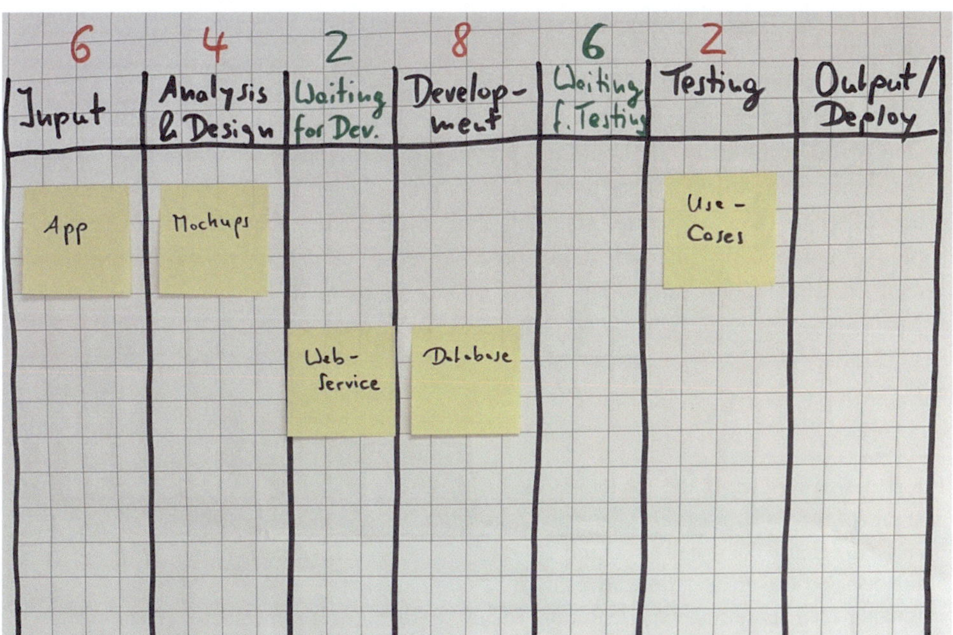

Fig. 6.2 Kanban board—principle

the web interfaces (web service) still have to wait. Mockups[8] are already being created for the app, but the app itself is not yet being worked on.

Of particular interest is the statement about the maximum "Work in Progress," the so-called WIP limit (see Sect. 6.1): Only 20 tickets[9] may be in progress or in the input at the same time. However, there are also 2 and 6 tickets, respectively, that can be in a "Waiting for" queue at most. The determination of the WIP limit and the queue sizes will be discussed in detail later (Sect. 6.6.2).

6.3 Kanban —The Four Principles

Kanban is much more than "just" the Kanban board. Kanban is "evolutionary change management." Kanban is based on four fundamental principles:

1. **Start with what you do now.**
   Kanban always starts with the status quo. The basic assumption is that the current state of the organization is not (only) bad, even if change is the goal.
2. **Agree to pursue incremental, evolutionary changes.**
   Evolutionary change means small steps! Only with patience can changes be successfully established.[10] Stakeholders must be brought on board early.[11]
3. **Respect current processes, roles, responsibilities, and job titles.**
   People often define themselves by their roles and job titles. Therefore, the status quo should not be disturbed here; instead, wait until the team itself wants to make changes.[12]
4. **Encourage acts of leadership at all levels.**
   Team members must be empowered to spontaneously take on responsibility ("leadership") within the team. It should not be the project manager assigning responsibility, but rather the team members themselves should take on responsibility in the project according to their own interests. This can involve, for example, responsibility for product components (increments) or process steps, but also for process improvement, team communication, and so on.

[8] Rough design sketches of the app interfaces.

[9] The sum of the red numbers above the phases (columns).

[10] What a difference compared to Scrum!

[11] Both decision-makers and those affected.

[12] From personal consulting experience, the author knows how team members can suffer from the abrupt change of roles and job titles in Scrum. This particularly affects project managers who suddenly (in their own perception) are "only" Product Owner or ScrumMaster.

6.4 The Six Core Kanban Practices

Kanban defines six core practices aimed at guiding the team and the organization in which it is embedded towards "Kaizen,"[13] the culture of continuous improvement:

1. **Visualize the workflow.**
   For Kanban, visualizing the workflow of work items is central! The Kanban board is therefore at the heart of all project activities. As already described in Sect. 6.2, all tickets pass through various phases until completion. Since the Kanban system is a "pull system," the team pulls tasks as tickets into the Kanban board when it has available capacity. Thus, the entire workflow in the project is visualized on the Kanban board. The Kanban board can be implemented "analogue" on a flipchart, a pinboard, or a whiteboard. However, digital Kanban boards are increasingly being adopted. These electronic project management boards[14] have the advantage that they can also be used by distributed teams or development organizations. It is important that they are visible to the entire team, centrally displayed on a sufficiently large screen. The whole team must be able to see and update the current project status at any time.
2. **Limit work in progress (WIP).**
   The WIP limit represents the maximum number of tickets that can be in progress simultaneously. The idea behind this restriction is that human teams cannot execute an unlimited number of tasks in parallel.[15] If we assume that most people can handle 2 work items at a high level simultaneously, and only allow tickets with a single assignee, then the initial WIP limit would be *2 x number of team members*. However, this calculation is almost always too simplistic, as not only the team itself but also its context, i.e., the organizational environment in which it operates, has a significant impact. In reality, setting the WIP limit is an "art," which will be discussed further below (Sect. 6.6.2).
3. **Manage flow.**
   Flow, i.e. the steady stream of project deliverables, is a central goal of Kanban. A regular value stream for the customer strengthens trust in the team. The workflow is continuously measured, deviations can be analyzed and eliminated. By ensuring a steady flow of tickets through the Kanban system, the project team demonstrates its reliability.

[13] For more on Kaizen, the culture of continuous improvement, see the book (Imai 1992), which provides a detailed description and derivation of Kaizen. Here, we will focus only on common practices such as the PDCA cycle or the "Seven Muda."

[14] There are now several good digital Kanban boards; an internet search is recommended. The author has had very good experiences with the Kanban board from *Jira* (Atlassian 2024).

[15] Context switching costs energy and time. This applies not only to operating systems, but also to human teams!

4. **Make process policies explicit.**
The "policies," i.e., the rules of collaboration within the team and the development organization, must be known and openly communicated. This includes both company policies, which typically form the project context, as well as the shared understanding of the process, such as when a ticket is considered done ("Definition of Done"), how many tasks the team wants to handle simultaneously (WIP limit), or what good error handling should look like. It is advisable to display the most important policies prominently on the walls of the team's workspace.[16] This way, changes or adjustments can be easily communicated to all team members.[17]
5. **Implement feedback loops.**
Feedback is a central concept in all agile process models (see Sect. 3.1.3). A famous feedback loop is the stand-up meeting, introduced by Kent Beck in Extreme Programming (Sect. 3.3.1.7) and made famous among developers as the Daily Scrum (Sect. 5.2.2.3). This meeting, ideally held daily, enables the team to exchange information about the project status and progress. However, it also makes sense to establish feedback loops for other questions defined by the team. Here are a few interesting questions that should be answered through feedback:
   - How satisfied is our customer really?
   - What is our most important task?
   - How can we optimize our process?
   - What are the internal and external impacts of such process changes?

   Many of these questions, of course, apply not only to Kanban but to all (agile) processes in general.[18]
6. **Improve collaboratively, evolve experimentally.**
Similar to the Sprint Retrospective known from Scrum (Sect. 5.2.2.6), the goal in Kanban is also to continuously improve. This includes trying things out, i.e., conducting "experiments." It makes sense to try out methods and models that fit the culture of continuous improvement (Kaizen). The following will take a closer look at the PDCA cycle and the "Seven Muda," the seven types of waste.

6.5 Practices for Process Improvement

Some practices used in Kaizen are also suitable for process improvement under Kanban and should be tried out by the agile team. The following will take a closer look at the PDCA cycle and the seven Muda (wastes).

[16] For example, above the coffee machine or in the meeting room; see Figs. 8.6 and 8.7.

[17] It is essential to prevent the "dusting off" of policies in a folder or on a drive that most team members are unaware of!

[18] And not just those!

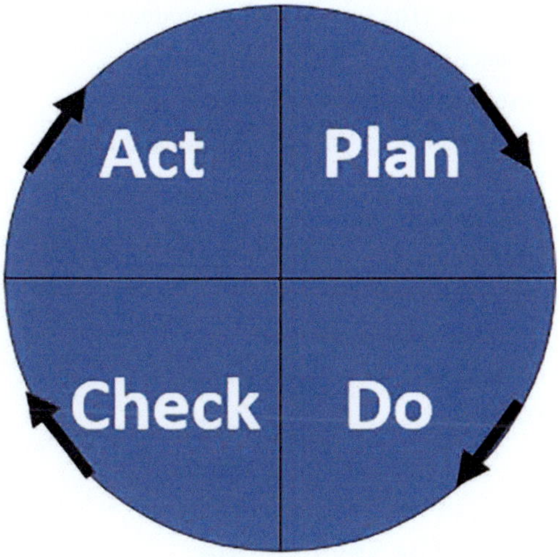

Fig. 6.3 The PDCA cycle ("Deming Circle")

6.5.1 The PDCA Cycle

The "Plan-Do-Check-Act" (PDCA) cycle describes an iterative, four-phase procedure for process improvement according to Deming (Deming Wheel, 1951[19]) (Fig. 6.3).

The four phases of the PDCA cycle can be described as follows:

Plan: The process step to be improved must be discussed and planned within the team.

Do: The plan must be tested and reviewed on a small scale[20]. Does everything work as intended? Are changes or adjustments necessary? The goal is to design the process step so that it can be introduced to the entire team or development organization.

Check: The process step, implemented and functioning on a small scale, is carefully reviewed again. Do the approach and results meet expectations, that is, the planning from the first phase?

Act: The newly developed process step is released and implemented for the entire project or development organization. This may involve extensive organizational adjustments and, if necessary, significant investments. The desired results must be checked regularly. If these "audits" reveal further need for improvement, the next iteration of the PDCA cycle is initiated.[21]

---

[19] See (Imai 1992) or also (Moen and Norman 2009).

[20] For example, with a few motivated team members.

[21] That is, the next "round" of Plan—Do—Check—Act.

Table 6.1 The seven Muda in production and their transfer to software development

Production	Software Development
Inventory (excessive *inventory*)	**Partially done work**
Overprocessing (inefficient manufacturing process)	**Extra process steps** (*additional development process steps*)
Overproduction	**Extra features**
Transportation (too many *material movement and handovers*)	**Task switching**
Waiting (*waiting times*)	**Waiting** (*waiting times*)
Motion (*unnecessary movements*)	**Motion** (*unnecessary handovers*)
Defects	**Defects**

6.5.2 The Seven Muda

The avoidance of the seven Muda, which in Japanese means "avoidance of the seven wastes," is a checkpoint of the *Kaizen Checkpoint System*[22] and the first principle of "Lean Software Development."[23] In this context, seven[24] potential wastes in production are transferred to software development (Table 6.1).

The seven main wastes in software development are identified as:

- too many incomplete intermediate products or unfinished work,
- additional, unnecessary process steps in the development process,[25]
- software features that are "nice-to-have" but not strictly necessary,[26]
- constant switching between different, often short-term assigned tasks by the developer, which leaves unfinished intermediate products with each switch and thus reduces value creation,
- inactivity due to waiting for the completion of other tickets needed for further work,

[22] The "Three Mu" are waste (Muda), overburden (Muri), and unevenness (Mura), see (Imai 1992).

[23] Kaizen, the culture of continuous improvement, is the foundation of the *Toyota Production System* (Monden 1998), on which *Lean Software Development* is based (Poppendieck and Poppendieck 2003).

[24] Depending on the company's quality system, the literature sometimes lists nine or eleven (or another number of) wastes. Ultimately, the number depends on the company context.

[25] The PDCA cycle can be applied here for process optimization (Sect. 6.5.1).

[26] But they consume developer time and are potential sources of errors.

- unnecessary handovers of tasks between team members but also between different development environments, etc.,[27]
- defects in software development.

The PDCA cycle and the seven Muda provide a good starting point for improving the software development process under Kanban. Many further practices can be found in the literature on Kaizen and "Lean Software Development."[28]

6.6 Kanban in the Project

During the course of the project, the agile project team identifies a variety of tasks to be completed. Each of these tasks is assigned a ticket[29]. As processing progresses, the tickets move from phase to phase.[30] As already described in Sect. 6.2, the maximum number of tickets on the board is limited to avoid overloading the team.

The condition ("signal") for pulling new tasks is the condition *WIP limit—work in progress > 0*, because then there is available capacity in the Kanban system. Typically, the stakeholders, i.e., the clients for the tickets, meet once a week to jointly decide which new tickets will be placed in the *Input Queue* column of the board. From there, the team "pulls them onto the board." Kanban is therefore a "pull system," because the team decides when to pull a new ticket from the input queue.[31]

Kanban does not have sprints or iterations. Kanban is "flow-oriented" and emphasizes the continuous development process without "timeboxing."[32] Consequently, Kanban also does not have discrete deployment dates.[33] However, the concept of "service classes" allows tickets to be given an end date (see Sect. 6.6.1).

---

[27] While in production the focus is on unnecessary movements, walking distances, or unpacking and rearranging tasks, in software development unnecessary handovers of tasks between team members or the transfer of source code between different development, debugging, or test systems predominate.

[28] See, for example, (Imai 1992) or (Poppendieck and Poppendieck 2003).

[29] That is, a Kanban card in the virtual Kanban system (Anderson 2011).

[30] That is, from column to column on the Kanban board.

[31] In the classic "push system," tasks were assigned to team members from outside! Incidentally, Scrum is also a pull system.

[32] Here, Kanban is the "countermodel" to Scrum! The author's experience shows that teams who struggle with Scrum love Kanban. While Scrum usually "turns the previous project process upside down," Kanban changes the existing project practice in small steps and gives the team more freedom.

[33] Comparable to the end of a Scrum sprint.

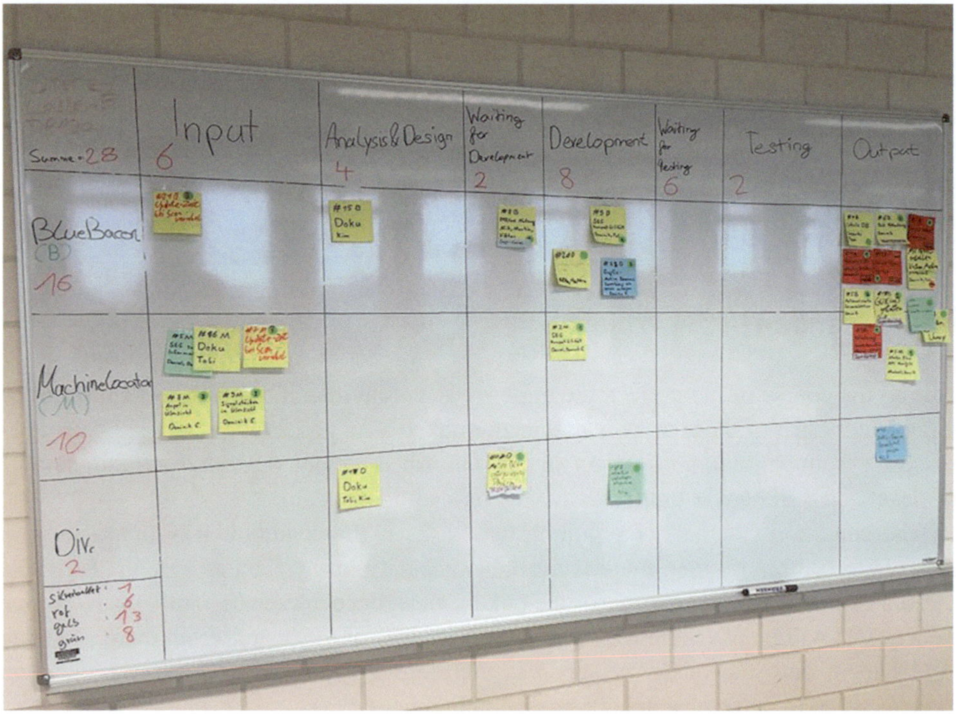

Fig. 6.4 Kanban board of a project with two sub-teams

6.6.1 A Kanban Board from Practice

Fig. 6.4 shows a Kanban board from a fourteen-member student group led by the author, which was divided into two (sub-)teams working on the topic of identifying machines in a factory hall using *Bluetooth Low Energy (BLE)*.[34]

The special feature of this project is that each sub-team works with Scrum (see Chap. 5), with the sprints running in temporal synchronization. However, there is also a joint working group that handles interface tasks, whose members temporarily switch from one of the two sub-teams to the working group. These team members therefore leave their original sub-team for one or possibly several sprints and are not available to it during that time. As a result, the team sizes of the sub-teams change repeatedly, which impairs their subproject progress and affects their release burndown chart (Sect. 5.3.3). On the other hand, the work of the interface working group is indispensable for the overall project progress.

[34] Student project 2017 at the author's *Center for Agile IT Projects* at DHBW Lörrach (https://dhbw-loerrach.de/kompetenzzentrumagileprozesse).

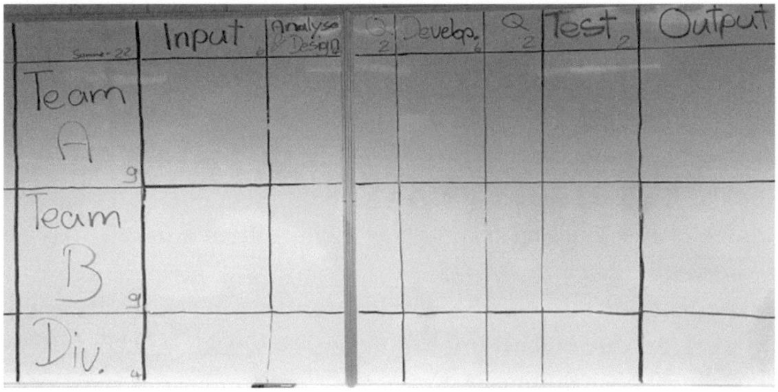

Fig. 6.5 Swimlanes of the sub-teams and the joint working group (*Div.*) as "rows" on the board (If you are wondering about the different labels on the Kanban board compared to Fig. 6.4: This is actually a simultaneous 2017 project with a similar task from another student team)

As can easily be seen, Scrum is not particularly well suited for such a constellation. On the other hand, the way the sub-teams work in Scrum sprints is indeed advantageous, among other things due to the synchronous availability of the current sprint results ("time-boxing") and the possibility of presenting the current project status simultaneously in a joint review meeting.[35]

6.6.1.1 Swimlanes

The solution in the project situation described above is to represent the tasks of the sub-teams and the joint working group in three so-called "swimlanes" (Fig. 6.5).

Here, evolutionary change management in small steps becomes apparent: The sub-teams can continue to use Scrum as their process model. Kanban initially does not change the existing process with its roles, but is limited to visualizing the overall process on the Kanban board. Only in the next step, by defining WIP limits in the swimlanes and phases, is the total number of open tickets restricted.[36]

On the boards in Figs. 6.4 and 6.5, in addition to *Input* and *Output*, the project phases *Analysis & Design*, *Development*, and *Testing* are found, as well as two *Queues* for tickets that have been analyzed or implemented and are waiting to be "pulled" into the next phase. Each handler or group of handlers for a ticket must update the ticket's phase on the Kanban board daily(!).[37] The function of the *Queues* "Waiting for Development" and "Waiting for Testing" (Fig. 6.4) is important. Here, tickets are placed that cannot yet

---

[35] In the literature, such a "hybrid" agile approach is also referred to as "Scrumban"; see, for example, https://www.atlassian.com/de/agile/project-management/scrumban.

[36] And thereby the quality of the team's work is increased.

[37] For whiteboards, this can also be done by a proxy. For an electronic board, this should not be a problem.

move on to the next processing step. They must wait! However, Kanban tries to minimize such queues (Sect. 6.5.2), which is why these queues also have a limit. If this is not sufficient, an increase in developer capacity must be considered!

6.6.1.2 Service Classes

The tickets on the Kanban board in Fig. 6.4 have different colors. These colors indicate different "service classes" of the tickets. This assigns them a priority. By default, there are the following *four service classes*:

Expedite: A ticket of this class is a "silver bullet".[38] The whole team must drop everything to work on this highest-priority ticket. This ticket temporarily overrides the normal flow of the Kanban system. A Kanban system can have at most one such active ticket at a time.

Fixed Date: These, usually red, tickets have a fixed delivery date. This is usually specified by stakeholders.[39] Since these tickets must be carefully estimated in terms of effort and time, the author's experience suggests that no more than one third of the tickets should belong to this service class.

Standard: This should be the normal case for a ticket. In the author's projects, typically half of the tickets are in the standard class.

Intangible: The effort is difficult to quantify and does not necessarily need to be estimated. What is usually important is that the task is completed by the end of the project and not forgotten.[40] According to the author's experience, usually no more than 10% of the tickets belong to this lowest service class.

It is important that the maximum number of tickets per service class is defined in advance. The distribution suggested above by the author provides an initial guideline for setting these limits (see also Fig. 6.6).

6.6.2 The Art of Limiting Work in Progress (WIP)

As can be seen in Figs. 6.4 and 6.6, in the student "BLE project" of Sect. 6.6.1, each *swimlane* of the sub-team ("row"), each *phase* ("column") of the Kanban board, and each ticket *service class* is assigned WIP limits. The sum of the rows, columns, and tickets per service class is 28 in each case. First, the limits in the different phases are considered. For this, a distinction is made between "active" and "passive" phases.

Analysis & Design, *Development*, and *Testing* are "active" because tickets in these phases require work from the team. Assuming a maximum of 2 tickets per team member,

---

[38] With the silver bullet, you take down "project werewolves" 😊. In Fig. 6.4 an active silver bullet can be seen in the *Development* phase.

[39] This could be, for example, a trade show date or the commissioning of an IT system.

[40] This could be project documentation, a training session, or something similar.

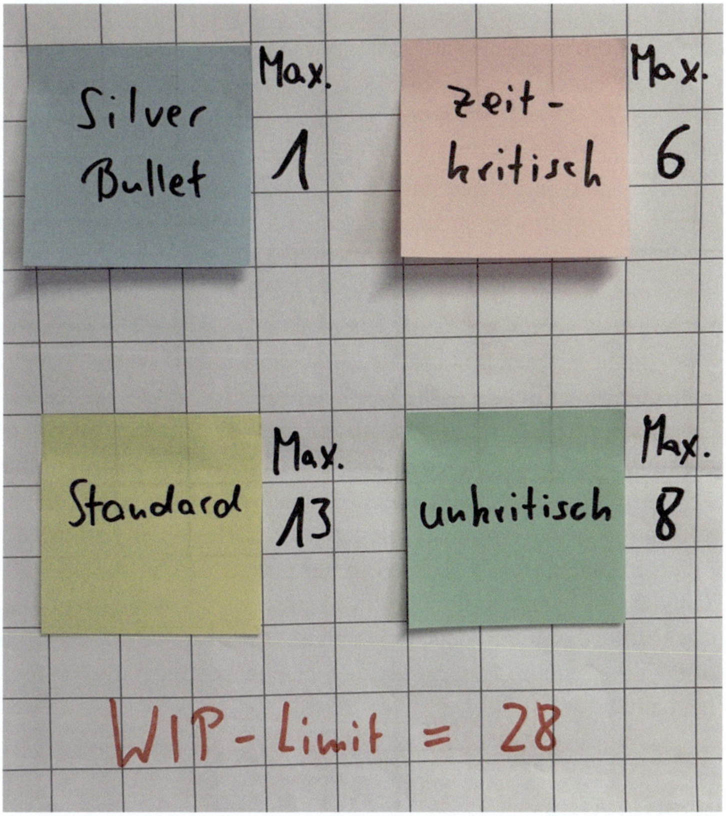

Fig. 6.6 Limits of the service classes in the student project in Fig. 6.4

a seven-person development team can work on the specified $4 + 8 + 2 = 14$ tickets simultaneously. However, this only applies if the team members can perform all required tasks—specification, development (coding), and testing—themselves. Additional administrative tasks in the project context must also be considered in this estimate.[41] This may increase the size of the team.

Input, *Waiting for Development*, and *Waiting for Testing*, on the other hand, are "passive" phases, as no work is performed by the project team here. Nevertheless, limits must also be set here, as becomes clear after a brief consideration:

The *Input* phase is the area from which the team can pull new tickets. Assuming that the relevant stakeholders refill the input queue once a week, the queue should not be larger than the amount of work the team can accomplish in a week. If the average time

[41] That is, what is handled by project managers, etc., in a traditional project.

a ticket spends in the system until completion is two weeks, that would be 7 tickets. The student team was a bit more conservative. Hence the limit of *6 tickets* in the input queue.

The two "queues" have a rather practical significance: When a ticket has passed through a phase, e.g., *Analysis & Design*, but cannot yet be processed further due to the limit in *Development*, it must be "parked". This corresponds in classical production to a workpiece being stored in an intermediate warehouse between two processing steps. An analysis according to the seven muda (Sect. 6.5.2) shows, however, that the muda *Partially Done Work* and *Waiting* should be avoided. On the one hand, the two queues *Waiting for Development* and *Waiting for Testing* are needed for process reasons; on the other hand, such queues should be avoided as much as possible. The author's experience shows that a pragmatic approach helps here: Let the Kanban system "run" for a while and measure the number of tickets in the two queues before setting the limits. The height of the limits reveals constraints in the system. For example, the limit of 6 for *Waiting for Testing* shows that the team has too few testers available. By increasing resources in testing, "inventory" is reduced and a "bottleneck" in the system is eliminated![42,43]

When introducing Kanban into an existing project, it is generally advisable to map the current state onto a Kanban board adapted to the project and let the project "run" for a few weeks. Only then—based on the current maxima of tickets (*current state*)—should suitable WIP limits for the subprojects, ticket phases, and service classes be derived after an analysis of the seven muda. These must then be checked regularly, preferably weekly at first, for their suitability.

6.6.3 Kanban Metrics

The first Kanban core practice, "Visualize workflow" (Sect. 6.4), requires the existence of a Kanban board to visualize the *flow* of tickets through the system (i.e., the project). This also makes it possible to measure this "throughput." This is done using the "Cumulative Flow Diagram," which allows two metrics to be determined: the current Work in Progress (WIP) and the average *Cycle Time*. The goal is to minimize WIP and keep the cycle time as predictably short as possible.

[42] A successful application of the seven muda with a clear statement about team structure! For these practical considerations, see also (Leopold and Kaltenecker 2018) in Sect. 17.3.2.

[43] The high WIP value in the *Waiting for Testing* queue is thus an indication of a bottleneck in the system, which can be eliminated by increasing resources. Such bottlenecks can be addressed using the "Theory of Constraints". A good summary of this Lean Development method can be found in (Kneuper 2018).

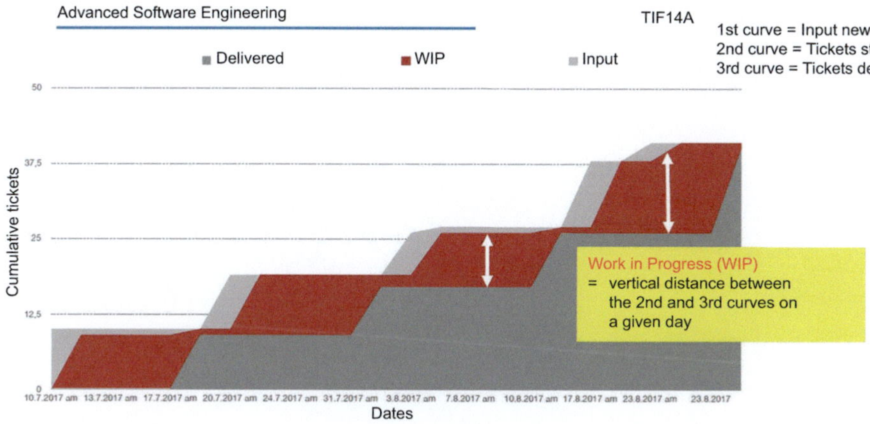

Fig. 6.7 The current Work in Progress (WIP) in the student BLE project

6.6.3.1 The Current Work in Progress

In the *Cumulative Flow Diagram*, the active tickets are plotted over time (Fig. 6.7). Typically, there are three curves: The first curve (the *topmost* light gray curve in the diagram) is the total number of tickets newly loaded into the system via *Input* at the given time.[44] The second curve (red) represents the tickets that have already been started. The third (*bottommost*, dark gray) curve is the number of tickets that have already been completed, i.e., "delivered" tickets in *Output*.

The vertical distance, the white arrow between the second ("started") and the third ("delivered") curve, indicates the *current Work in Progress (WIP)* on the day in question. In a simple Kanban system without subprojects using Scrum, one expects a *steady flow*,[45] as sketched in Fig. 6.8: Only the input tickets are loaded in a block by the stakeholders. The processing of the tickets takes place more or less evenly.[46] The "stepping" in Fig. 6.7, on the other hand, is rather unusual for Kanban projects. The explanation is the two subteams in the upper swimlanes of Fig. 6.4. They work internally with Scrum using synchronized sprints. This is reflected in the Cumulative Flow Diagram (Fig. 6.7), where the number of started tickets naturally decreases towards the end of the sprints.

However, it does not go all the way to zero, because the joint work in the lowest swimlane is not processed in sprints and therefore, for the most part, remains open beyond the sprint boundaries.

---

[44] In the example considered, new tickets are loaded into the Kanban system by stakeholders approximately every 14 days.

[45] That is, WIP arrows of roughly equal length!

[46] See also (Leopold and Kaltenecker 2018) in Sect. 7.2.

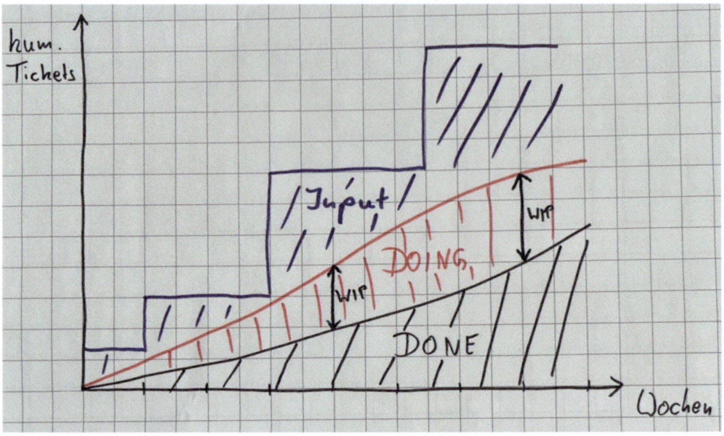

Fig. 6.8 Cumulative Flow Diagram of a simple Kanban system (sketch)

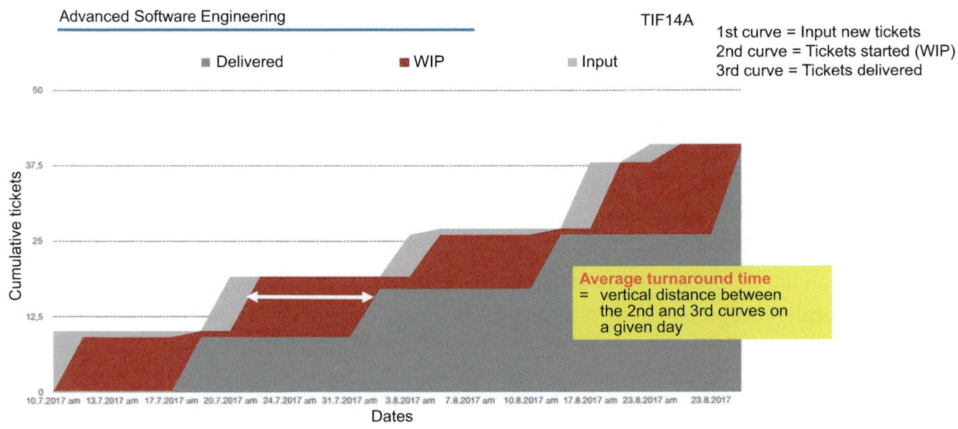

Fig. 6.9 The current cycle time of the tickets

6.6.3.2 Cycle Time

If you look at the Cumulative Flow Diagram along the time axis (Fig. 6.9), the average *cycle time* of the tickets can be determined as the horizontal distance between the second and third curve, i.e., between started and delivered tickets.[47]

If you analyze the tickets in detail, you can determine their distribution (Fig. 6.10). As can be seen, in the student BLE project most tickets could be completed in 9 hours.[48]

---

[47] White horizontal arrow!

[48] This is a net value, as the student teams worked on the project as part of a lecture course. This value is, of course, project-dependent!

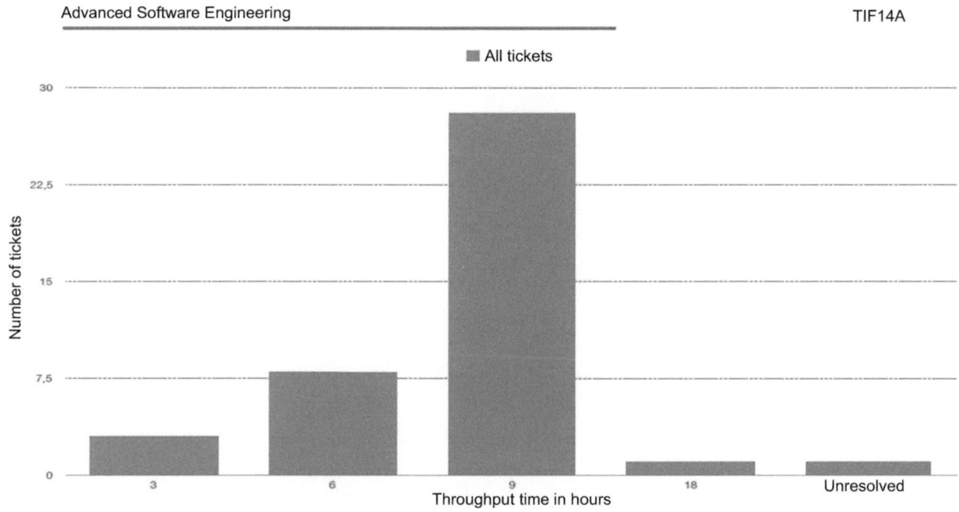

Fig. 6.10 Cycle time of the tickets—distribution

Interestingly, about a quarter of the tickets could be completed more quickly, while only 2 tickets took more than twice as long, and one of them could not be resolved within the specified time!

References

Anderson D (2011) Kanban—Evolutionäres Change Management für IT-Organisationen. Heidelberg: dpunkt Verlag

Atlassian (2024) Jira. https://www.atlassian.com/de/software/jira, Zugriff August 2024

Imai M (1992) Kaizen. Der Schlüssel zum Erfolg der Japaner im Wettbewerb. München: Langen-Müller

Kneuper R (2018) Software Processes and Life Cycle Models. Cham: Springer Nature Switzerland

Leopold K, Kaltenecker S (2018) Kanban in der IT. München: Hanser

Moen R, Norman C (2009) Evolution of the PDCA Cycle. In Proceedings of the 7th ANQ Congress. Tokyo: Asian Network for Quality

Monden Y (1998) Yasuhiro Monden (1998), Toyota Production System, An Integrated Approach to Just-In-Time. Norcross (GA): Engineering & Management Press

Poppendieck M und Poppendieck T (2003) Lean Software Development: An Agile Toolkit. Boston: Addison-Wesley Professional

Rook A (2013) Kanban einführen—aber richtig! In „CIO-Handbuch", Band II. Düsseldorf: Symposion

DevOps

7

In contrast to the models discussed so far, DevOps is not a process model. Rather, it is a holistic approach that aims to bring together software development and the management of the finished production system within the same team or through close collaboration between departments. By applying various shared "best practices," it is ensured that operational aspects of the production system are already considered during the design and development of the software, in order to shorten the time to productive deployment.

DevOps is a portmanteau of ***Dev**elopment* (software development) and ***Op**erations* (software deployment in the production system). The first documented appearance of DevOps in the IT industry was in 2009. The need to minimize the time from the development of a software system to its productive deployment was first addressed at the *Velocity Conference* in San José and shortly thereafter at the *DevOps Days* in Ghent, initiated by Patrick Debois.[1] DevOps seeks to achieve this by involving specialists from different disciplines, such as development and operations, as early as possible, so that potential issues between specification and commissioning can be identified and avoided early on. In particular, the "silo mentality" of the different disciplines is to be broken down in this way (Hüttermann 2012; Halstenberg et al. 2020).[2]

[1] However, the author already encountered the term as a job title *DevOps Engineer* in the pharmaceutical industry in the 1990s. Here, it referred to the transition from laboratory scale to pharmaceutical-chemical production and was only marginally related to IT.

[2] Developers usually have "more agile" processes than operators from the data center. The challenge is to align these different mindsets!

E. Hanser, *Agile Processes—Agile Teams*, https://doi.org/10.1007/978-3-662-72726-3_7

7.1 CALMS—The Core Principles of DevOps

DevOps is based on the following core principles:

- **C**ulture
- **A**utomation
- **L**ean
- **M**easurement
- **S**haring

The five core principles are fundamentally nothing new. All of them have already been described in this book. What is new is that they are to be practiced in *cross-functional* teams consisting of development, IT operations, business, and others. The following sections briefly examine the principles and their relation to the process models already described.

7.1.1 Culture

Culture is already known as a central concept from agility. The Agile Manifesto with its four principles (Chap. 2) or Extreme Programming with its five values (Sect. 3.1) are important components of software development processes. In DevOps, culture refers more generally to collaboration at *all* levels of the company, not just in development, but also with IT operations and other areas. Everyone contributes to the whole, across different units of the organization. Decisions are made at the appropriate (the "right") level.[3] The same values, norms, and guiding principles must apply throughout the organization. Important points include

- No silo mentality!
- Willingness to take responsibility
- Error culture: positive handling of mistakes, learning from mistakes
- Agile team structure in the various units of the organization
- Systems thinking: understanding teams and the organization as systems!

This list is exemplary and must be expanded as needed in individual cases.

---

[3]This is also known as the "subsidiarity principle." A principle that is also important in political decision-making!

7.1.2 Automation

The software pipeline must be extended from development to production, i.e., to IT operations. This should be done as automatically as possible. This results in a new model of close collaboration between development and IT operations. The goal of developing new software is only achieved when the entire production system goes live! The associated DevOps practices of Continuous Integration, Continuous Delivery, and Continuous Deployment are discussed in Sect. 7.2. Continuous Integration is already known from Extreme Programming (Sect. 3.5.4).

7.1.3 Lean

The origins of Lean are based on the *Toyota Production System (TPS)* from the 1950s.[4] The goal is to increase production efficiency by reducing waste, thereby making work more "meaningful." Important practices for process improvement derived from this are already used in Kanban (Sect. 6.5).

7.1.4 Measurement

DevOps is based on reliable metrics. Only in this way can "gut-feeling decisions" be avoided. Important metrics certainly include the number of errors occurring in the system and their resolution time, or the availability of the IT system. But Kanban metrics (Sect. 6.6.3) can also be applied to IT operations by extending Kanban tickets. This allows the flow of a software change ticket from the input queue to going live in the production system to be measured.

7.1.5 Sharing

Information, best practices, but also background on failures should be shared among all participants. The focus is *not* on assigning blame, but on a culture of improvement. *Sharing* is therefore closely linked to *culture*.

As can be seen, the five core principles are known from various software process models. What is new is their application to the entire "deployment pipeline"!

[4] Lean Management, Lean Thinking, see also https://www.toyota-europe.com/about-us/toyota-vision-and-philosophy/toyota-production-system.

7.2 DevOps Life Cycle

The goal of DevOps is to cover the entire life cycle from requirements to the "operation" of the software system. Typically, eight phases from development and IT operations are identified, which are to be considered "holistically" under DevOps.[5]

In Fig. 7.1, five phases are shown that are originally assigned to software development and three phases that typically belong to IT operations. What is new is that these eight phases, which are part of the value chain for a new software feature or a software modification, must be carried out with equal importance.

The associated DevOps practices *Continuous Integration*, *Continuous Delivery*, and *Continuous Deployment* "automate" the processes in the DevOps life cycle, with Continuous Integration already being advocated by Kent Beck in Extreme Programming (Sect. 3.5.4), thus originating as a software development practice. This integration at short intervals—usually daily and with automated unit tests (Sect. 3.3.3.3)—serves the purpose of always having an up-to-date codebase. Good version management is a prerequisite for this. In Continuous Integration, it is already a first success if the software system can be translated into code without errors. Typically, this code should also pass automated unit-level tests without errors. If not, this signals to the software developers that rework is needed.

Continuous Delivery extends the Continuous Integration approach by creating a "release candidate" that also passes automated acceptance tests. The challenge here is the automation of these tests "against" the high-level specification. If necessary, automated testing must be supplemented by "manual" tests.

Continuous Deployment is the most far-reaching DevOps practice. The release candidate is not only automatically tested but also made available in the production environment, ideally without manual intervention. Of course, it must first be ensured that the desired features are "built into" the release (or not). The goal is a deliverable product!

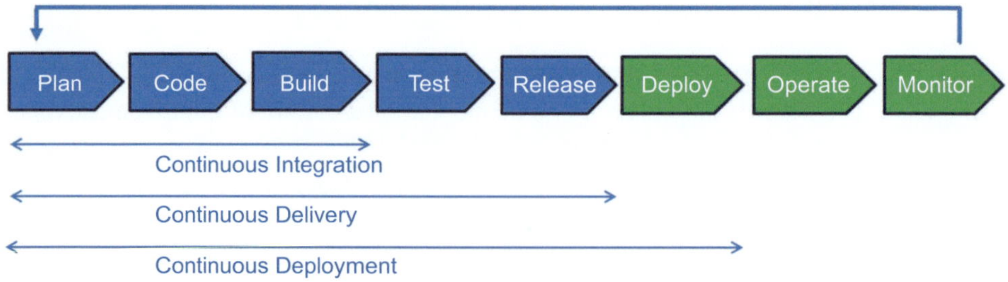

Fig. 7.1 DevOps life cycle with 8 phases

[5] The division into eight phases is not consistent in the literature. Modified representations can be found in (Halstenberg et al. 2020) or (Kneuper 2018).

Continuous Deployment also requires precise knowledge of the target platform. If this is a cloud solution, its configuration and all necessary resources must be defined in configuration files. These are often JSON or YAML files that can be read by cloud management software. An example of this so-called *Infrastructure as Code (IaC)* can be found in (Mustafa 2023).

7.3 The Three Ways

"The Three Ways" describe the three approaches to optimizing the "value stream." They are described in the cult novel "The Phoenix Project" as the DevOps perspective on the "IT factory" (Fig. 7.2).

The "1st Way" *Flow* deals with minimizing the "lead time" of a task through the IT system. This is comparable to the flow of a ticket in Kanban (Sect. 6.6.3.2), but now the focus is on the *entire* IT system. As already discussed in Chap. 6, bottlenecks must also be identified and eliminated here.[6]

If, for example, a new feature is to be added to a software system, the flow is measured from specification to going live in the production system. Using the seven muda (Sect. 6.5.2), all types of delays due to "waste" can be analyzed and eliminated. Many of the lean techniques already known from Kanban can be applied here (see, for example, Sects. 6.6.2 and 6.6.3). The important thing is to keep the entire DevOps life cycle (Fig. 7.1) in view.

The "2nd Way" *Feedback* complements the flow analysis of the first way with feedback loops for continuous improvement. This principle is known, for example,

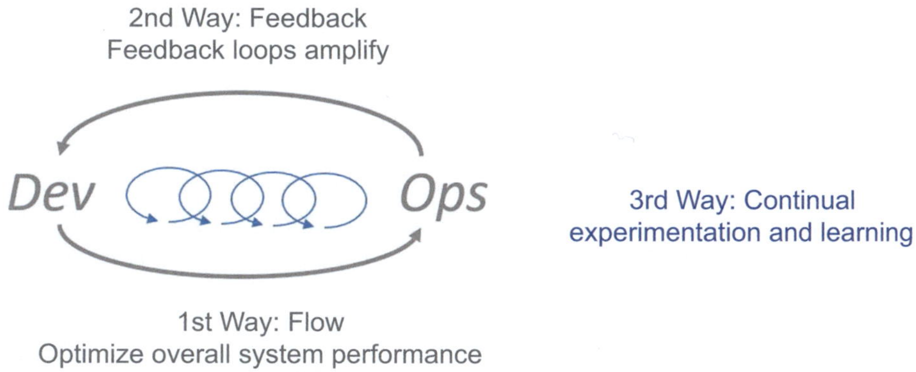

Fig. 7.2 DevOps—The Three Ways, after (Kim 2012)

[6] See also Chap. 6, where the theory of constraints is discussed in the context of limiting work in progress (Sect. 6.6.2). For the "Theory of Constraints," see also (Goldratt and Cox 2004).

from Scrum, where the team gives feedback on the process in the sprint retrospective (Sect. 5.2.2.6). Here, too, the generalization to the *entire* DevOps life cycle applies.

The "3rd Way" complements flow analysis and feedback with *continual experimentation and learning*. Here, the PDCA cycle (Deming cycle) known from Kanban (Sect. 6.5.1) can be applied. Of course, it must be clear that experimentation also involves mistakes or misjudgments. A positive error culture is a prerequisite for this (Sect. 7.1.1).

7.4 A Critical Perspective

DevOps addresses the critical question of how to minimize the time from the development of a software system to its productive deployment. Considering the DevOps Life Cycle (Fig. 7.1) with all its phases from software development and IT operations within a team composed of specialists from both areas is intended to break down the silo mentality of the individual departments within an IT organization. However, what is neglected here is the human factor! The author's experience shows that those who develop software and those who operate data centers or clouds are completely different types of people. Even the timeframes they operate on are entirely different.[7] Implementing a new software feature may take several days, but if an IT system is "down," it may be a matter of minutes or less! Every IT manager is familiar with this problem. In academic studies, these are different areas of focus! Therefore, great care must be taken when assembling such an interdisciplinary team with members who operate on different time scales. Ideally, "boundary crossers" between the different "silos" of Dev and Ops are involved. For current experiences in a corporate context, see (Hanser 2024).

The different team types are discussed in Chap. 9. There, a new systemic approach is presented that assembles teams not based on the "fields of activity" of their members, but on their types.

References

Goldratt E, Cox J (2004) The Goal: A Process of Ongoing Improvement. New York: Routledge

Halstenberg D, Pfitzinger B, Jestädt T (2020) DevOps—Ein Überblick. Wiesbaden: Springer Vieweg

Hanser E (2024) Der VM-Blog—praktische Erfahrungen mit aktuellen Vorgehensmodellen. https://map-model.de/vm-blog.php, Zugriff Oktober 2024.

Hüttermann M (2012) DevOps for Developers. New York: Apress Media

[7] The author repeatedly emphasizes to his students that "the smallest unit of time for a developer is a day" 😉.

Kim N (2012) The Three Ways: The Principles Underpinning DevOps. https://itrevolution.com/articles/the-three-ways-principles-underpinning-devops/, Zugriff August 2024
Kneuper R (2018) Software Processes and Life Cycle Models. Cham: Springer Nature Switzerland
Mustafa O (2023) A Complete Guide to DevOps with AWS. New York: Apress Media
Sampson C (2018) What is DevOps. https://theagileadmin.vom/what-is-devops/, Zugriff August 2024

Experimental Software Engineering in the Student Laboratory

8

In the student software engineering lab of the *Competence Center for Agile IT Processes (KAP)* (Hanser 2014) at the Baden-Württemberg Cooperative State University Lörrach, each student cohort (referred to as a *course*) jointly carries out a software project as a team. In doing so, questions regarding agile project practices and their success in practice are specifically addressed. This allows agile process models known from the literature to be put to the test. In this context, the author wonders whether the approach of process models is even the right one. Does this not restrict the team too much?

The student software engineering lab at the Baden-Württemberg Cooperative State University Lörrach is part of the computer science degree program. Each student cohort (referred to as a *course*) jointly carries out a software project as a team. Thus, the number of team members naturally results from the number of students plus the instructor. In approximately 60 course hours, each project team typically consists of 5 to 6 members, but in some projects up to 20 team members participate. In two courses, this results in up to 300 effective project hours per team or more.

The IT lab has existed in this form since 2004. The author, as one of the instructors, assumes the role of the customer (and occasionally that of the consultant), while the roles of project manager and quality manager—if they are filled—are either assigned by him or elected by the team (Hanser 2006).

E. Hanser, *Agile Processes—Agile Teams*, https://doi.org/10.1007/978-3-662-72726-3_8

In addition to the primary goal of developing stable software that meets the specifications, more in-depth questions about project organization are also explored:

1. Are there agile project practices that *do not* work without intervention from (project) management? Which agile practices are *not* the result of the team's self-organization? Here, particular attention is paid to the group of XP practices described in Sect. 3.5, which still form the basis for current agile models and—as already mentioned—give rise to discussion.
2. Practical experience shows that teams with more than about five members split into "mini-teams":
   - In XP, such a mini-team is called a "pair." It consists of two members. Are these pairs successful in reality?
   - Is there an ideal size (greater than two) for successful mini-teams?
   - What is the member structure of such (successful) mini-teams?

In addition to the author's personal experiences, various contributions in the literature also give rise to these questions. It is known that the "initial project" of XP, the *Chrysler C3* project mentioned in Chap. 3, did not end successfully. It was only a success in the first phase up to 1997. As the project progressed, it encountered increasing difficulties and was discontinued in 1999. Kent Beck himself admits that even XP is no guarantee for a successful project (Fowler 2005; Beck 2009). Alistair Cockburn, the founder of the *Crystal* family of methods (Chap. 4), is also critical. In this context, the well-known XP caricature on his website shows two programmers in front of a screen, reminiscent of Edvard Munch's painting "The Scream" (Cockburn 2008).

In this context, the author increasingly wonders whether the approach of process models is even the right one. Does this not restrict the team too much? More on this in Chap. 9.

8.1 The Projects in the Student Lab

From 2004 to 2008, an email marketing software was developed in the author's student lab. Newsletter content is read from an underlying database and sent in personalized form to subscribers who have previously signed up for the respective newsletter. The software features a web-based graphical user interface and an administration interface. Figures 8.1 and 8.2 show some input screens of the newsletter system. The system is now fully functional after more than 3000 project hours and has been ported to Linux servers with the help of the Mono project. The project was completed in 2008.

In 2009, as part of a field trip, a room planning software for groups with physical disabilities was developed for a real client in the field of vocational qualification (Fig. 8.3). The project lasted eight full working days with a team consisting of a Product Owner,

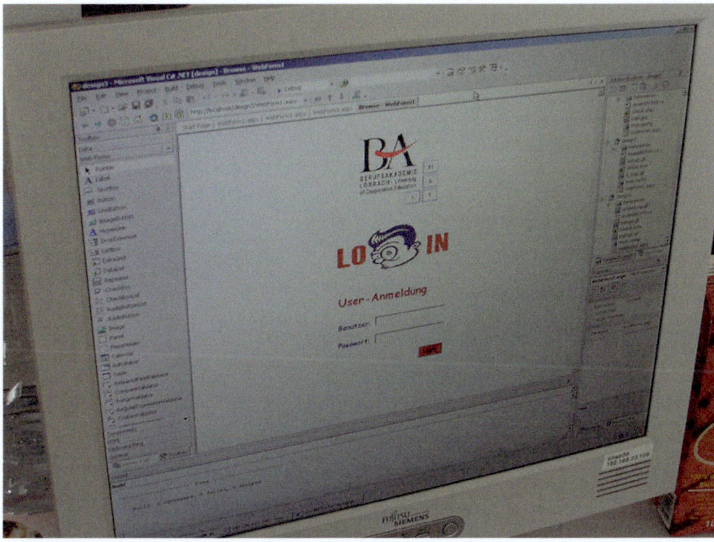

Fig. 8.1 Newsletter system, login screen

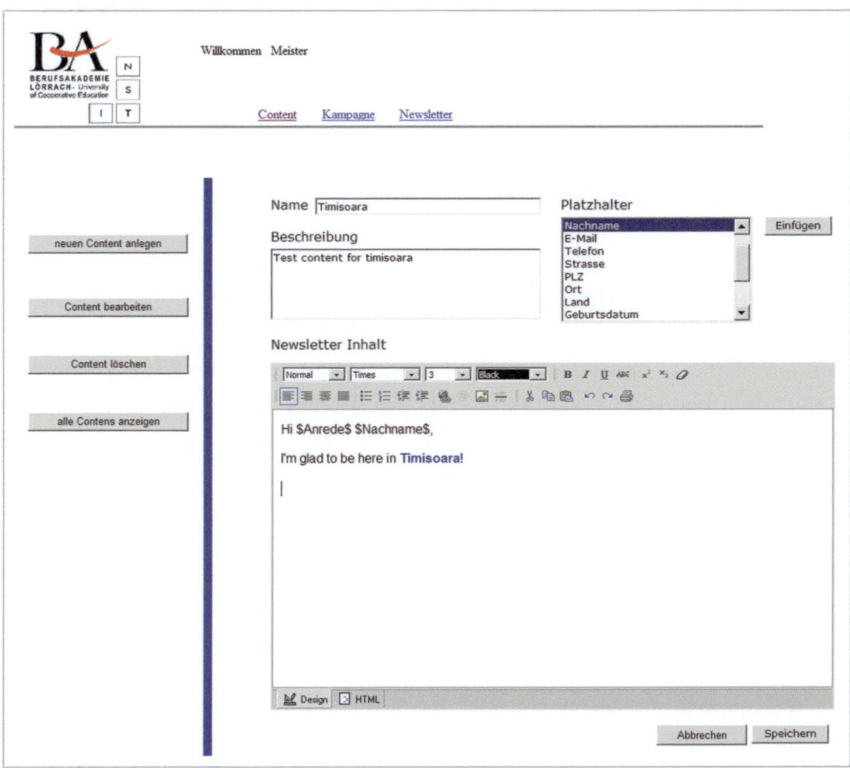

Fig. 8.2 Newsletter editor

Fig. 8.3 Room planning software “TeRaPlan”

ScrumMaster[1] and a ten-person team.[2] Three of these days were spent on-site with the client as part of the field trip. This student project was part of the *Life Science Informatics* (Applied Computer Science) degree program.

8.2 Boundary Conditions of the Student Sessions

Each session of the IT laboratory at the Competence Center for Agile IT Processes is subject to certain boundary conditions set by the instructors (Hanser 2014). This allows for targeted examination of issues arising from the use of agile process models. These boundary conditions are also based on experiences from previous years. In particular, various agile process models are “tried out” in the first six sessions[3]:

- In 2004, no specific agile process model is emphasized. The team is to develop its own agile process based on the Agile Manifesto.

[1] This role is assumed by the author.
[2] This corresponds to approximately 600 project hours.
[3] Currently, the teams mainly work with Scrum and Kanban, but also use practices from XP and Crystal.

- In 2005, the team is supposed to practice XP. The actual agile process ultimately deviates from this.
- 2006: Starting from an agile approach, a hierarchical process develops. Interestingly, the project manager who establishes this process was previously elected by the team.
- In 2007, the team is supposed to practice Crystal. As in 2005, the actual agile process deviates here as well.
- 2008: The starting process is again XP. Here too, the agile process is modified and adapted.
- 2009: For the first time, Scrum is the starting process. This agile management method is also adapted or extended. For the first time, development is carried out for a "real" client outside the university. The project is very successful.
- From 2009 onwards, Scrum and Kanban are offered as alternative team processes, but also the heavyweight V-Model.

Of particular interest is the change in boundary conditions between the first two sessions of the student laboratory. The following Table 8.1 compares the boundary conditions of 2004 and 2005.

Table 8.1 Year 2004 vs. 2005

IT Laboratory of DHBW Lörrach	Session 2004	Session 2005
Prerequisites	The instructor assigns the positions of project manager and quality manager to suitable students	The instructor assigns the positions of project manager and quality manager to suitable students
	The rest of the team (class) is initially divided into groups of three (mini-teams)	The team (class) is initially unstructured, but is tasked with forming mini-teams in the form of XP pairs
	The team members have background knowledge of process models, especially agile programming	The team members have background knowledge of process models, especially Extreme Programming (XP)
	The client (the instructor) is a team member	The client (the instructor) is a team member
Development Platform	Microsoft Visual Studio.NET 2003	Microsoft Visual Studio.NET 2003
Project Goal	Successful product, successful project	Successful product, successful project
	Business logic and graphical user interface are to be developed by competing mini-teams in C# and Visual Basic, respectively	Joint implementation of a fully functional email marketing system in C#
	The team is to choose a suitable agile process	XP is required by the instructor
Session Success	Only the minimum requirements for product and process are met	In the end, a successful product and a successful process

How can the different outcomes of the two sessions be explained? What are the necessary "ingredients" for a successful project? Of course, the strength of the team members plays a major role, but both cohorts had strong programmers. The key to success must therefore also lie significantly in the organization of the team. To support this, the roles of project manager and quality manager will first be examined. Do these classic project roles still make sense in an agile environment, or how do they change?

8.3 Change of Classic Project Roles in Agile Projects

The classic project roles are project manager and quality manager. These roles in particular undergo a transformation in agile projects.

8.3.1 The Project Manager in the Agile Project

The "classic" project manager leads his or her team and monitors project progress. He or she creates the project manual, which describes the project, and the project plan for effort, time, and resources. The project manager sets the course for a successful project. In an agile project, however, this classic project role is not clearly defined. Therefore, in the 2005 student laboratory, it was decided that a student should take on this role in order to redefine it within the agile team. The project manager at the time described his role as follows (Hanser et al. 2006):

Impact of Project Progression on the Role of the Project Manager

"In an agile project, the role of the traditional project manager is actually not defined. The team is supposed to be self-managing. Every member shares responsibility for all areas. This principle is also reinforced by the five values of XP. However, from the perspective of XP, this project was somewhat special: The number of project members was well over twelve. The client had concrete ideas regarding the scope of functionality, while the team members first had to familiarize themselves with the subject matter. As a result, there were few to no change requests from the client, while the team members' understanding only grew over time. Therefore, the XP approach was adapted for the first time right at the start of the project. These adaptations led to an initial definition of the project manager's role:

1. Creating short user stories.
2. Coordinating the team until everything runs smoothly (everyone is committed to XP).
3. Monitoring the overall project.

Goals in the first project phase:

1. Conducting team training to improve programming skills.
2. Dividing the overall project into iteration steps lasting about three weeks each.
3. Developing the foundations for the project, including design templates for the website and defining the database structure.
4. Not prescribing any fixed rules or procedures.

In collaboration with the client, user stories were developed and posted on a pinboard each morning. The team was to independently form groups and work on a corresponding user story. If a story was incomplete, the group was to independently develop or improve a new user story with the client or the project manager and post it on the pinboard. The team was thus expected to manage the project independently.

Problems in the first project phase:

1. The varying programming skill levels among team members led, from a quality management perspective, to either very good or very poor implementations of individual user stories. To achieve a high-quality end product, some groups had to be enlarged.
2. A lack of willingness to communicate proved to be a very difficult hurdle to overcome. Restrictions identified by groups for the development of forms were not or only partially communicated further and thus not adhered to by all groups. Inquiries to the client were made only by the quality manager or the project manager.
3. Established rules were not followed, and there was no sign of "Collective Code."

After a few weeks, the team became disillusioned when it was realized that a lot of "junk" had been developed. As a result, a *redefinition* of the project manager's (PM) role was established:

1. The PM became the communications manager between the individual groups and ensured that important information was shared among the groups.
2. The PM facilitated contact between team members and the client.
3. This resulted in a shift toward a traditional project manager, i.e., more guidelines (user stories could no longer leave so much freedom to the developer).

Goals of the second phase:

1. Prevent the project from failing.
2. Finally get the first iteration "up and running."
3. Re-motivate team members.

Result of the second phase:
Key modules began to take concrete shape and functionality. The team's morale improved. Team members adapted rules, for example, by introducing a stand-up meeting to improve communication. In these meetings, each team reported on successes and problems encountered while working on a user story. Furthermore, change requests from the client regarding user stories were planned and implemented by the individual team members themselves. At this point, the team was successfully practicing "its" own form of XP. However, it also became apparent that productivity was not equally high in all groups: the difficult modules were implemented very well, while the simpler modules continued to be rather poorly executed, which can be explained by the heterogeneous team structure. (Good people are naturally drawn to the challenging topics.)

In the final phase of the project, the diploma exams were approaching, and thus the number of team members decreased. However, productivity did not suffer from this, as there were now a more manageable number of teams. During this phase, a project wiki was introduced for documentation, which was very well received by the individual team members. In it, all source code was briefly explained and any special features were highlighted. This documentation was available online everywhere and facilitated collaboration. The only issue was that it was introduced too late. An earlier introduction could have resolved some inconsistencies sooner. Integrating the individual subprojects on the target platform presented unexpected difficulties. Therefore, a very skilled programmer had to be assigned to this task. The inadequate adherence to quality management rules meant that it was not possible to compile or integrate a group's source code on another PC without significant effort. Due to the time lost as a result, it was not possible to implement all modules to complete satisfaction. As a substitute, beta versions had to be used.

In the end, the client was presented with the basic functions, and the project could be considered a success."

It is noticeable that the project manager in 2005 (Fig. 8.4) considered the project to be a special case from the XP perspective: Even the number of team members greater than twelve (there were up to 20 students) places increased demands on communication

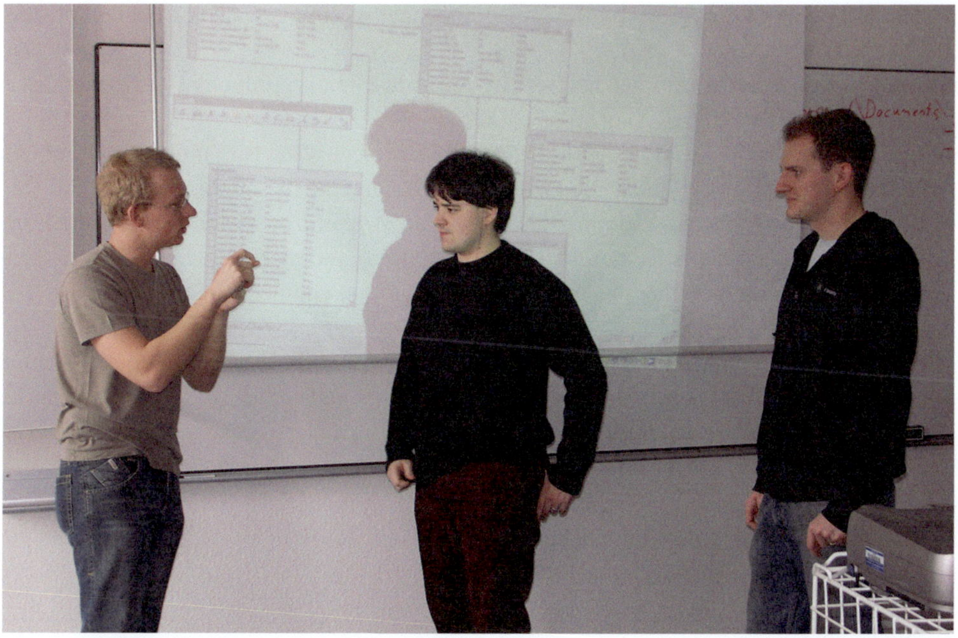

Fig. 8.4 Agile project manager (in the middle)

within the team. The lack of willingness to communicate is also explicitly mentioned as a problem in the first project phase. Lack of discipline and varying programming skills among team members make it difficult to establish the agile process. Collective Code Ownership is not observed (at least not on a voluntary basis).

Only through a redefinition of the project manager's role by the team were the most serious problems resolved. The "redefined" project manager

- acts as a communications manager between the individual programmer groups (mini-teams),
- maintains contacts between team members and the client, and in this context is also a key co-designer of user stories,
- motivates the mini-teams in the face of setbacks.

The agile project manager himself perceives the partial "regression" to the traditional project manager role, which imposes more and more guidelines on the team and monitors their compliance, as a step backward. However, the successes of the second project phase demonstrate the efficiency of this approach.

The following observations by the project manager in 2005 are also of interest:

- Fewer team members do not necessarily mean less team productivity. It depends on the team's performance!
- Documentation, for example with the help of a project wiki, is extremely helpful. An earlier introduction could have resolved some disagreements sooner.
- Integrating the individual subprojects on the target platform presents unexpected difficulties and must be delegated to a very skilled programmer. This leads to the introduction of a corresponding project role, the integration engineer (Sect. 8.4).

Finally, it should be noted that the project manager in 2005, due to his above-average programming skills, also acts as a.NET expert and is sought after for technical troubleshooting.

In summary, the role of the *project manager* can be described as follows:

- Coordinator of the project
- Problem solver
- Communicator
- .NET expert
- Co-designer of user stories

8.3.2 The Quality Manager in the Agile Project

The role of the quality manager, who in a "classical" project measures project quality and is responsible for creating the quality assurance plan, risk analysis, and test plans, is not defined in the agile project. As with the project manager, it was also decided in the 2005 student lab that a student should take on the role of quality manager in order to individually define this new agile role. The quality manager at that time describes his role as follows (Hanser et al. 2006):

Impact of Project Progress on the Role of the Quality Manager

"There is no classical quality manager in an agile project. So what are his tasks in an XP project?

At the start of the project, all project members had to be 'initiated' into XP, because no one on the team really knew what to expect, except perhaps that development would be done 'in pairs.' There was therefore a great need for clarification at the beginning regarding exactly how the project should proceed. To make things easier for the members, fixed rules were defined for how work should be carried out in the project.

New for everyone was that after each user story, the teams had to be changed, or that reviews between two teams should be conducted simultaneously, with one member from one group conducting a review with a member from the other group. All these rules were recorded on large posters that were hung on the walls of the IT lab.

The problems that arose from a quality assurance perspective were that some user stories were not implemented satisfactorily. There were mainly two reasons for this: on the one hand, team members were allowed to form teams themselves. This often resulted in teams with too great a disparity in know-how, both in terms of programming skills and knowledge of the.NET framework. On the other hand, many teams found testing and peer reviews to be a nuisance, so these important activities were neglected.

As the project progressed, the XP quality manager took on, in addition to the traditional roles of a quality manager—being responsible for testing, reviews, or code conventions—other roles that overlapped significantly with those of the project manager.

Through constant direct contact with the customer, the quality manager is also involved in specifying the user stories. However, since user stories are not detailed documentation but only mini-specifications in the customer's language, he, like the project manager, is a constant point of contact for developers to answer questions about the background and details of the implementation.

The quality manager, like the project manager, has a good overview of the status and problems within the project. He often also takes on the role of a *problem solver*. For example, when there are problems with implementation or integration, he tries to help himself or coordinates the next steps. He also works directly on particularly important tasks, such as database design, due to his experience, or reviews the developed concept. In situations where XP does not work, he develops new approaches together with the project manager, in line with Kent Beck's words, 'Fix XP when it breaks.'

Overall, it can be stated that, in addition to his traditional activities, the quality manager in an XP project also takes on other roles, some of which overlap significantly with those of the project manager.

In summary, for the entire project, it can be said that the project was only completed on time because XP was adapted in the way that was best suited for the team."

It is interesting that the quality manager in 2005 (Fig. 8.5), in addition to his "classical" quality assurance tasks, also has to handle tasks outside the usual role description. Essentially, he also takes on the role of process owner, training the other team members in XP.[4]

[4] And this, even though the other students had already learned about XP in a lecture. There really is a difference between theory and practice, isn't it?

Fig. 8.5 Agile quality manager (standing)

In the initial phase of the project, quality assurance tasks predominate, such as:

- Writing the quality assurance plan and risk analysis,
- Developing templates for test plans,
- Defining and disseminating project rules and code conventions (Fig. 8.6),
- Training in the review process and initial supervision of the same.

As the project progresses, the tasks arising from the project increasingly overlap with those of the project manager:

- Due to constant contact with the customer, the quality manager is part of the "core team" that develops the user stories. From this perspective, it becomes clear that *not all* team members are interested in creating user stories!
- Just like the project manager, the quality manager also sees himself as a constant point of contact for developers to answer questions about the user stories.

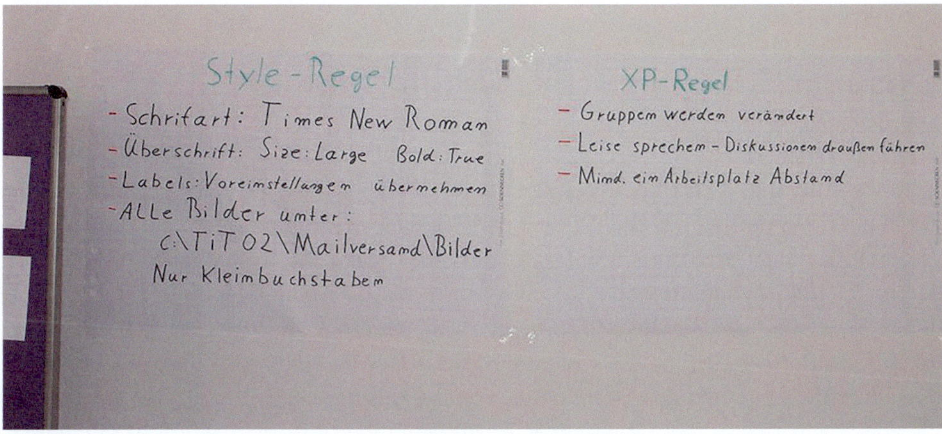

Fig. 8.6 Project rules as posters on the wall (1)

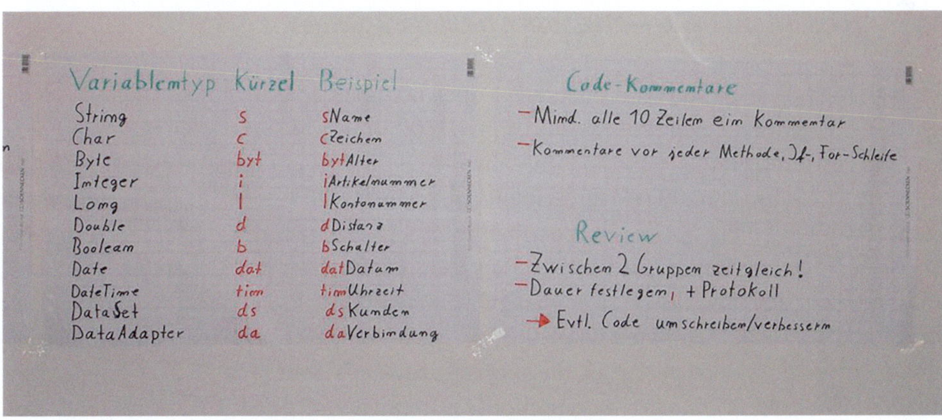

Fig. 8.7 Project rules as posters on the wall (2)

Since the quality manager in 2005 also has very good programming skills, his know-how as a.NET expert and his abilities as a technical trouble-shooter are also gladly used by the mini-teams.

In summary, the role of the *quality manager* can be described as follows:

- responsible for product and project quality
- defining project rules (Figs. 3.8, 8.6 and 8.7)
- conducting reviews
- tester

- problem solver
- communicator
- .NET expert
- co-designer of user stories

It is noteworthy that both students define their *new* role in a very similar way. They differ only in the first point, i.e., in the “classic part” of their new agile project role. Most of the time, both students perform similar activities: they teach the team (agile) project rules and support its implementation, especially in terms of communication. They set up a wiki as a central, simple archive for project documentation. They monitor the team structure and, if necessary, adjust the structure of the XP pairs. As part of the agile approach, the team, with these two *communication managers* at the helm, “fixes” XP for the first time and adapts one of the XP practices by allowing the self-organization of the pairs to be influenced by the two communication managers in the future.

8.4 New Team Role—the Integration Engineer

The path to successful software integration does not open up on its own. Negative experiences from the first session of the student lab (2004), in which the team was allowed to choose its own integration steps and only integrated on the very last(!) day, prompted the customer to require three-week integration cycles in the 2005 session. Although this is significantly more than is usually specified in XP projects (Sect. 3.3.1.5), it is still challenging for a young team. Even these integration cycles are not independently adhered to by the team. Continuous or at least regular integrations do not seem to matter to the team. Each mini-team works on its own issue. Massive intervention by the customer and a more “classic” understanding of the project manager’s role (Sect. 8.3.1) improve the situation. The role of “integration engineer” is created and filled by a very good (but) developer who prefers to work alone. This “lone wolf,” who always keeps some distance from the rest of the team with his integration computer, integrates very successfully. By filling this position, continuous integration becomes possible after about five weeks (Fig. 8.8).

All sessions of the IT lab have the same result: integration is *not* the result of the team’s self-organization, but the outcome of central planning by the project manager. There must be only *one* integration engineer with *one* integration computer! Integration by equal pairs, as is strongly advocated in XP (Sect. 3.3.3.5), has so far not led to success in the student lab!

Fig. 8.8 Integration engineer as "lone wolf"

8.5 Changing Agile Practices and Processes in Practice

As already indicated in the description of the changes to classic project roles (Sect. 8.3), some (especially "famous") agile practices are not sustainable in practice or need to be adapted. The practices considered below mostly originate from XP (Chap. 3), but are so universal that they are also used in Scrum, Kanban, and partly in DevOps. The following presents the results from the student lab.

8.5.1 Design of User Stories

In all sessions of the student lab from 2004 to 2008, creating user stories does not attract much interest among team members. The customer is hardly acknowledged as a team member. Only the project and quality managers (in their new understanding of their roles) and a few team members seek contact with the customer to achieve maximum quality and understanding of the user stories. Often, completed user stories are "interpreted" without asking questions. Only when developer mini-teams take responsibility for a user story do they become active and create a detailed low-level design.

8.5.2 Collective Code Ownership

Collective responsibility for the entire code is not very popular within the team in any of the sessions (see also the project manager's experience report in Sect. 8.3.1). Apart from the project and quality managers, only the few team members who were already involved in the user stories are able to understand the entire code—and not just the comparatively small part they developed themselves. A willingness for collective code ownership is not evident in any session from 2004 to 2008. Only the fear of making serious mistakes that could negatively impact the product prompts at least the aforementioned team members to "try out" collective responsibility for the code.

8.5.3 Mini-Team Size: Are XP Pairs Successful?

An interesting parameter for a process model is the size of the "subgroups" within the team (mini-teams) in which individual user stories are worked on. In XP, "pairs" are required: two developers sit at the same computer, one developer thinks strategically, the other operationally (Sect. 3.3.3.4). To analyze the "stability" of such pairs, in the 2004 session, teams of three are formed at the start, while in the 2005 and 2008 sessions, pure XP pairs are used from the outset. The question of how mini-team sizes change over time, as documented in Table 8.2, is of particular interest.

The following sequence of images (Figs. 8.9, 8.10, 8.11, 8.12, 8.13, 8.14 and 8.15) from the 2005 student lab shows the "decay" of XP pairs in favor of larger mini-teams, recorded from the project start at two-week intervals:

Table 8.2 Comparison of pair programming over the years 2004, 2005, and 2008

Session 2004	Session 2005	Session 2008
6 mini-teams with 3 members at the start	9 XP pairs as initial mini-teams	6 XP pairs as initial mini-teams
Over the course of the project, *no* XP pairs form spontaneously	The number of XP pairs decreases	3 XP pairs "survive"
The smallest team size remains 3	Most mini-teams grow. The number of members increases to 3, 4, and more	50% of the teams are XP pairs
The most successful mini-team has *4* members ("super-team" 1)	In special phases, e.g., during *integration*, there are team sizes with up to 6 members ("super-team" 2)	Integration: several pairs form an *integration team*

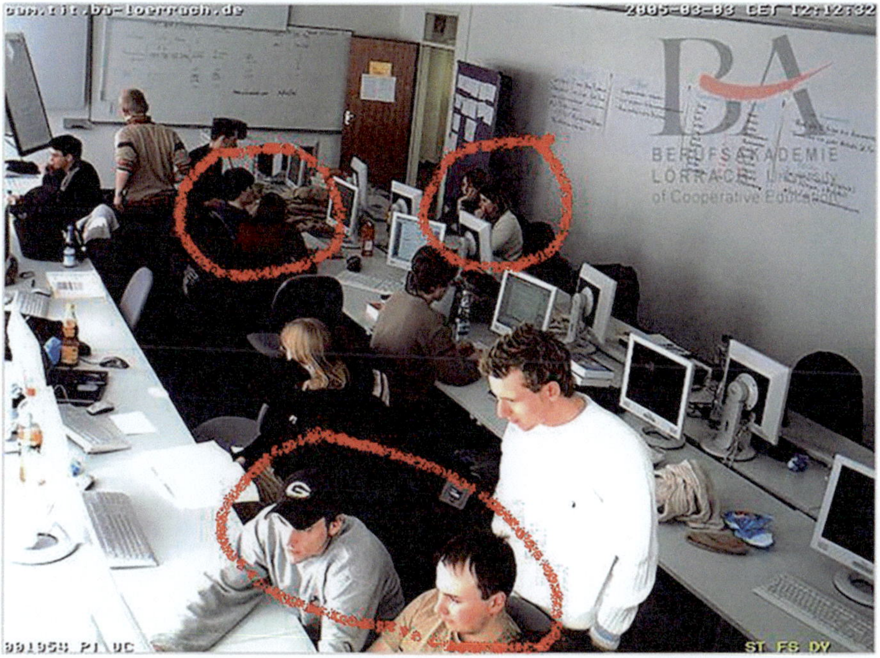

Fig. 8.9 Session 2005, project start: Three XP pairs can be seen …

Fig. 8.10 … plus another, making four XP pairs

Fig. 8.11 Session 2005, project start: A women's triplet can already be seen

Fig. 8.12 2 weeks later: Three XP pairs can be seen …

Fig. 8.13 … but also already a "super-team" supporting the integration engineer

Fig. 8.14 Four weeks later: only one "classic" XP pair remains …

Fig. 8.15 … but the super-team remains "stable"

Thus, it appears that XP pairs are "unstable." The size of the mini-teams changes constantly, depending on the task at hand. According to the author's experience, there is no reason for a team size of two, i.e., for pairs. For cross-cutting tasks, such as preparing for integration, a group of six is not uncommon. And even when pairs do form, this by no means implies that they are XP pairs. Often, "pairs" consist of a stronger and a weaker partner, where the first develops the structure of the solution while the other handles the details.

To better understand the internal structure of XP pairs in practice, a "fortunate circumstance" can be taken advantage of: in 2008, after four years, the first student lab with *three* stable XP pairs emerged, who also consciously identified as such. These XP pairs were required to fill out a form at the end of each project day, recording with which other team members or pairs they had collaborated (Fig. 8.16).

Both the completed form and the photos (Figs. 8.17 and 8.18) show that, even here, the composition usually resembles more of a team of three or four than "classic" XP pairs. This is not surprising: even when stable pairs form, they work intensively with other pairs, sometimes splitting up when one partner temporarily forms a "triplet" with another pair. It can happen that, during this time, one partner works in isolation. This is evident from the analysis of the "interaction form" of a typical XP pair (Fig. 8.19):

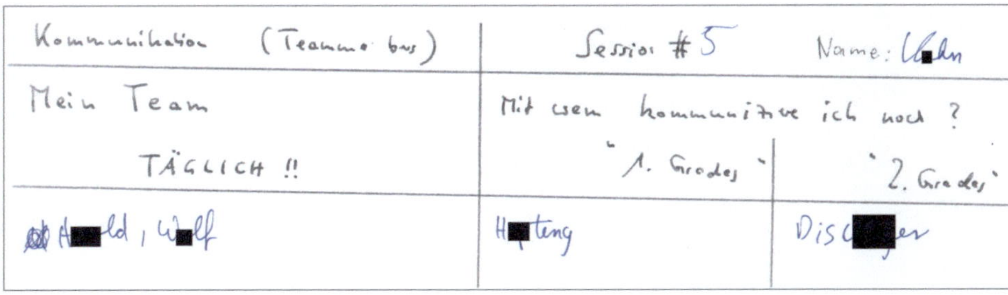

Kommunikation (Teammembers)	Session #5	Name: [redacted]
Mein Team	Mit wem kommuniziere ich noch?	
TÄGLICH !!	„1. Grades"	„2. Grades"
[redacted], [redacted]	[redacted]	[redacted]

Fig. 8.16 Form "Interaction between two pairs" (2008) (names redacted)

Fig. 8.17 Interaction between two pairs (back and front)

Conclusion: XP pairs are generally not stable, but rather change their structure toward larger mini-teams that form for specific tasks, such as integration. Of course, it is not impossible for the pairs to "reunite" after the specific task is completed, but it is more likely that they "dissolve" (Fig. 8.9, 8.10, 8.11, 8.12, 8.13, 8.14 and 8.15). The fact is that only in one out of five sessions in the student lab were multiple XP pairs stable and also identified themselves as XP pairs (Session 2008). "Classic" XP pairs tend to require similar types, since both pair members are supposed to alternate between strategic and tactical actions. Especially among men, this constellation fosters rivalries, which in turn jeopardize the pair's success. In the context of the student lab, well-functioning, equal

Fig. 8.18 Short-term formation of a triplet

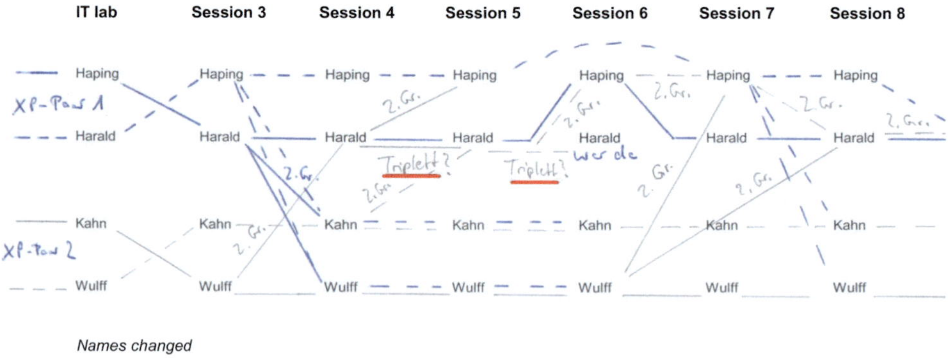

Fig. 8.19 Interaction between two pairs (2008)

XP pairs were found—apart from Session 2008—according to the author's observation, only among female students!

Figure 8.19 can certainly also be interpreted as the "inner workings" of a successful four-person mini-team. In the author's opinion, the "compulsive" division of successful mini-teams into XP pairs is not beneficial for the success of a project!

In the following chapter, the inner workings of a particular mini-team will be examined more closely, using the software integration phase as an example.

8.5.4 The Path to Successful Software Integration

XP requires that each pair integrates their code themselves (Sect. 3.3.3.5). However, this can only be done by one pair *at a time*. If pairs want to integrate their code one after the other and notice mutual dependencies in their code, they begin to communicate: What adjustments need to be made in the code programmed by each pair so that everything "fits together," i.e., so that neither syntactic nor semantic problems arise during integration. The pairs move closer together! The example from Session 2008 (Figs. 8.17, 8.18, and 8.19) shows that the pairs still see themselves as such, but work closely together. The "super-team" from Session 2005 demonstrates an even higher "degree of fusion." After only two weeks of the project, it forms (Fig. 8.13) and remains stable thereafter (Fig. 8.15), which can be seen, among other things, by the fact that it works on new user stories together. At the latest after the completion of integration, it should have "broken up" again into XP pairs! However, the members seem to enjoy working together in this group. Obviously, there is sufficient technical and social competence in the mini-team to tackle challenging user stories. Whenever such super-teams emerge, it can be observed that they take on demanding tasks. The super-team is therefore more than the sum of the original smaller units (XP pairs).[5]

It is important that, especially during the integration phase of one or more user stories, larger mini-teams form (or already work together successfully). There is a great need for communication here, which requires larger developer units.

Unfortunately, such super-teams are still not sufficient to guarantee regular and efficient integration. The reason is simple: even super-teams only see "their" user stories and their integration. If they see no reason for integration, none takes place. The solution here is the new role of the *integration engineer* described in Sect. 8.4 (Fig. 8.8). This person implements an integration plan devised by the project manager in consultation with the customer. The integration engineer is usually respected within the team—his or her technical competence is undisputed. He or she has the necessary "standing" in the team to demand code for pending integrations.

Based on the author's experience, developers tend to release only perfect code for integration. They try to keep the integration engineer waiting as long as possible until the "finished" code is ready. This code may indeed be error-free within the module, but inter-modular errors (i.e., errors at the interfaces between classes or modules) are often still undiscovered. Errors, for example, that result from the interaction between user stories, often remain undetected for a long time. The task of the integration engineer is therefore also to demand code *early*, i.e., to repeatedly make it clear to developers that it is better to submit code with minor method-level errors (of course, with a note about the error!) in order to speed up integration. During integration by the integration engineer, the affected mini-team can simultaneously eliminate the local "bug" and include

[5] Organizational psychology can explain why such team structures are so stable (Chap. 7).

the corrected method in the next integration step. Experience in the student lab shows that integration is massively accelerated in this way.

The student lab in recent years shows that super-teams form on their own, especially to solve integration problems, but that integration itself and its frequency must be managed by the project manager. The actual integration is the responsibility of the specifically created role of the integration engineer.

The following chapter (especially Fig. 8.21) shows that super-teams are also formed for other reasons, e.g., to accomplish complex porting tasks.

8.5.5 Crystal and Reflected Improvement

2007 is a special session: Here, a student can be recruited to accompany the team's process throughout the semester as part of his thesis. For him, the role of *process owner* is created (Hättich 2007).

The task of the 2007 project team is to port the existing email marketing software to Linux using the Mono project[6]. The process model specified by the author is *Crystal Clear*, the agile process model for smaller teams by Alistair Cockburn (2005). At the same time, a small subgroup forms during the second meeting, which deals exclusively with agile documentation (content management system Joomla[7] plus use of a wiki from previous teams), thus establishing its own small project.

In Figs. 8.20 and 8.21 you can see the project team evenly distributed in the room at the start of the project, which, at the first major task (porting the existing system to Linux), forms the first larger mini-team just three days later—a super-team with four developers. Thus, Session 2007 demonstrates the mini-team behavior already observed in previous sessions: larger mini-teams that focus especially on "mission-critical" tasks (in this case, a porting task).

By creating the new role of process owner, the 2007 team can be questioned much more intensively and, above all, in a documented manner regarding the process as it is actually practiced. As already described in Sect. 4.3, Crystal Clear, in contrast to XP, requires only a few mandatory characteristics:

1. regular delivery of the current, tested code,
2. reflected improvement of the process, achieved through regularly held meetings,
3. osmotic communication, i.e., information exchange within the team that takes place "incidentally," without additional effort (usually due to physical proximity).

[6] www.mono-project.com

[7] www.joomla.de

Fig. 8.20 Session 2007—Assignment of tasks (project start)

Fig. 8.21 Just three days later, the first larger mini-team forms (super-team for porting to Linux)

Are these requirements being met by the team? In a survey, team members are asked to assign school grades indicating the extent to which they have achieved the three objectives mentioned above. The responses are compared with the analyses of the process owner and the author (Fig. 8.22):

In particular, the process owner criticizes the irregular code deliveries and the lack of process reflection.

The team, on the other hand, gives itself the following average school grades regarding fulfillment of the Crystal Clear requirements (Hättich 2007):

This survey, conducted after about three-quarters of the project duration, is repeated at the end of the project for points 1 and 2, resulting in even better scores:

Process owner and author can only explain the good grade for osmotic communication (Tables 8.3 and 8.4). The other grades are not comprehensible from the perspective of Crystal Clear. Therefore, the team members are specifically asked again how they arrived at their grading:

For point (1) *Regular deliveries*, the following emerges (Hättich 2007):

How crystal-clear-compliant is the project team?

Project	Ideal	IT lab 2007
Number of employees	• 6 (max. 12)	• 11
Reflection workshop	• < 1 month	• never
Daily stand-up meetings	• Yes	• Never
Regular delivery	• End of semester	• Was adhered to
Osmotic communication	• Yes	• Yes, without problems
Iteration length	• 3 weeks	• Irregular
Easy contact with end users	• Yes	• Not often at the beginning • During the project, repeatedly as needed
Frequency of integrations	• Continuous	• Not possible at the beginning due to porting problems • Towards the end, integration was more frequent, although not regular

Fig. 8.22 Session 2007—Project team survey (Hättich 2007)

Table 8.3 Fulfillment of the Crystal Clear requirement from the team's perspective (1st survey)

	Crystal Clear Property	Grade
1	Regular code delivery	3.0
2	Reflected process improvement	2.9
3	Osmotic communication	1.7

Table 8.4 Fulfillment of the Crystal Clear requirement from the team's perspective (2nd survey)

	Crystal Clear Property	Grade
1	Regular code delivery	2.5
2	Reflected process improvement	2.3

Regular Deliveries

"Since the project was a porting task, it was hardly possible or very difficult to deliver finished code at the beginning. Toward the end, deliveries increased in both quantity and frequency. *Due to the nature of the task, regular deliveries were not possible*."

However, this is only partially correct. It is more likely that the team did not see the necessity for regular deliveries and therefore tacitly adapted the process model.

For point (2) *Reflected improvement*, the following emerges (Hättich 2007):

Regular Deliveries

"Here, the team did not interpret reflected improvement as a meeting, but rather as the *many improvements achieved through discussions in small groups* with the project manager, quality manager, and also with the customer."

While one might still speak of an "interpretation" of the Crystal property in the case of *regular delivery*, the team clearly took its own path with *reflected improvement*. The process as practiced is *no longer* Crystal Clear!

Session 2007 demonstrates the risk of *unspoken* process adaptation. The student lab clearly shows here that the team is not even aware of the process adaptation (or, even worse, does not care at all). In this way, the quality of the process gradually deteriorates, which, in the author's experience, very often leads to a decline in product quality as well. The consistently practiced role of the *process owner* can prevent this. In smaller projects, this role can also be assumed by the project manager or the quality manager, provided they still have sufficient capacity.

8.5.6 Scrum in the student lab

In the 2009 session, Scrum is "experimented with" in the student lab. After extensive training in the agile project management method, the role of Product Owner is filled by a student.[8] As part of an excursion, a room planning software for groups with physical disabilities is developed for a real client from the field of vocational qualification.

The project spans eight full working days with a team consisting of a Product Owner, ScrumMaster[9] and a ten-person team. The first three days take place as part of an excursion at the client, *Berufsförderungswerk Bad Wildbad (BFW)* (Figs. 8.23, 8.24, and 8.25).

The project workflow of the BFW project is described in the ScrumMaster's "diary" (excerpt):

Fig. 8.23 Session 2009—The client in discussion with the product owner and team

[8] The selection process, involving self- and peer-assessment, is examined in more detail in Sect. 9.5.4.

[9] This role is assumed by the author.

Fig. 8.24 Product owner with sprint backlog as user stories

Fig. 8.25 Clients of the Berufsförderungswerk Bad Wildbad (BFW) waiting for the sprint review

From the "Diary" of the Scrum Master

Day 1 (BFW)

Afternoon: After the announcement of the task (in the morning), the team organizes itself. Initial conflicts arise regarding the coding conventions. A "speaking token" is introduced to channel the discussion.

A "User Story Core Team" quickly forms, consisting of the customer, Product Owner (PO), and five team members. Thus, Scrum is already being "extended" for the first time.[10]

The User Story team "overdoes it." They try to find the "optimal" solution, i.e., to specify the final solution. This does not succeed; the ambition is too high.

The ScrumMaster (SM) points out the principle of *Simplicity*. The Product Owner identifies three user stories to start with, which are estimated by three mini-teams. The sprint length is set to two days.[11]

A mini-team of one to four developers takes care of the coding guidelines.

Day 2 (BFW)

Morning: Intensive coaching of the Product Owner. It is not so easy to get into this complex and initially unfamiliar role.

10:00 to 10:15: *Daily Scrum*: Mini-teams report on their progress. The seating arrangement is criticized. The seating arrangement is changed. Some team members have trouble adhering to the conventions (order of speaking).

11:30: The customer discusses requirement details with the PO.

Afternoon: Dividing the first sprint into three large user stories proves to be too "coarse." Some developers get bored because there are no additional user stories available for them to work on.

13:30: Two and a half hours remain until the end of the first sprint. The sprint review meeting is scheduled for 4:00 p.m. The integration computer is provided by the customer and is ready for use.

15:55: The Integration Engineer (IE) hesitated too long to install the first release of the software on the integration computer. Shortly before the start of the sprint review meeting, the application is still not running on the integration computer.

16:10–16:45[12] **:** *Sprint Review No. 1* begins with a ten-minute delay. The demo has to be run on the IE's notebook. Thus, the requirement that the demo must run on the integration computer is not met. The team demonstrates the features of the first release. The PO announces that the team has successfully implemented 66% of the user stories. One reason for the deductions is that the demo did not run on

[10] The ScrumMaster lets the team proceed and observes the approach.

[11] This is very short, but justified given the short project duration of eight days in the student lab.

[12] Since sprints are quite short in the student lab, the meetings also end more quickly.

the integration computer. This problem is to be solved by the end of the next sprint. The customer praises the team; his expectations are met! In the discussion, the IE develops into the "spokesperson" of the group.

Day 3 (BFW)

8:30–9:45: *Sprint Retrospective*. The unanimous opinion of the team is that the first sprint went "pretty well" (pleasant atmosphere). The team is satisfied. IE would like better time management for integration and also addresses technical aspects (how is the shared codebase managed? New story card *Versioning/shared project server*). The team criticizes: code could be submitted earlier. Collective code ownership should be "lived" better in the future. Some team members wish for better communication between the mini-teams working on the individual story cards. Others feel this is already the case.

There is disagreement about the code documentation language. Although English was previously chosen (coding conventions), German is now selected, but English parts remain (new story card *Improve comments in the code of Sprint 1 if necessary*).

The team discusses how to prevent duplication in the design. This leads to the story card *Refactoring groups/rooms* for the next sprint.

In the following sprints, idle time for team members should be avoided. This results in a *process change/extension* and thus an *adaptation* of Scrum:

From now on, team members with free resources or new ideas can formulate potential story cards and "feed" them into the system. For this, there is a new role in the team: the *Story Coordinator* (SC). The team member discusses the new idea/story card with the SC. The SC makes a preliminary selection and passes the selected story cards on to the PO. The new story cards are considered in the next sprint. However, there is also a *new* possibility to add a new story card to the current sprint, but this should be the *exception*. The end of the sprint does not change as a result!

Other new roles are agreed upon: Quality Assurance/Tester (QA) for functional testing of the sprint increments on the integration computer.

10:15–10:30: The *Daily Scrum* starts a bit late. It is brief, as many topics were already addressed in the retrospective meeting.

10:30–13:50 (excluding a one-hour lunch break): *Sprint Planning Meeting*. This time, the PO clearly takes on *too much* work: 37(!) user stories for the next sprint. An objection from the SM triggers a discussion in the team. Opinions are divided. Story cards are grouped by topic. The PO defines the three most important user stories for the next sprint. There is a controversial debate about whether complex stories should be handled by larger mini-teams. The sprint length is again set to two days.

The fourth to eighth project days take place in the student lab. The following problems arise:

Overview

Day 5

9:15: In the middle of the second sprint, a fundamental discussion begins between the PO and two team members about the project's goal. This discussion is important, but does not belong in the sprint. The SM blocks the discussion and postpones it to the next sprint planning meeting.

9:45: SM coaches PO to define realistic final goals for the software (concept of spatial proximity of training rooms).

16:00–17:00: *Sprint Review No. 2.* Although the PO accepts 85% of the user stories in the sprint backlog as completed, the discussion with the customer[13] gives the impression that the implementation misses the customer's wishes. The customer again explains his wishes in detail (manual room variations and simulations with additional groups, calculation of the resulting room utilization). PO and the team "readjust" their goals.

Interestingly, in the subsequent retrospective meeting, the division of the team into two rooms is not criticized. The resulting quiet is seen as a benefit. The team does not perceive a lack of osmotic communication.[14] It is also interesting that the team constantly needs feedback from the Product Owner. He is often involved in conversations with team members. It is obviously very difficult to bring the requirements fully into the team during the sprint planning meeting.

A one-time rescheduling of the Daily Scrum on day 6 to 1:00 p.m. shows how quickly the team has become accustomed to 10:00 a.m. It is important to always hold daily meetings at the same time. The "diary" of the ScrumMaster from day 7 and the last day (excerpt) is again interesting:

From the "Diary" of the Scrum Master

Day 7

15:45: Sprint Review starts in half an hour. The team is busy and restless.

16:15–17:00: *Sprint Review* proceeds very professionally. IE demonstrates the current release of the software in a professional manner. During the demonstration, he occasionally finds minor issues. Perhaps detailed test plans are needed after all.

[13] The customer is connected via a web-based conference tool.

[14] Here, the ScrumMaster, i.e., the author, has a different opinion.

Ad-hoc testing does not catch all errors. *Conclusion:* Successful sprint, but since not all story cards were implemented, only 50% fulfilled (PO). The customer is impressed by the solution. Minor issues still need to be fixed in the final sprint.

Day 8

8:45: SM has to intervene because the PO is "wasting" too much project time trying to keep track of all remaining open user stories in the final phase. This blocks the team, as it cannot yet work on the open user stories. This standstill costs one developer hour every six minutes! And the final submission deadline is set for 14:00. PO finally releases all priority 1 user stories, even without estimates from the respective mini-teams. The estimates must be provided later by the respective mini-team.

14:00–14:45: The final *Review Meeting* starts on time. The whole team worked surprisingly calmly and focused on the final touches. The state of the software is impressive, the software runs stably. A few minor things still do not work, but are to be corrected after the review session. The customer sees his expectations met, in large part even *exceeded*, and is very satisfied.

14:45–16:15: The team eliminates the last bugs, organizes tests with test plans, and conducts them together.

16:15: The software is submitted by email including documentation[15]. The focus was not on documentation, but all working documents, backlogs, code conventions, etc. were collected and centrally archived.

16:20: ---END OF PROJECT--- The project had about 580 project hours, that is, 4.8 programmer months. Great achievement!

The reasons for the project's success are

- the consistent assignment of project roles,[16]
- the use of Scrum for regular sprints with a *defined delivery date*,
- a small and motivated team!

However, during the course of the student project, Scrum had to be extended by the role of the *Story Coordinator*, which allows team members with free resources or new ideas to formulate these as potential story cards and "feed" them into the system, i.e., after pre-selection by the Story Coordinator, to present them to the Product Owner (see "Diary—Day 3").

[15] Link to the project wiki.

[16] For the assignment procedure with self- and external assessment, see Sect. 9.5.4.

Finally, some comments from the students, collected in a survey at the end of the project, are summarized:

- By a large majority, the usefulness of the *Daily Scrum* meeting is confirmed. In just fifteen minutes, the whole team could get an overview of the current state of the project. The division of the project into fixed sprints was also perceived as effective.
- There was one XP pair in the team. The remaining team members worked on user stories in mini-teams of varying sizes.
- The usefulness of the formal sequence of the various Scrum meetings is questioned (with the exception of the Daily Scrum).

It should also be noted that there is a risk of overburdening the Product Owner. He must be seen as a "bottleneck," since he is mainly responsible for contact with the customer, which puts a heavy time burden on him. There is a risk that the team will have to wait for his user stories, which actually happened in the student lab. In a real project outside the lab, he must be given the opportunity to plan and prepare the project several days in advance. This will generally be the case. The Product Owner comments on the usefulness of the process requirements as follows:

Thoughts of the Product Owner on Implementing the Process Requirements
Positive/effective:

- The *role distribution* used in the project seemed sensible to me. The integration of the individual software modules, communication with the customer, goal formulation, and process monitoring cannot be regulated democratically by the entire team. For this, there were the roles of integration engineer, product owner, and process observer.
- The daily reflection on one's own work by each team member during the *Daily Scrum* was a good opportunity to reconsider strategies and to recognize possible conflicts with other teams at an early stage.

Negative/problematic:

- The *independent selection of tasks by the mini-teams* in combination with a very heterogeneous developer team could lead to inexperienced programmers overwhelming themselves with highly complex tasks, while experienced mini-teams dealt with rather simple tasks. Here, a system for coordinated task distribution may be lacking, e.g., during the sprint planning meeting. However, this would come at the expense of time.

- The *Product Backlog*[17] proved to be too time-consuming and, as it grew, simply not flexible enough to be updated regularly, especially regarding prioritization. Instead, it increasingly degenerated into a pool of ideas, which was only skimmed during release planning and when creating user stories for the next sprint. It only became helpful when the individual items were sorted by category to provide a better overview. But does this really have to be in table form? A pen and a few sheets of notes serve the same purpose, at least in such a short project with correspondingly short sprints and limited preparation time.

These statements clearly show the absolute necessity of the team's *experience* with agile approaches. Nevertheless, after some familiarization, this student team was also able to apply Scrum.

For more on team composition and the distribution of project roles, see Sect. 9.9. Possible extensions and adaptations of Scrum will be discussed there.

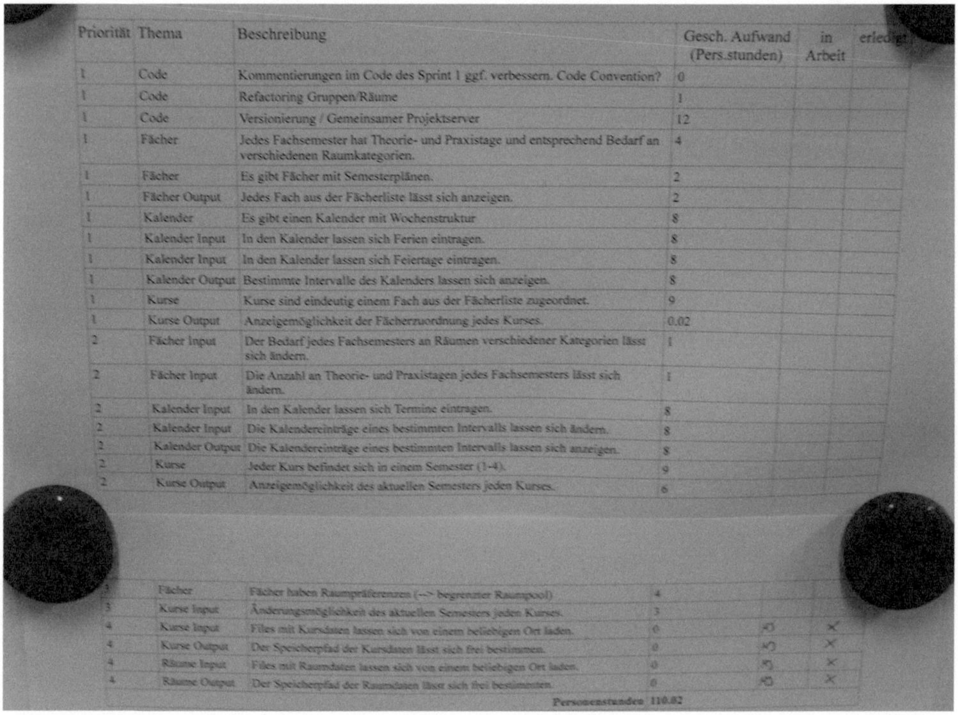

Priorität	Thema	Beschreibung	Gesch. Aufwand (Pers.stunden)	in Arbeit	erledigt
1	Code	Kommentierungen im Code des Sprint 1 ggf. verbessern. Code Convention?	0		
1	Code	Refactoring Gruppen/Räume	1		
1	Code	Versionierung / Gemeinsamer Projektserver	12		
1	Fächer	Jedes Fachsemester hat Theorie- und Praxistage und entsprechend Bedarf an verschiedenen Raumkategorien.	4		
1	Fächer	Es gibt Fächer mit Semesterplänen.	2		
1	Fächer Output	Jedes Fach aus der Fächerliste lässt sich anzeigen.	2		
1	Kalender	Es gibt einen Kalender mit Wochenstruktur	8		
1	Kalender Input	In den Kalender lassen sich Ferien eintragen.	8		
1	Kalender Input	In den Kalender lassen sich Feiertage eintragen.	8		
1	Kalender Output	Bestimmte Intervalle des Kalenders lassen sich anzeigen.	8		
1	Kurse	Kurse sind eindeutig einem Fach aus der Fächerliste zugeordnet.	9		
1	Kurse Output	Anzeigemöglichkeit der Fächerzuordnung jedes Kurses.	0.02		
2	Fächer Input	Der Bedarf jedes Fachsemesters an Räumen verschiedener Kategorien lässt sich ändern.	1		
2	Fächer Input	Die Anzahl an Theorie- und Praxistagen jedes Fachsemesters lässt sich ändern.	1		
2	Kalender Input	In den Kalender lassen sich Termine eintragen.	8		
2	Kalender Input	Die Kalendereinträge eines bestimmten Intervalls lassen sich ändern.	8		
2	Kalender Output	Die Kalendereinträge eines bestimmten Intervalls lassen sich anzeigen.	8		
2	Kurse	Jeder Kurs befindet sich in einem Semester (1-4).	9		
2	Kurse Output	Anzeigemöglichkeit des aktuellen Semesters jeden Kurses.	6		
3	Fächer	Fächer haben Raumpräferenzen (--> begrenzter Raumpool)	4		
3	Kurse Input	Änderungsmöglichkeit des aktuellen Semesters jeden Kurses.	3		
4	Kurse Input	Files mit Kursdaten lassen sich von einem beliebigen Ort laden.	0	[illegible]	×
4	Kurse Output	Der Speicherpfad der Kursdaten lässt sich frei bestimmen.	0	[illegible]	×
4	Räume Input	Files mit Raumdaten lassen sich von einem beliebigen Ort laden.	0	[illegible]	×
4	Räume Output	Der Speicherpfad der Raumdaten lässt sich frei bestimmten.	0	[illegible]	×
		Personenstunden	110.82		

Fig. 8.26 Scrum product backlog on the wall

[17] See also Fig. 8.26.

8.5.7 Hierarchical Processes under the Agile Veil

In the 2006 session, something strange happens due to a change in the framework conditions: The author actually wants to try out which type of project manager a team would choose if given the opportunity. In practice, this almost never happens,[18] but in the student lab, this scenario practically suggests itself. Will the team choose a moderator or an "autocrat"?

The team indeed selects a strong, hierarchically oriented project manager,[19] who approaches his task with zeal and diligence. He organizes the creation of user stories with the customer, selects the participating team members, and formulates the user stories. In a daily meeting (which actually takes place sitting down), he assigns the user stories to individual mini-teams. However, he only influences the composition of the mini-teams when he deems it necessary. The result is a "classic" iterative-incremental process, which is *successful* in terms of achieving the project goals! However, this success is bought at the cost of an excessive and, from the author's perspective, *unhealthy* workload for the project manager. In the end, both the project manager and the author agree that it would have been better to distribute the work among several shoulders (i.e., to proceed in a more "agile" manner).[20]

In retrospect, the author is certain that the project team, which knew and could assess the future project manager well from several years of courses, consciously made this decision to save themselves work. They were obviously confident that the project manager's high level of commitment would save the team effort. The approach of letting the project manager be chosen is no longer pursued by the author in the student lab.

The formation of the mini-teams, however, is unaffected by the hierarchical project structure. Pairs and triplets form, which also dissolve or change their composition. Interestingly, no super-team forms (Figs. 8.27 and 8.28).

Based on all the experiences described in the student lab, the author is left with the central question of whether the approach of process models is even the right one. Does it not restrict the team too much? Would it not be better to merely define the framework conditions for the process and let the team find the appropriate agile team process?

[18] At least, the author is not aware of any such constellation.

[19] Who, according to the author, also comes from a correspondingly hierarchical company.

[20] Nevertheless: great respect for the project manager's performance, which could not even be graded within the context of the student lab.

Fig. 8.27 Session 2006—Pairs and triplets in the hierarchical process

Fig. 8.28 No super-team forms in the hierarchical process

References

Beck K (2009) https://wiki.c2.com/?CthreeProjectTerminated, last edited June 19,2009. Zugriff September 2024

Cockburn A (2005) Crystal Clear: A human powered Methodology for small Teams. Pearson. Dt. Übersetzung: Crystal Clear: Agile Software-Entwicklung für kleine Teams. mitp-Verlag

Cockburn A (2008) alistair.cockburn.us. Zugriff August 2009

Fowler M (2005) https://www.martinfowler.com/articles/newMethodology.html#id2251638. Zugriff September 20024

Hättich N (2007) Das agile Prozessmodell Crystal, Studienarbeit, DHBW/BA Lörrach, Studiengang Informationstechnik

Hanser E (2006) Extreme Programming in Real World at the „IT Laboratory“ of BA Loerrach, ISTC Conference Proceedings. Vaal University of Technology, South Africa

Hanser E, Brecht U, Michelbach A (2006) Agile Software-Entwicklung: Extreme Programming im IT-Labor der BA Lörrach. BA Dialog Nr. 6

Hanser E (2014) Kompetenzzentrum für agile IT Prozesse (KAP), https://dhbw-loerrach.de/kompetenzzentrumagileprozesse. Zugriff Dezember 2024

MAP—Meta Agile Process Model 9

The experiences described in the student laboratory provoke the central question of whether the approach of continually developing new process models is actually the right one. The Meta Agile Process Model (MAP), developed by the author and first published in 2009, therefore takes a different path: MAP is a systemic model that defines the framework conditions for the process but gives the team enough space to find the appropriate agile team process themselves. In particular, an organizational-psychological perspective of the team is taken into account.

Is the approach of continually developing new process models the right one? This central question arises from the experiences described in the student laboratory of the Competence Center for Agile IT Processes (KAP).[1] Does the strict adherence to a prescribed process model not restrict the team too much? Even in the student laboratory, it was repeatedly observed that members of the team were not familiar with the required process model (despite having previously attended a lecture on the subject). Isn't it generally better to define only the framework conditions for the process and let the team find the appropriate agile team process themselves?[2]

9.1 Team Psychology—Map of Team Behaviors

Organizational psychology identifies six behaviors of team members that, according to the author's experience, are essential for a successful team: communicators, idea generators, subject matter experts, and team workers, who are important for the mini-team, as

[1] Baden-Württemberg Cooperative State University (DHBW) Lörrach, https://www.dhbw-loerrach.de/kompetenzzentrumagileprozesse (KAP).

[2] But to be absolutely clear: knowledge of process models is indispensable, as it allows team members to use the rules and practices described there as a "toolbox" for daily use.

E. Hanser, *Agile Processes—Agile Teams*, https://doi.org/10.1007/978-3-662-72726-3_9

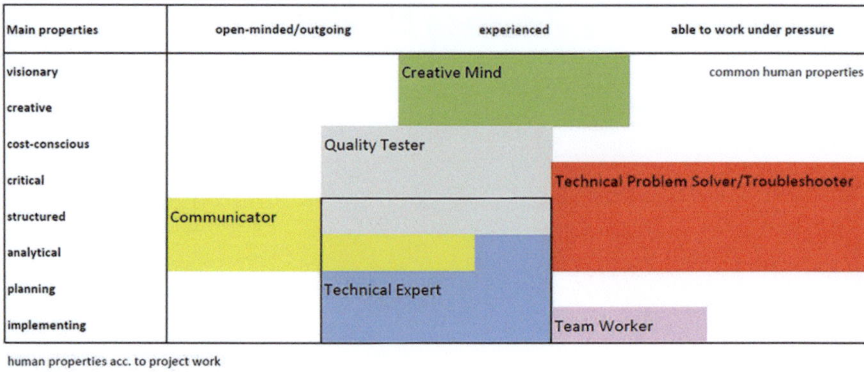

Fig. 9.1 "Map" of team behaviors

well as problem solvers and quality assessors, who are (additionally) significant for the entire project team (Fig. 9.1).[3] The mix of these different behaviors forms the foundation for the team's success.

The map of team behaviors (Fig. 9.1), referred to as *MAP*[4] for short, is to be "read" as follows:

In the top row, from left to right, are general human properties. With respect to project work, the following are particularly important here:

- ready to communicate
- experienced
- resilient (i.e. able to work under pressure)

In the front column are human properties that play a particularly important role in projects:

- visionary
- creative
- cost-conscious
- critical
- structured
- analytical

[3] Highly recommended on this topic are also (Baldegger 2004) or (Baldegger and Gotsmann 2001). The above figure was created in discussion with Mr. Baldegger.

[4] In addition to being the acronym for Meta Agile Process Model, this is another reason for the naming of the agile meta-model; see also (Hanser 2009).

- planning
- implementation-oriented

The types of team members, or more precisely their *behaviors*[5, 6] in the team, result from the combination of these human properties.[7] In the map, the resulting behaviors partially overlap:[8]

- The *Communicator* must participate in the project with open eyes and recognize and resolve communication problems. He must analyze a problem in a structured way and communicate it to the team. For example, he does not need to be visionary or implementation-oriented, nor does he need to excel at working under pressure.
- The *Creative Mind* is experienced and ready to communicate, as well as visionary and creative. Typically, he lacks a critical, questioning attitude. Costs usually play little role in his considerations. He does not need to be resilient.
- The Technical *Expert* has strengths in structured, analytical, and planning approaches. He is experienced, generally open to other opinions, but also has a clear preference for "doing," for implementing the solution.
- The *Technical Problem Solver/Troubleshooter* performs at his best under pressure. His experience and his critical, structured, and analytical thinking help him to "pull the cart out of the mud" in difficult situations. "Normal" project tasks, such as planning iterations or cost estimation, usually interest him less.
- The *Team Worker* is the "implementer"[9] in the team. Together with his mini-team, he takes on a user story and implements it independently with his colleagues. He is often experienced and usually quite capable of achieving his goals under pressure. However, these traits are not the main focus. Experience in the student lab shows that the team worker is generally less interested in participating in cross-team tasks, such as creating user stories.

---

[5] For the sake of linguistic clarity, the term "MAP types" will be used hereafter, with the understanding that these are not personality types in the psychological sense. The assignment of a person to their "MAP type" can certainly change over the course of life (especially in younger years)!

[6] For simplicity, the masculine forms are used here, with the clear understanding that women make a significant contribution to the team's success and also improve the team climate.

[7] It should be noted, however, that people can also embody several such behaviors. Moreover, behaviors change over the years. The world is not just black and white!

[8] Each behavior thus represents a colored rectangle in the "MAP." The behaviors of quality tester, communicator, and technical expert overlap due to the partially matching underlying human traits.

[9] Caution! In discussions with psychologists, the term Team Worker often causes confusion. Psychologists often see the Team Worker as a "worker on the team process" (Baldegger and Gotsmann 2001). Here, the Team Worker is understood as a "worker" on the product (e.g., as a programmer implementing a user story).

- The *Quality Tester* has only one goal: to ensure the maximum quality of product and process. He is experienced and critical, thinks in a structured way, and keeps an eye on costs. He is often "orthogonal" to the team, making him well-suited for the role of quality assurance. Unlike the classic project role, however, he needs more communication skills in the agile team.

9.2 Existence of All MAP Types in the Team

If the existence of all outlined MAP types is the foundation for a team's success, then in a successful team, one must find the MAP types in a "reasonable," complete mix. It therefore makes sense to examine the super-team from the 2005 student lab (Sect. 8.5.3) for the behaviors present among its team members.

9.2.1 The Super-Team in the Student Lab

The super-team from the 2005 session at the author's *Competence Center for Agile IT Processes* (Hanser 2014) originally formed in response to an integration task and initially worked in support of the integration engineer (Fig. 8.13). The super-team is of great importance for the project's success! In particular, its successful coordination of the sub-activities prior to the first integration made the success of the 2005 session possible in the first place. What is special is that the super-team remained stable even after completion of the integration task. The members realized that this form of organization brought them advantages. In contrast to the overall team, this sub-team did not need an internal quality reviewer, as this role was taken over by the project team's quality manager. Likewise, the super-team did not need its own troubleshooter. In the 2005 session, this role was assumed by the project and quality manager (Sects. 8.3.1 and 8.3.2). According to MAP (Fig. 9.1), the super-team as a project sub-team therefore needs the four MAP types (behaviors): communicators, creative minds, subject matter experts, and team workers. Fig. 9.2 shows the actual composition of the super-team from the 2005 session:

As can be seen, all behaviors required by MAP are present in the super-team. It should be explicitly emphasized once again that this sub-team formed *spontaneously*. The trigger was an important integration task after the customer (the author) had vehemently demanded adherence to the delivery deadline. The successful super-team thus formed under external pressure and without management intervention—simply out of necessity—and remained together after successfully completing the task! The super-team was "looking for" members with the behaviors necessary for success[10]!

[10] It should also be noted that the author developed MAP (the map of behaviors) in parallel with the formation and existence of the super-team. MAP therefore came first, and there was great satisfaction when all behaviors identified as necessary for the team's success could also be isolated in the super-team. Incidentally, Fig. 9.2 was later confirmed by the then project manager.

Fig. 9.2 "MAP types" (behaviors) in the super-team of the 2005 session

This is a successful confirmation of the map of behaviors (Fig. 9.1). To enable a project's success, it is therefore sufficient to provide the project team with enough (but not too many) members who possess the behaviors necessary for success. The successful mini-teams needed to solve a tricky task will then form on their own.[11]

9.2.2 Comparison with Belbin's Team Roles

Although the MAP types or MAP behaviors can be derived from the analysis of the super-team, it is also possible to derive the MAP types from Belbin's nine team roles (Belbin 2004, 2007). However, it must be taken into account that Belbin analyzed management teams, not development teams.

The complete mapping of Belbin's team roles to the MAP types shown in Table 9.1 is also strong evidence for the completeness of the six MAP types for a successful team. All Belbin team roles are represented in the MAP team! Experience to date shows that the six MAP types are sufficient to predict team success[12] (Fig. 9.13).

[11] Nevertheless, the existence of an integration engineer, the "lone wolf," is indispensable, as this task can only be managed centrally (Sect. 8.4).

[12] So far, in no discussion has the absence of a MAP type been demonstrated.

Table 9.1 Mapping of Belbin's team roles to MAP types (behaviors)

Belbin's Team Roles	MAP Types
Coordinator & Resource investigator	Communicator
Plant	Creative Mind
Completer & Monitor evaluator	Quality Tester
Shaper	Technical Problem Solver (Troubleshooter)
Specialist	Technical Expert
Teamworker & Implementer	Team Worker (Developer)

9.3 What is MAP?

Over the course of (project) years, the author has become increasingly convinced that the approach of constantly developing new process models is misguided. While it is important to provide students and trainees with fundamental process models as a project "toolbox," it is even more important in project practice to identify the minimal "ingredients" required for a successful, agile team and thus a successful process. The author refers to this approach as the "Meta Agile Process Model." MAP is therefore a *meta-model*. The focus is not on defining an agile process, but on defining the *framework conditions* for the agile process:

Based on the author's experience in the student lab, a successful *MAP team* (with up to 20 team members) requires the following agile *project roles*:

- A *customer* who takes their role seriously and is available to the team not necessarily always, but often enough.[13]
- One or two good and flexible *communication managers* who divide up project and quality management tasks, but above all ensure communication within the team and with the customer.
- An *integration engineer* who, while solely responsible, is monitored by project management, demands and guarantees continuous project integration.
- A well-balanced *MAP team* with a healthy psychological process, in which all *types* known from organizational psychology are sufficiently represented.
- A *process owner (MAP observer)*, who documents the actual process as practiced and its changes, and monitors compliance with agreed rules and practices. (This can also be handled by the quality manager!)

[13] The customer can also, as in Scrum, be replaced by a Product Owner.

If these roles are filled, the choice of software development process model plays a subordinate role according to findings from the student lab. The *MAP team* will find the appropriate process within the project's boundary conditions.

The approach of describing the framework conditions for a project rather than process steps is certainly unusual for the reader. However, it arises from the problem that a process, which is constantly changing anyway, cannot form an *invariant* in the life of the team:[14] How is a team member supposed to remember a process that is constantly changing! It is better if the team draws on its knowledge of process models to select rules and practices that *fit* the current project or project situation, rather than wasting energy following a certain process that, at least in the student lab, has always proven to be suboptimal over time.

It is also true, however, that all student groups over the years have followed a kind of *minimal process*. This will be presented in Sect. 9.6.

9.4 The MAP Team as a System—Integration into the Viable System Model

The "Meta Agile Process Model" (MAP) places the team, with all its internal and external interactions, at the center of the pursuit of project success—and not the chosen (agile) process! The MAP team is a social[15] system, which, through the existence of suitable MAP types (see Sects. 9.1 and 9.2), possesses control and regulation mechanisms that enable a successful project course. These mechanisms can be observed, with the help of the Viable System Model (VSM) developed by Stafford Beer (Beer 1979, 1981), on three recursion levels of interaction within the project: communication at the company level (client and contractor), communication of the MAP team with its immediate environment, and the interaction of the individual team member with their environment.

The Viable System Model is a suitable neurocybernetic model that can describe the MAP team and its interactions "systemically": While the MAP teams of a company are integrated at level 1 like other agile project teams into the company (see Hanser and Wehinger 2012), the MAP team can also be represented within the VSM at the team level (level 2) and at level 3 of individual behaviors (MAP types, see Fig. 9.1) with their interactions, as well as control and regulation mechanisms (Hanser and Wehinger 2012).

The Viable System Model forms the basis of the "St. Gallen Management Concept" (see also Schwaninger 2000). It describes a company with its structures and project

[14] Since the author studied physics, his life has been shaped by the search for conservation laws and invariants;-).

[15] The author also likes to use the term "societary" to express that it is a social system that exists purely as a "contractual society" within the framework of a project (see also the definition in DWDS 2023).

teams as a viable system and is strongly oriented towards the structure of the central nervous system: The *operational subsystems* (in a biological organism, these would be, for example, muscles or organs) interact with their *environment*, monitored by a *metasystem*, which in biology corresponds to the nervous system and the brain (Walker 2020). The metasystem is divided into *systems 2 to 5*, while the operational subsystems are referred to as *system 1*. While system 2 coordinates the systems 1, system 3 is the operational management, which is extended by the audit and monitoring functions of system 3*. System 4 interacts with the environment and houses strategic management, while system 5, the normative management, is responsible for the value system of the team and its members.

Figures 9.3, 9.4 and 9.5 show different recursion levels of the Viable System Model (Hanser and Wehinger 2012): Figure 9.3 shows recursion level 1: The MAP teams are integrated as agile project teams into the company with its control and monitoring subsystems and act as parts of their organization with the company environment. Figure 9.4 shows recursion level 2: The MAP team members are the operational systems 1, which are coordinated by system 2, consisting of internal communication managers. In software production, the coordination function is performed by the integration engineer (system 2). System 3, the operational management, is the team itself, which manages itself within the framework of its planning meetings, etc. It is supported by the MAP observer (system 3*), who coaches the team. The external communication manager(s) maintain contact with the customer to identify and develop new or changing specifications (user stories). The normative system 5 corresponds to the "MAP culture" of the team, which is maintained and further developed in the team's reflection meetings (Hanser 2015).

Figure 9.5 shows recursion level 3 of the Viable System Model, i.e., the individual *MAP team member* with their various identified MAP behaviors. As an example, this figure shows a team member who is suitable to represent the customer's interests within the team, i.e., to replace the customer.[16] Accordingly, this person has three personal MAP system 1s (also called MAP types), the MAP behaviors *Communicator*, *Quality Inspector*, and *Expert* in decreasing order of importance, as indicated by the decreasing size of the system 1 boxes. Each system 1 represents important characteristics for specific tasks, which together correspond to the tasks of a Product Owner. The team member coordinates their behaviors (system 2) and manages themselves through reflection on their own agile working methods (systems 3 and 3*). The team member communicates and interacts with the other team members, where expectations can lead to conflicts. The team member has a strong "agile" value system with a high degree of personal responsibility and self-organization, as is generally observed in members of agile teams.

[16] In Scrum, this team member would be a suitable *Product Owner* (Schwaber 2004).

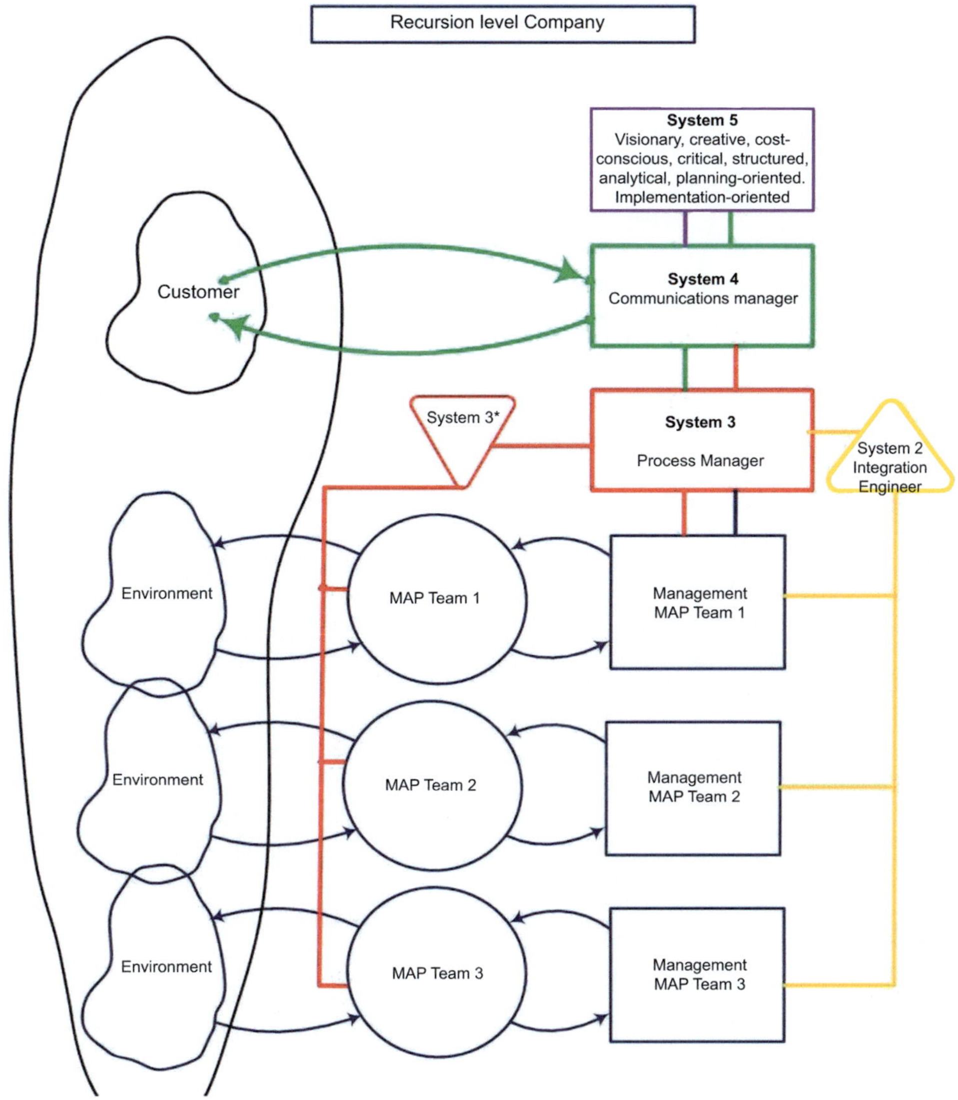

Fig. 9.3 VSM recursion level 1—the company level

The seamless integration of MAP into the Viable System Model at three recursion levels[17] shows that MAP fits well into the VSM. MAP teams thus form, in the sense of the VSM, viable systems that possess the "organizational intelligence" necessary to successfully carry out projects that are critical in terms of time and requirements.

---

[17] Without any adaptation of MAP!

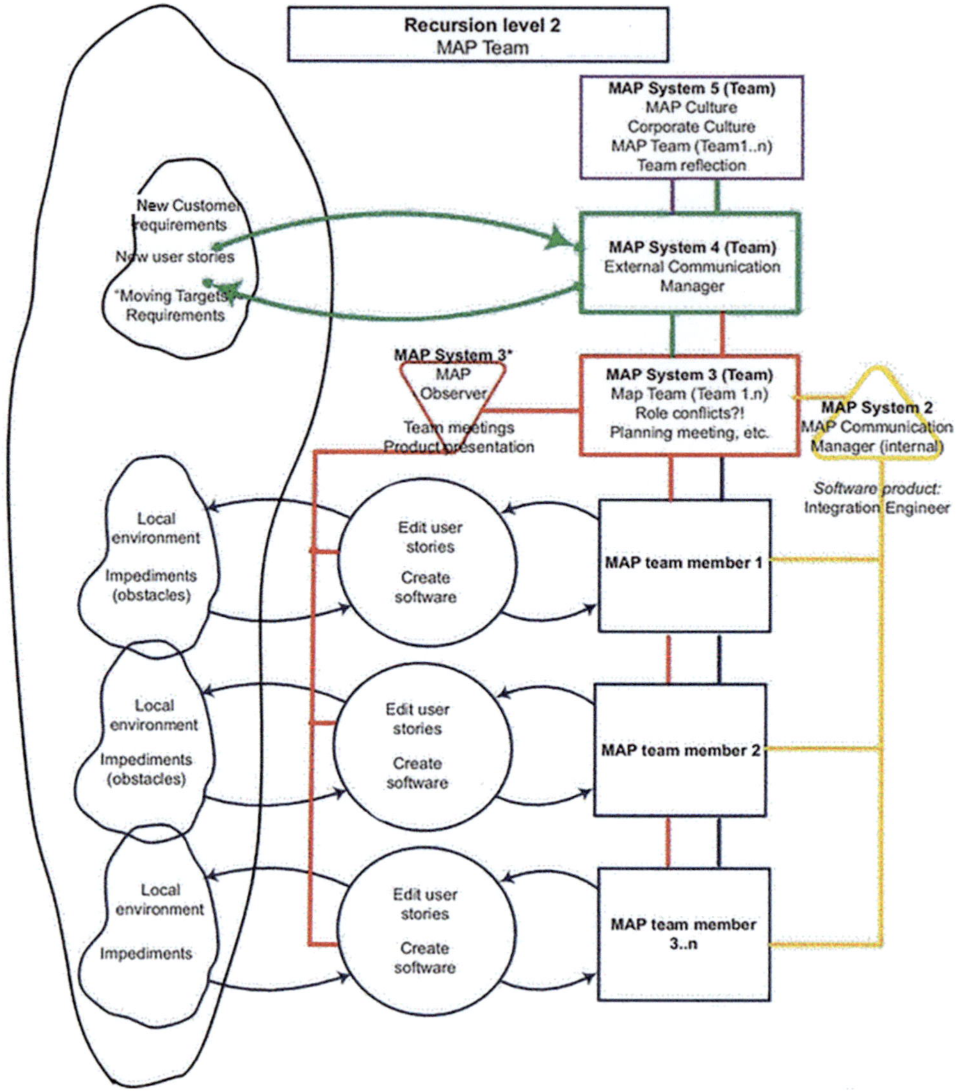

Fig. 9.4 VSM recursion level 2—the MAP team (Figs. 9.3, 9.4 and 9.5 were developed together with Jan Wehinger (Volkswagen Group Research, Foresight and Trend Transfer) (Wehinger 2013))

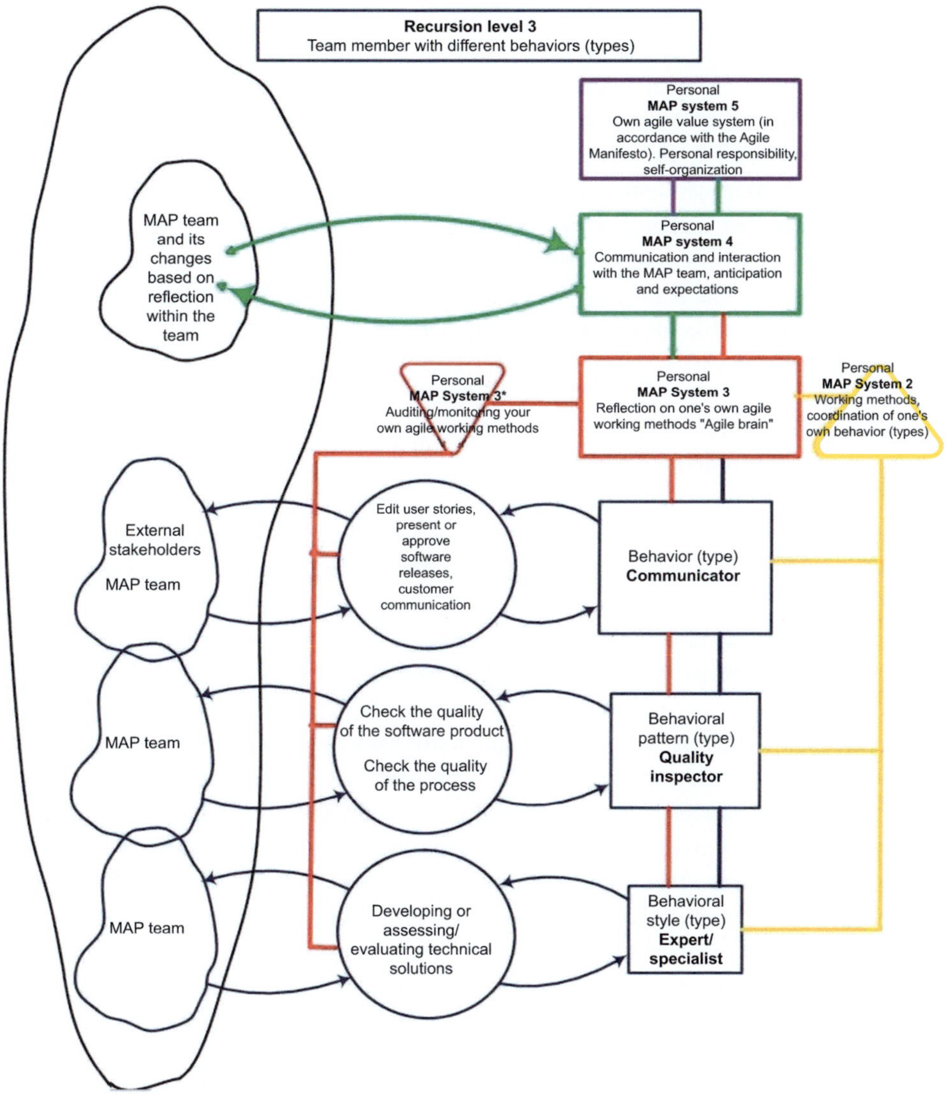

Fig. 9.5 VSM recursion level 3—MAP team members with their different behaviors (types)

9.5 MAP—the Project Roles in the Team

Since MAP is a meta-model, special importance should be attached to the project roles. The team members who take on these roles must be carefully selected. As the student lab in 2006 showed, otherwise a hierarchical process can easily develop under the guise of agility (Sect. 8.5.7).

9.5.1 Customer

The *customer* must keep a close eye on the final product to be created. He alone is responsible for ensuring that the finished product is *of value* to the client. Thus, he *validates* the product.[18] His professional qualifications must be particularly strong, but so must his assertiveness within the customer organization, that is, on the client side. Nothing is worse than a change to the product initiated by the customer within the team, but rejected by other users of the software product! The *central* factor is the availability of the customer. The team must be guaranteed a response time when questions arise. Therefore, it is advisable to support the customer with a *Product Owner*, as known from Scrum (see Sect. 5.1.1).

9.5.2 Communications Manager

Experience from the student lab shows that most projects suffer from a lack of communication (Sect. 8.3.1). Communication fundamentally takes place in two directions:

1. Communication within the team
2. Communication between the team and the customer

Communication *within* the team is fundamentally osmotic (Cockburn 2005). By having all developers present in the same office, it is ensured that everyone notices when a topic concerns several developers (and thus might be of interest to the whole team). In the student lab, the author usually just strolls through the rows of desks and is then generally well informed about the team's current problems. This must apply to every developer as well. Nevertheless, communication between the mini-teams is sometimes limited. Since they usually work on different user stories, from the perspective of the mini-teams there is often little need to be informed about *all* the concerns and issues of the project team.[19] This is where the communications managers come in. By holding *stand-up meetings* or similar gatherings, the flow of information is promoted. In critical project situations, all team members are immediately informed. During integrations, a shared knowledge base regarding the functionality of the targeted version is established. This can also be achieved by initiating a short presentation by a subject matter expert (Fig. 9.6).

---

[18] However, usually without the elaborate validation process known, for example, from the V-Model.

[19] Of course, this also has to do with the size of the team: Teams with fewer than five people do not report communication problems to the author.

Fig. 9.6 Presentation in the student lab (Session 2007)

According to experience from the student lab, communication *between* the team and the customer is even more critical.[20] It is hard to believe how often the customer is "interpreted" instead of simply being asked. In the student lab, there was rarely a team that did not occasionally succumb to this temptation. Interestingly, the attempt to interpret the customer can be found even when the customer is present with the team in the same project rooms throughout the entire project. Here, the communications manager must intervene. He maintains the connection with the customer and tries to recognize when a mini-team needs information from the customer. It is also important that the team is informed in a timely manner about any changed project constraints.

Thus, a communications manager, in the team's "external relations" with the customer, takes on tasks that are classically found in project management. It is therefore not surprising that in MAP teams with more than five people, several communications managers usually share project and quality management tasks. In the student lab, it has proven effective for two communications managers to take on project management and quality management, respectively. It is important that these classic project roles are filled separately, as their goals sometimes conflict: while the project manager must keep an eye on deadlines and costs, the quality manager can focus entirely on the demand for optimal quality.

[20] Or Product Owner.

9.5.3 Integration Engineer

The role of the integration engineer is already discussed in Sect. 8.4. Negative experiences in the first student lab were the trigger for introducing this role. It is simply not enough, as required in XP for example (Beck 2000), to provide an integration machine; you also need the corresponding responsible person, the integration engineer. While it is true that this can create a bottleneck in the project workflow, experience in the student lab shows that the advantage of having an expert and troubleshooter in a central position outweighs this. It is clearly defined who is responsible for integration. To make it clear once again: each mini-team is responsible for assembling the code to be integrated and handing it over to the integration engineer. But the actual integration on the integration machine is carried out by him alone. In doing so, he must resolve any problems that arise with the involvement of the affected mini-teams.

Interestingly, the V-Model XT (see Sect. 1.4.1) has a comparable project role, the *system integrator* (role *D.1.28* in Weit 2019). However, in the "heavyweight" context of the V-Model, this role also takes on additional tasks in the area of testing (e.g., providing a test environment), acceptance of external units, or creating documentation. Such tasks can also be taken on by an integration engineer as needed. Thus, his range of tasks may correspond to that of a system integrator in the V-Model XT.

9.5.4 Team

The team is at the center of MAP. This is not unusual in agile projects per se. What is new is that, according to the "map" of behaviors within the team (Fig. 9.1), MAP sets clear requirements for the behaviors[21] that must be present in the team.[22] As outlined in Sect. 9.1, a successful MAP team needs the following MAP types:

- Communicators
- Creative Minds
- Technical Experts/Specialists
- Technical Problem Solvers/Troubleshooters
- Team Workers
- Quality Testers

[21] As already mentioned in Sect. 9.1, for the sake of clarity, the term "MAP types" is preferred, fully aware that these are not personality types in the psychological sense.

[22] Thus, MAP sets requirements for team psychology!

Main characteristics		Ready to communicate	experienced	resilient	General human characteristics
MAP	Cross set		X	X	
Visionary					
creative					
cost-conscious					
critical/inquisitive	X				
structured	X				
Analytical	X				
planning					
Implementation-oriented	X				

Project-related Human qualities

Fig. 9.7 Self-assessment form (completed)

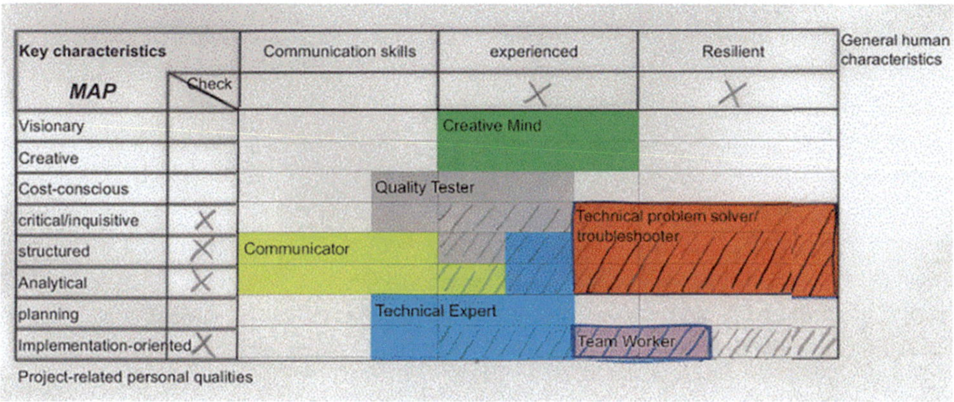

Fig. 9.8 Self-assessment form (manual evaluation)

The "super team" in Fig. 9.2 shows that in a small, successful team, each MAP type is simply present. Larger teams naturally require several individuals of the same type in a balanced ratio. An interesting question is how this team composition can be achieved:

The starting point is the assessment[23] of potential team members with regard to their behavior in the team—the "MAP type." In the student lab, a combination of self-assessment and two external assessments has proven effective. For this purpose, the author developed a form[24] that is suitable for both types of assessment (Figs. 9.7 and 9.8).

[23] In companies, the works council should be involved in such assessments. It is important that such information *must not* be used for employee evaluation under any circumstances.

[24] Of course, the evaluation is now "automated." Teams can register for free and perform self-assessments on the research website https://map-model.de.

Figure 9.7 shows a completed self-assessment form. If this assessment is confirmed by at least one external assessment, it forms the basis for assigning one or more MAP types.

In Fig. 9.8, a transparency with the MAP types (i.e., the team behaviors) is placed over the self-assessment form. [25]As can be easily seen, in this example the self-assessment matches *Technical Problem Solver* or *Team Worker* with one hundred percent agreement. The match with *Quality Checker* and *Expert* is about 50%. There is no apparent match with *Communicator* or *Idea Generator*. Thus, in this example, the team member is very well suited as a *Technical Problem Solver* or *Team Worker*.

With this method, the team can be assembled in a balanced way by ensuring that all MAP types are sufficiently represented.

9.5.5 Process Owner—the MAP Observer

A *process owner* is the person who documents the process as it is actually practiced and its changes, and monitors compliance with agreed rules and practices. (This can also be handled by the quality manager!) They must have in-depth knowledge of fundamental "prototypes" of process models and must not hesitate to modify and adapt the process model in use. (This is always necessary!)

In case of doubt, however, the project and thus the fulfillment of the assignment take priority! Nevertheless, in the student lab it has proven advantageous to have a team member who insists on adherence to the agreed rules and practices, such as holding regular team meetings and implementing reflective improvements. A project manager is rather unsuitable for this task. Here, there is a conflict of interest with achieving the project goal.

9.5.6 Project Roles in the Map of Behaviors

Figures 9.7 and 9.8 show how self-assessment and external assessment can be used to assign one or more MAP types within the team. What is still missing is the mapping to the other defined MAP project roles. For this purpose, the author developed a second slide that can be placed over the self-assessment form.[26] Here, in addition to the behaviors, an assignment to the MAP project roles is made (Fig. 9.9).

[25] Once again, reference is made to the research website https://map-model.de, where teams can register for free and perform self-assessments.

[26] See also https://map-model.de.

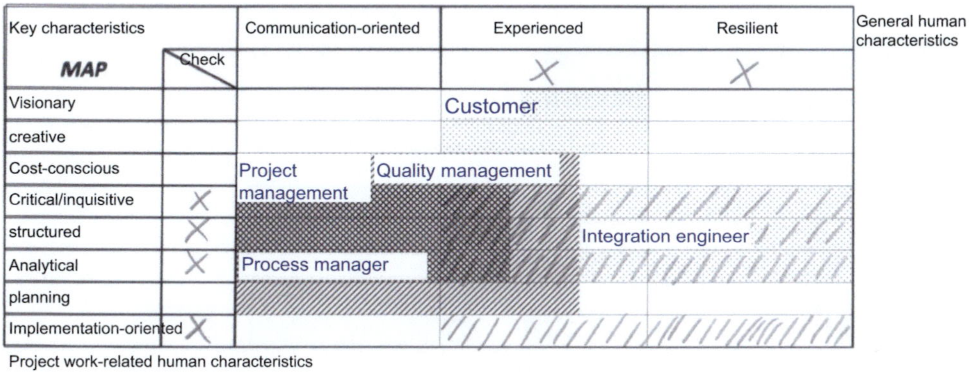

Fig. 9.9 Assignment to project roles (manual evaluation)

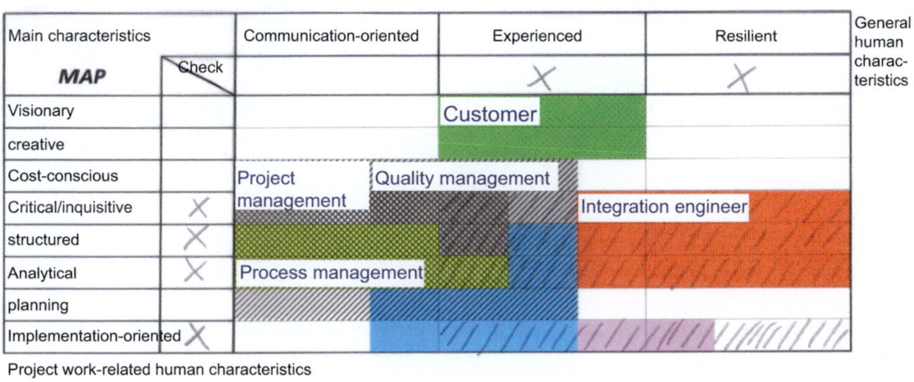

Fig. 9.10 Behaviors and corresponding project roles

In the example, one can see the potential suitability for the *integration engineer* role.

It is important to note that this is a *potential* suitability. Professional qualifications and assertiveness must confirm this suitability.

Figure 9.10 shows MAP types and project roles superimposed:

9.6 MAP Cycle—the Reference Process

Based on the experiences from the student lab, a “MAP minimal process” can be defined (Fig. 9.11). It is *important* to understand that this *reference process* itself is also just a *best practice*. The experiences in the student lab simply showed that all student teams

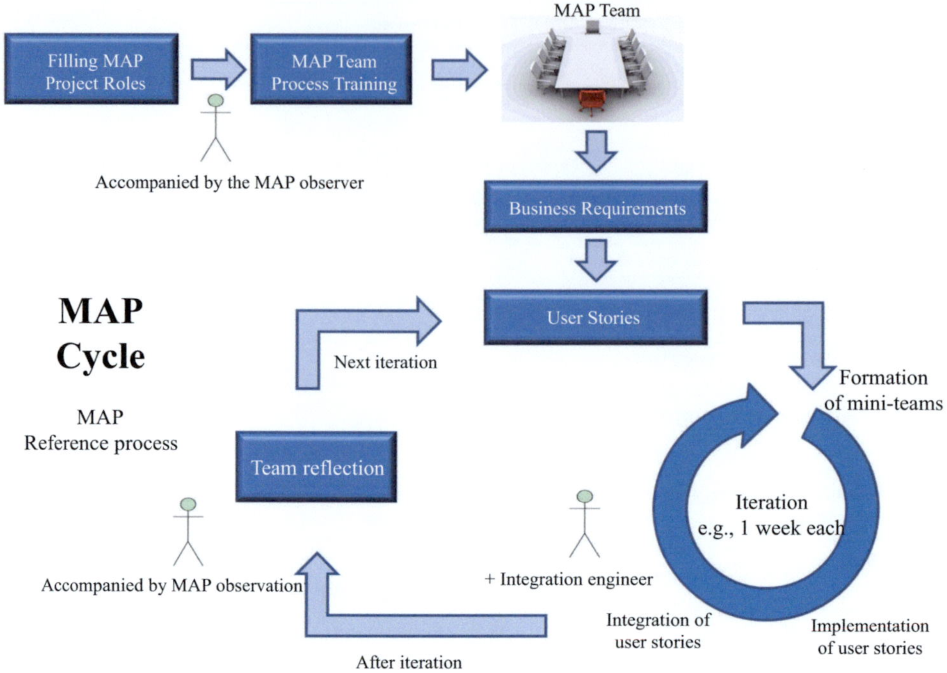

Fig. 9.11 MAP reference process (minimal process, best practice)

more or less followed this process. This is certainly also related to their knowledge of iterative-incremental processes.

At the beginning of the project, the essential project roles must be filled. Experience in the student lab shows that it is indeed possible to assign at least the *project manager* and *quality assurer* in a completely "classical" way by management.[27] What is new is that management relies on the self-assessment forms of the applicants (Fig. 9.7).

The *MAP observer* (Sect. 9.5.5) is often brought into the project from outside in practice, e.g., as an external consultant and coach. In the student lab, this role is assumed by the author, at least for inexperienced teams. The *integration engineer* should be elected by the team based on their "application documents" (self- and peer-assessment forms), but can also be appointed by the project manager and quality assurer.[28]

[27] In the student lab, the author assumes the management role.

[28] This strengthens the role of the quality assurer compared to "classical," non-agile projects. Of course, self- and peer-assessment forms must also be taken into account here.

In the next step of the MAP cycle, the team[29] is "sworn in" to the process or meta-process.[30] Afterwards, user stories are written based on the business requirements. As already mentioned, this work is carried out by a "core team" (Sect. 8.3.2)—in the student lab, team members can choose whether or not to participate. (In practice, team members who do not wish to participate join the team later.)

With the distribution of user stories, the actual development cycle begins: First, the effort for each user story is estimated by the mini-teams. Then, the user stories are implemented and integrated on a computer with the help of the integration engineer. The result—the release—is presented to the customer in a formal presentation (review). Deviations from customer requirements are immediately identified and documented as new user stories. As is typical in agile projects, the integration cycles last about one to two weeks.

After integration, a *reflection phase* is mandatory. This is the responsibility of the MAP observer. It can be very brief and may, for example, take the form of a *stand-up meeting*, but it should not be omitted. It is important that team members briefly discuss the current process—that is, their daily collaboration in the project—highlight strengths, and identify weaknesses. It is also important to immediately name countermeasures.[31] The MAP observer documents the results and makes them available to everyone.[32]

The 2007 session of the student lab (Sect. 8.5.5) clearly shows that many discussions in small groups do not lead to process improvement. This is because not all team members are informed about the intended improvements! The team needs a *joint* reflection session. Only in this way is everyone informed and able to "live" the discussed process improvement.

After the reflection session, the team works on the next user stories. These may either be leftover from previous iterations or newly created from the customer demonstration of the current software release. This marks the beginning of the next cycle.

It should be explicitly emphasized again that the MAP cycle is a *reference process* (minimal process).[33] The focus is on fulfilling the conditions of the meta-model *MAP*. However, it has been shown in the student lab that the participating teams followed the

[29] A note on the team: In the student lab, the students' course is the team; in practice, developers should have the opportunity to apply for a position on the team—naturally with completed self- and peer-assessment forms.

[30] Even for students in the lab, a brief review is beneficial—despite a prior lecture!

[31] Weaknesses for which no countermeasures can be named (e.g., "political" conditions in the company environment) paralyze the team and should not be the focus. However, it does no harm to document them.

[32] It has proven effective to create a dedicated section in the project wiki.

[33] The MAP reference process is quite similar to Scrum, but is significantly more flexible, especially regarding sprint length.

MAP cycle process without much intervention from the author. Nevertheless, in line with Kent Beck (Wells 2009): "Fix the actual MAP process if it breaks." A chosen process is therefore only valuable as long as it moves the project forward—and does not hinder it!

9.7 MAP in Practice

Since 2004, analysis of student projects at DHBW Lörrach,[34] teams from other universities, as well as corporate teams[35] has shown that social extensions of development projects according to MAP increase the quality of both the project *and* the product. A correlation between project success and a good team role assignment according to MAP can be demonstrated (see Fig. 9.13). Notably, the corporate projects show no deviations from the student projects! This is to be expected, since the "young professionals" who typically work in agile corporate projects generally do not differ much in behavior and training from the students in the student projects, especially as these students are already in higher semesters during the projects and, due to their dual studies, have already gained practical experience in corporate projects.

The great success of the projects studied is based on the consistent implementation of the "project ingredients" required by MAP. In advance, team members underwent a self-evaluation and two external evaluations. From this, the project-specific "map" (MAP) of behaviors in the team was determined and the project roles were assigned.

As shown in Fig. 9.12, two separate calculations are performed when assigning behaviors or *types* to the project members. Therefore, each team member (represented by the numbers 1 to 7) is assigned two bars. In principle, the height of the bar is a measure of the affinity to the respective type. The smaller, blue bar (left) only takes into account evaluation results if they appear in at least two out of three evaluations. Everything else is disregarded. The good assignment of team member no. 2 to the communicator type thus means that the corresponding project-related and general human characteristics were checked in two to three evaluations and thus appear dominantly. Single mentions are not considered. The affinity to the respective type is calculated from the overlap of the "crossing areas" of the project-related and general human characteristics with the types in the "map" of behaviors in Fig. 9.1. The situation is different with the higher, red bar (right). Here, all mentions of the characteristics are taken into account. Thus, each team member forms a pair of bars, which, in comparison with the other team members, clarifies the assignment to the corresponding project type:[36] For example, team members no. 2 and 5 are well suited as communicators!

[34] The more recent ones in a corporate environment (Sect. 9.11).

[35] Now with several hundred participants.

[36] Here, the red bar is always as high or higher than the blue bar, since the red bar also includes less pronounced characteristics.

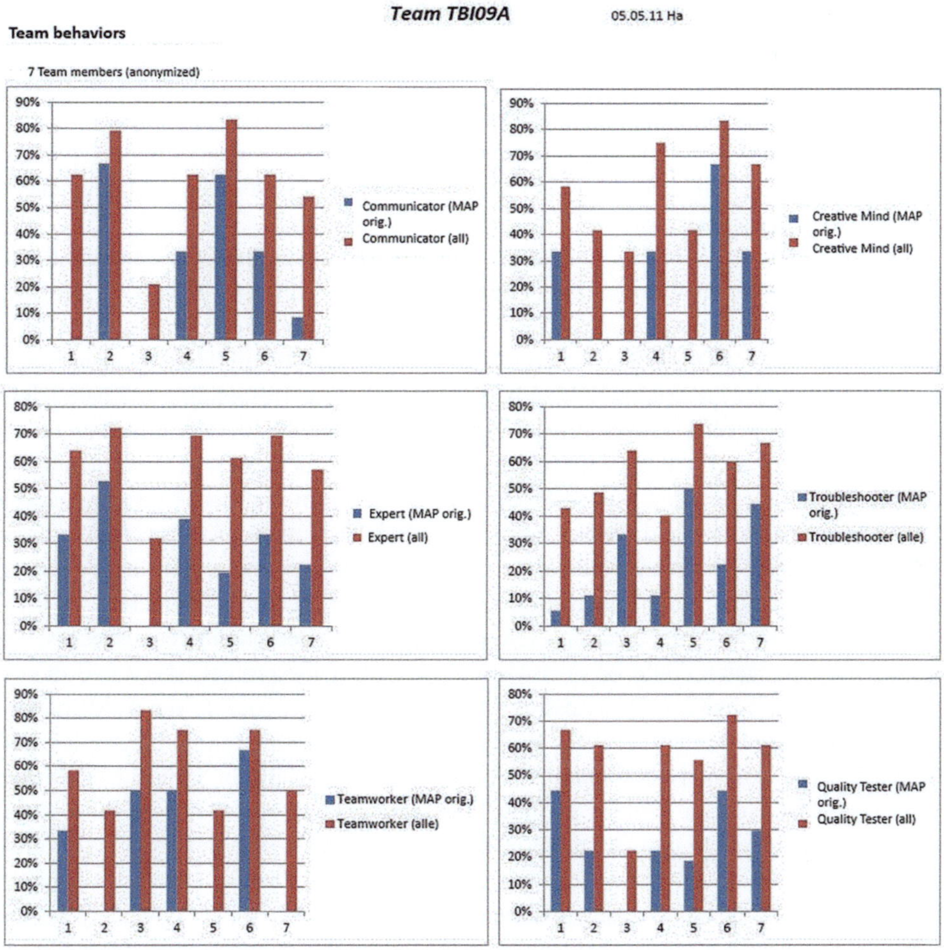

Fig. 9.12 Behaviors in the team—Evaluation Project 2011

However, Fig. 9.12 also shows team members for whom the development of a type is not very pronounced. For team member no. 3, for example, the "sharper" left, blue bar is zero for the assignment to four types. The corresponding right, red bar shows a height between 20% and 30% four times. This team member is therefore quite balanced and "unremarkable" with regard to the four behaviors Communicator, Idea Generator, Expert, and Quality Checker. However, there is an affinity to the team member (Teamworker) and—less pronounced—to the Troubleshooter.

9.8 Competing Teams—Predicting Team Success with MAP

To be able to compare project success, it is interesting to observe teams that have to complete a project in a competitive situation under the same conditions. This situation, which rarely occurs in companies, is more often observed in university projects. It is also important for these university teams to have a certain degree of technical homogeneity, which facilitates comparison.

Table 9.2 presents an initial comparison of the MAP evaluation of three student Scrum teams from the Baden-Württemberg Cooperative State University (DHBW) and their measured project success (Hanser 2013). For simplicity, to determine simple "MAP coefficients" for Product Owner (PO), ScrumMaster (SM), and Team (TE), the mean values are calculated from the "sharper" blue bars (left) and the corresponding red bars (right) known from Fig. 9.12. The overall team values incorporate the MAP coefficients for PO with a factor of 2, SM with a factor of 1.5, and TE with a factor of 4 (4 team members!). This takes into account that a good Product Owner has more influence on team success than the ScrumMaster—and the ScrumMaster, in turn, has more influence than a "regular" team member. However, it should be noted that in this example, four team members are working in parallel, so the team's influence on project success is very large.

As Table 9.2 shows, in the case presented, MAP can indeed predict team success! The project success, which could be measured at the end of the project, about two months after the MAP evaluation, by assessing the product, corresponds to the MAP ranking of the teams at the beginning of the project, according to which the project roles were assigned.[37] The extremely important role of the team (especially in Scrum) is confirmed by the fact that even the ranking of "just" the team characteristics matches the project success of the teams. In particular, TE in Team1 dominates with a very high MAP coefficient of 81%. However, Team1 also has the most suitable Product Owner according to MAP, at 60%. It is also interesting that the quality of the ScrumMaster obviously has less influence on project success. This can be explained by the rather "administrative" tasks in the project. If the project comes under pressure, the importance of the ScrumMaster role will increase and have a greater impact on project success.

Table 9.2 MAP ranking of three competing student teams at DHBW

	PO	SM	TE	MAP-Index	MAP Ranking				Project Success
					PO	SM	TE	Total	
Team1	60%	49%	81%	69%	**1**	3	**1**	**1**	97%
Team3	56%	36%	50%	49%	2	4	2	2	92%
Team2	38%	58%	42%	44%	3	**1**	3	3	82%

[37] With the goal of maximizing the MAP index.

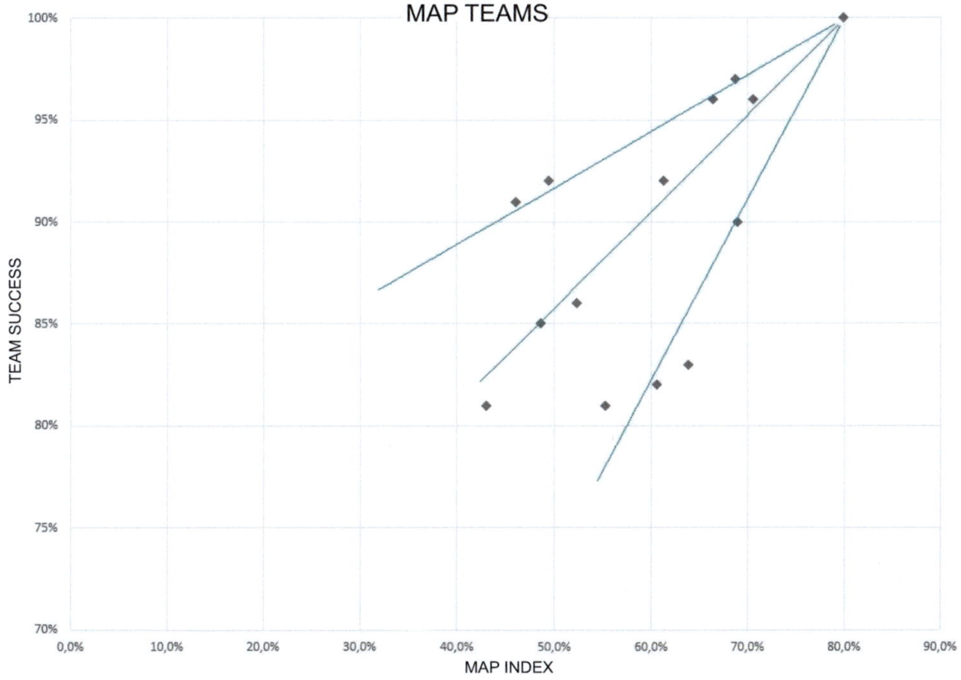

Abb. 9.13 MAP index vs. team success—comparison of 14 competing student teams at DHBW

Figure 9.13 shows a more detailed, current comparison of *14* competing student teams at DHBW, also with the same project assignment. In this representation, each point represents *one* team. As in the first case (Table 9.2), the "MAP index" (X-axis) is calculated for each team. The Y-axis is the measure of project success. Figure 9.13 clearly shows that teams with a better "MAP index" (i.e., further to the right on the X-axis) generally also achieve greater project success. This correlation becomes more pronounced with the level of the MAP index, that is, with the increase in the team's "social quality".

However, Fig. 9.13 also shows that in the mid-performance range there are teams with a lower MAP index and better team success than comparable teams.[38] This is a result of the MAP algorithm, which can better capture clearly pronounced behaviors (types) than those that are less distinctly perceived. MAP is intended to identify the top teams and optimize their role distribution! Therefore, the "predictions" are better in the top range (high MAP index).

This "systemic" view of the project team shows that "empowering" the team by optimizing its team structure (maximizing the MAP index) is more important in project

[38] Smaller x-value with simultaneously higher y-value than the competing team.

practice than the choice of process model. For the MAP team, the chosen process model is merely the "starting process," which may and should be changed and adapted within the framework of the MAP rules. The (admittedly provocative) question may be asked as to whether development processes are needed at all: Is a team well-trained in process practices, whose key positions are filled through a MAP evaluation, not sufficient for project success? Does it therefore hold true for modern development teams that the system (i.e., the structure of the team) is more important than the chosen process? The author's previous findings suggest this conclusion.

9.9 MAP and Scrum

MAP is a meta-model. Although the previous chapter touched on the question of whether a defined (agile) process is still needed, many teams find it more comfortable to follow a defined process with its prescribed rituals and documents. This also has advantages in communication with the customer. The following will therefore address the question of whether the MAP team can also follow *Scrum* as a widely used development process[39].

To answer the question of whether Scrum is compatible with MAP, the differences must first be examined: MAP is an agile meta-model. MAP fundamentally assumes that bringing the right people together in the team is crucial for success. This is more important than any chosen process model (Sect. 9.8). Scrum, on the other hand, is an agile process management method. Here, the focus is on which project roles interact in what way to drive the project—and thus the product—forward. Scrum does not address developer practices, the "rules and practices" of the team. This leaves room for the integration of, for example, the new MAP role of *Integration Engineer* (Sect. 9.5.3). The question, therefore, is whether Scrum can serve as the agile management process beneath MAP, or what adjustments may need to be made.

9.9.1 Comparison of Roles

As an agile meta-model, MAP requires the following roles in the team:

- Customer
- Communications Manager
- Integration Engineer
- Team
- Process Owner—the MAP Observer

[39] In the HELENA survey, in which the author participated with dual partner companies of DHBW Lörrach, Scrum already accounted for over 50% of development processes in practice (Kuhrmann et al. 2017).

As an agile management method, Scrum requires the following roles:

- Product Owner
- Team
- ScrumMaster

The following are mentioned as additional roles (Sect. 5.1.4):

- Customer
- User

The roles that match are:

- Team
- Customer/User

The following will compare the roles and check them for "compatibility."

9.9.1.1 Team and Integration Engineer

In both approaches, the team plays the central role. However, as a meta-model, MAP is very much concerned with the composition of the team from an organizational psychology perspective (Sect. 9.5.4). Team formation is the primary focus of the meta-model.

The role of the *Integration Engineer* is unique to MAP. Scrum, as an agile management process, does not address practices and roles in software development. Therefore, there is nothing to prevent retaining this role in the agile process. Experience from the student lab even shows that this role is indispensable for the success of the project (Sect. 8.4).

9.9.1.2 MAP Observer and ScrumMaster

MAP Observer and ScrumMaster are clearly corresponding roles. Both are the "friend of the team," supporting and coaching it, removing obstacles in the process. The differences are in the details. While the ScrumMaster "watches over" the process and checks its correctness, the MAP Observer "observes" the process. Of course, both are responsible for the process. However, since MAP allows for a changing process, the MAP Observer does not necessarily have to intervene. His task is more to moderate and document the change process.[40] In the student lab, it has proven very useful for the MAP Observer to

[40] If we compare this to CMMI, we have, in effect, achieved a much higher "maturity level." We are not only concerned with the process (maturity levels 2 to 4), but with process change management (maturity level 5). (See also Kneuper 2005).

repeatedly prompt the team, through small surveys and provocative remarks, to reflect on their process and bring unconscious practices to awareness (Sect. 8.5.6).

If MAP and Scrum are to be combined, the ScrumMaster's perspective on the process must be broadened. He must begin to understand "pure" Scrum as a starting process that will undergo changes over the course of the project. No process in the student lab "survived" in its pure form. All processes were adapted by the team. However, it is important that this adaptation happens *consciously*.[41] For example, in the student lab in 2009, Scrum was *extended twice* (Sect. 8.5.6):

- On the very first day, a "User Story Core Team" was formed, consisting of the customer, Product Owner, and five interested team members, who supported the Product Owner in understanding customer requirements. This is not provided for in pure Scrum.[42]
- On the third day, the team created the possibility for team members with free resources or new ideas to formulate potential story cards and "feed" them into the system. The new team role of *Story Coordinator* was created, whose task was to preselect these ideas and forward them to the Product Owner. An interesting variant was that such "subsequently added" story cards could be included in the ongoing sprint without affecting the end of the sprint.

The ScrumMaster must be able to accompany such process changes and ensure their orderly and conscious implementation. In doing so, he expands his role to that of the MAP Observer.

9.9.1.3 Customer, Communications Manager, and Product Owner

This is the area where the greatest need for clarification exists regarding the representation of these roles. The Product Owner (Sect. 5.1.1) is responsible for the product and represents the perspective of the end customer. In this respect, the Product Owner does correspond to the customer in MAP. The difference is that the Product Owner is not the customer *themselves*. In MAP, a real customer is involved, as is also required in XP (Sect. 3.5.5). The MAP customer has no project responsibility, apart from being responsible for the user stories. They do not manage the software development. This task is usually taken on by one of the MAP communications managers, who assumes the role of *project manager*. This role does not exist in Scrum. Its responsibilities are divided among the Product Owner, the team, and the ScrumMaster (Pichler 2008).

However, MAP does not necessarily require the role of project manager. Discussions by the author, particularly with small development teams from companies, show that

[41] See Sect. 8.5.5 for a rather negative example.

[42] Although, in the design workshop, the team may certainly raise questions of understanding that prompt the Product Owner to make further inquiries with the customer.

good project results can certainly be achieved without a project manager. Thus, a MAP project team can also distribute the tasks of the project manager among the team members and MAP roles. A *communications manager* can take on the role of *Product Owner*, especially since communication is explicitly mentioned as one of the Product Owner's tasks (Sect. 5.1.1). Requirements and release management, which are classic project manager tasks, can also be handled by the communications manager.

The question, however, is where the knowledge about the requirements comes from. For this, the Product Owner must have *customer knowledge*. They must obtain this from the customer and users.[43] Here there is a significant difference between the MAP reference process and Scrum. In the MAP reference process, in principle, any team member can participate in creating the user stories together with the customer. Usually, a mini-team ("User Story Core Team", Sect. 8.3.2) takes on this work of the Scrum Product Owner. The author sees the reduction of this important task to a single person, the Product Owner, as a disadvantage, since there is a risk that the Product Owner becomes a "bottleneck" for the project. Even in the student lab in 2009, where Scrum was used as the process, this "User Story Core Team" formed *spontaneously* on the first day (Sect. 8.5.6).

The "social pressure" to form such a User Story Core Team to support the Product Owner naturally decreases if the Product Owner has sufficient product-specific knowledge and can competently answer the team's questions about the requirements. In this *special case*, reducing the original (and usually spontaneous) "specification core team" to a single role, the Product Owner, is possible and justifiable. A combination of MAP as a meta-model and Scrum as the "underlying" agile management process is possible under these conditions.

9.9.2 Determining the Product Owner

As already demonstrated, choosing a suitable Product Owner is essential for the success of an agile project.[44] Usually, the Product Owner is "appointed," either due to their excellent product knowledge or because they bring certain management experience. This

[43] The author generally wonders, in the context of Scrum, how the Product Owner manages to acquire such detailed knowledge of the product requirements as the customer possesses: The author's experience from practical projects shows that the person who has the knowledge about the future product (the customer) and the person who has the knowledge about managing the project (usually the project manager) are rarely the same person. Therefore, a transfer of knowledge must take place without any loss of information. The author believes it is better if the team obtains this information directly from the customer and not (filtered) through the Product Owner. This view is also supported by experiences with the spontaneous formation of the "User Story Core Team" in the student lab in 2009 (Sect. 8.5.6).

[44] Of course, this applies not only to *agile* projects!

Key characteristics		Communication-oriented	Experienced	Resilient
MAP	Cross set	X	X	
Visionary				
creative	x			
Cost-conscious	x			
Critical/inquisitive	X			
structured	X			
Analytical	X			
planning	X			
Implementation-oriented				

General human charact-eristics

Project work-related human characteristics

3 mentions

2 mentions

Fig. 9.14 Form for self/external assessment in the student lab (weighted)

chapter will use an example to illustrate how MAP can be used to systematize the search for a good Product Owner.[45]

In the 2009 student lab, where Scrum was prescribed as the process, MAP was used to preselect candidates for key roles, especially the Product Owner.[46] As described in Sect. 9.5.4, students were able to assess themselves using the form developed by the author (Fig. 9.7). They also asked two of their fellow students for an external assessment of themselves.[47] These three completed forms were consolidated: All attributes checked on all three forms were marked dark gray, those checked twice were marked light gray. Attributes mentioned only once were not considered. Figure 9.14 shows the attributes weighted in this way[48] of the eventual Product Owner.

In the next step, the "map" of team behaviors from Fig. 9.1 was overlaid onto the assessment form created in this way (Fig. 9.15).

By simply counting the overlapping "boxes" in the assessment form and weighting the light gray areas with 2/3, the following results were obtained in this case:

[45] In the student lab, the author is constantly faced with the decision of identifying the suitable Product Owner from among the students in the course.

[46] In addition, there was the important MAP team role of integration engineer.

[47] Of course, participation in the self/external assessment was voluntary.

[48] During the process, there were discussions about the meaning of the main attribute "experienced." Since it is listed under general human qualities, it was agreed to interpret it as general life experience or wisdom.

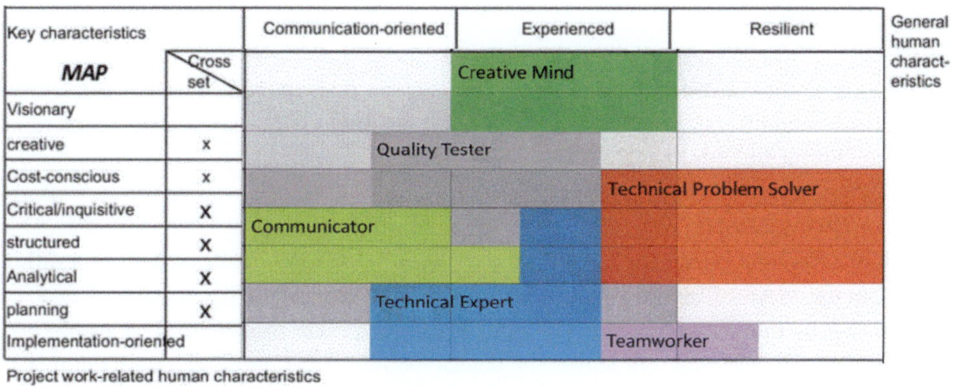

Fig. 9.15 Map of the behaviors of the eventual Product Owner in the student lab

- 100% suitability as a *Communicator*
- 90% suitability as a *Quality Tester*[49]
- 75% suitability as an *Expert*

If one weights the ability to communicate at 50%, suitability as a quality inspector at 30%, and good troubleshooting skills at 20% for a good Product Owner, this results in a suitability of 77% for the Product Owner in this case.[50] If this analysis is carried out with all participants, a ranking of the most suitable Product Owners emerges.

However, this analysis does not take product knowledge into account. It is assumed that potential candidates have sufficient product knowledge. In the student lab, projects are chosen so that usually no student has proven product knowledge.

To avoid misunderstandings: The author is a declared opponent of "pseudo-accuracy." This simple analysis should never be more than an indicator for filling a project role. However, ranking participants according to their suitability for a project role using MAP can help to objectify the decision. In the student lab, the ranking was presented to and discussed with all participants. By interviewing those involved, the first impression was refined and confirmed by acclamation from the team.[51] The success of the 2009 project subsequently confirmed the selection.

[49] This was rounded up slightly.

[50] The attribute "resilient" was checked only once in an external assessment. Initially, the author was unsure whether this might be a limitation for filling the Product Owner role. However, these concerns were dispelled during the extremely successful project: What matters most is the resilience of team members during a sprint. The Product Owner is less affected by this type of "stress."

[51] The author is aware that so much "democracy" is not common in most companies. However, an in-depth conversation with the candidates can reinforce the first impression gained through MAP—or not confirm it (which can also be very important).

9.9.3 Process

If you look at the Scrum flow (Fig. 5.2), you can see that after the Product Backlog is created, the actual iterative process begins—the Sprint. How do the specific characteristics of the Sprint fit with MAP?

9.9.3.1 Sprint Length

What is special here is that the Sprint has a fixed duration, e.g., 30 days. This is a difference from the MAP reference process, as well as from other agile approaches. However, the fixed Sprint duration does *not* contradict MAP. As a meta-model, MAP does not take a position on this question, but leaves the determination of the iteration length entirely to the team. While Scrum requires a fixed Sprint duration, MAP does not. But if the team decides on this, it is not a problem within the MAP meta-model framework[52]!

9.9.3.2 Sprint Planning Meeting

In every iterative-incremental process, planning for the next iteration must take place. In the student lab, this happens through the interaction of customer, communication manager, and team. As is known from the comparison of MAP and Scrum roles (Sect. 9.9.1), this is not a contradiction. Sprint planning meetings are also a sensible practice within the MAP meta-model framework.

9.9.3.3 Daily Scrum

The Daily Scrum is a daily, time-boxed team meeting (Fig. 9.16). Such meetings also exist in other agile practices. XP prefers a standup meeting (Wells 2009). The MAP teams in the student lab also held such meetings regularly (usually in the morning), regardless of the process chosen. The daily coordination of the team was considered very effective. Integrating this practice into a MAP project therefore poses no problem at all.

9.9.3.4 Sprint Review

This practice must be central to *every* agile project. The customer must be informed about the current state of the software product at short intervals—after each iteration—by means of a demonstration. If this does not happen, the feedback loop to the customer cannot function.[53] Integrating this practice into an agile process under MAP is essential.

The only new aspect is the time limitation. Scrum requires *timeboxing* to a maximum of four hours.[54] MAP, of course, does not specify any times here. That would be odd for

[52] In the student lab, the fixed Sprint length is well received. It provides students with a temporal orientation—a point in time to work towards.

[53] One must always keep in mind that the specification of the product in agile projects is rather sparse!

[54] Depending on the Sprint length (Chap. 5).

Fig. 9.16 Daily Scrum in the student lab 2009

a meta-model. The MAP team, based on its competence, knows how long the review meeting should last. However, since it is also known that meetings longer than four hours are hardly productive, this Scrum requirement is not fundamentally a "killer argument" against linking MAP and Scrum.

9.9.3.5 Sprint Retrospective

The idea of regularly reflecting on the process is not new and is also known from the agile process model Crystal (Chap. 4). It is even *absolutely* necessary and is regularly applied in the student lab (Sect. 8.5.5). Process reflection serves to optimize the process and does not contradict MAP. Again, the only new aspect is the time limitation to a maximum of three hours. For the reasons discussed above, however, this is not a restriction to including the Sprint Retrospective as a practice in an agile process under MAP.

In the student lab, only the regular occurrence of the Sprint Retrospective after *every* Sprint was criticized. The team adapted the process so that they reserved the right to keep the meeting *very* short if necessary. However, the MAP observer/ScrumMaster (i.e., the author) insisted on holding the retrospective meeting after every Sprint.

9.9.4 Artifacts

Finally, the required Scrum documents (Sect. 5.3) are checked for "MAP compatibility."

9.9.4.1 Product Backlog

In the student lab, a Product Backlog is created as a collection of user stories (already known from XP). Basically, these stories must be prioritized and estimated in every agile process. The Product Backlog is thus a specific agile requirements document and can be integrated into any agile process under MAP.

In practice in the 2009 student lab, however, there were critical objections from the Product Owner regarding the required up-to-dateness of the Product Backlogs. In a statement at the end of the very successful project, he wrote (Sect. 8.5.6):

The *Product Backlog* proved to be too time-consuming and, as it grew, simply not flexible enough to be updated regularly, especially with regard to prioritization. Instead, it increasingly degenerated into a pool of ideas, which was only skimmed during release planning and when creating user stories for the next Sprint. It only became helpful when the individual items were organized by category to provide a better overview. But does this really have to be in table form? A pen and a few sheets of notes serve the same purpose, at least in such a short project with correspondingly short Sprints and limited preparation time.

In fact, for him, the Sprint Backlog was the control instrument of choice, which was not perceived as disruptive during the project.

9.9.4.2 Sprint Backlog

During iteration planning, the requirements to be implemented in the iteration are identified. The team defines the activities necessary to implement these requirements and keeps the activity list, the Sprint Backlog, up to date. There is nothing to prevent integrating this practice and the associated document into an agile process under MAP.

In the 2009 student lab, the variant *Sprint Backlog as User Stories* was used exclusively and with great success (Wirdemann 2009).

9.9.4.3 Release Plan and Burndown Chart

Agile projects also have to plan releases, as far as this is possible. To track project progress, it makes sense to do this by creating a Release Burndown Chart (Fig. 5.6). Here, too, there are no problems integrating this practice and the associated documents into an agile process under MAP.[55]

9.9.5 MAP and Scrum—is that possible?

The preceding analyses of project roles and the comparison between Scrum and the MAP reference process show that it is possible to implement Scrum as an agile process "under" the MAP meta-model. Initial, very positive experiences with this approach have already been made in the student lab in 2009. However, it is important to ensure that the following conditions are met:

[55] These artifacts were described as helpful and well received by the Product Owner in the 2009 student lab.

The ScrumMaster's Perspective on the Agile Process must be Broadened
The MAP observer, now acting as ScrumMaster, must understand "pure" Scrum as a starting process that may undergo changes that deviate from Scrum. In the Sprint Retrospective, the team has the opportunity to introduce new practices that are *not* Scrum. This is permitted in agile processes under MAP. The team, by virtue of its composition and knowledge, has the competence to do so. The MAP observer expands the classic ScrumMaster role in such a way that he does not prevent this change process, but rather moderates it. However, he will help the team to assess the meaningfulness of the change and will document the change.

Closeness Between Customer and Team must be Maintained
By introducing Scrum, the *specification core team* known from MAP is reduced to a single Scrum role, the Product Owner. This places the Product Owner between the team and the customer. Therefore, in the spirit of MAP, it is important that the contact between customer and team remains sufficiently close so that the team's questions about requirements can be answered competently and first-hand.[56] This way, ambiguities regarding specifications can be clarified quickly and directly. It is acceptable for only the Product Owner to create and prioritize the Product Backlog, but not for the Product Owner to stand between the customer and the team when it comes to clarifying requirements for the software product.

Length of Sprint Review and Retrospective is not set in stone
The durations of the sprint meetings prescribed by Scrum, especially the Sprint Review and Sprint Retrospective, must not become dogma. The MAP team, due to its composition, is itself capable of deciding whether the prescribed meeting length is sufficient in each individual case. However, it is also clear that meetings that are too long are unproductive. The ScrumMaster (represented by the MAP observer) expands his role by supporting the team in deciding whether to continue, pause, or end a Scrum meeting.

If the discussed conditions are met, there is nothing standing in the way of combining the agile MAP meta-model with Scrum as the underlying agile process.

9.9.6 Advantages for Scrum Users

Scrum power users may ask themselves what the advantage is for them in installing MAP as a process "superstructure." Doesn't Scrum already provide everything an agile project needs?

[56] It does not make sense for the team to ask the Product Owner, and for the Product Owner to ask the customer (the "telephone game" phenomenon).

No, says the MAP advocate. Scrum is an agile project *management* method. Scrum says nothing about the actual development process, nor is there a clear practice regarding team composition. MAP, in addition to team psychology, also manages the incredibly important role of the *integration engineer*. As has been known from the student lab since 2004, the proper staffing of this important project role is crucial for the positive course of a project: The integration phase is the weak point of agile projects! Here, the new agile role of the integration engineer provides a counterbalance! MAP explicitly emphasizes the team's relationship with the customer (especially regarding the customer's skills and availability). In addition, communication within the team is actively strengthened by appointing one or more communication managers. Of course, the Product Owner is also a communication manager in this sense, but the MAP project team usually has several of them.[57]

It is clear, then, that MAP and Scrum place their *emphases* differently. While Scrum focuses on the agile management process with clear role distribution, clear process flows, and documents,[58] MAP's focus is on team composition, always following the motto: *A properly composed team knows what it has to do!* This explicitly includes the possibility of adapting and optimizing the process being followed.[59]

9.10 MAP in Regulated Environments

Even in environments regulated by authorities, such as pharma IT projects—especially in research—there is a great need for agile techniques.[60] There, too, there is often a customer or user of the software system whose requirements change over the course of the project or are fundamentally not yet fully defined. However, the documents required by authorities pose a challenge: It is common practice to write comprehensive user specifications, so-called *User Requirement Specifications (URS)*, at the beginning of the project, which can then be used for testing. Until a few years ago, authorities often required the V-model as a process model (Sect. 1.4.1). This has changed in recent years. In principle, there is nothing against agile approaches as long as legal requirements and guidelines for the validation of computerized systems are met (GAMP 5©[61]). With Scrum4LS,

[57] This too is an experience from the student lab in recent years.

[58] From the perspective of classic project managers, the new roles are certainly somewhat unconventional.

[59] See the case studies in Sect. 8.5.

[60] For a detailed analysis, see Zurzevic 2015.

[61] Good Automated Manufacturing Practice, see ISPE 2022 Appendix D8 as well as Zurzevic 2015, Ch. 6: "Agile GMP-compliant Software Development".

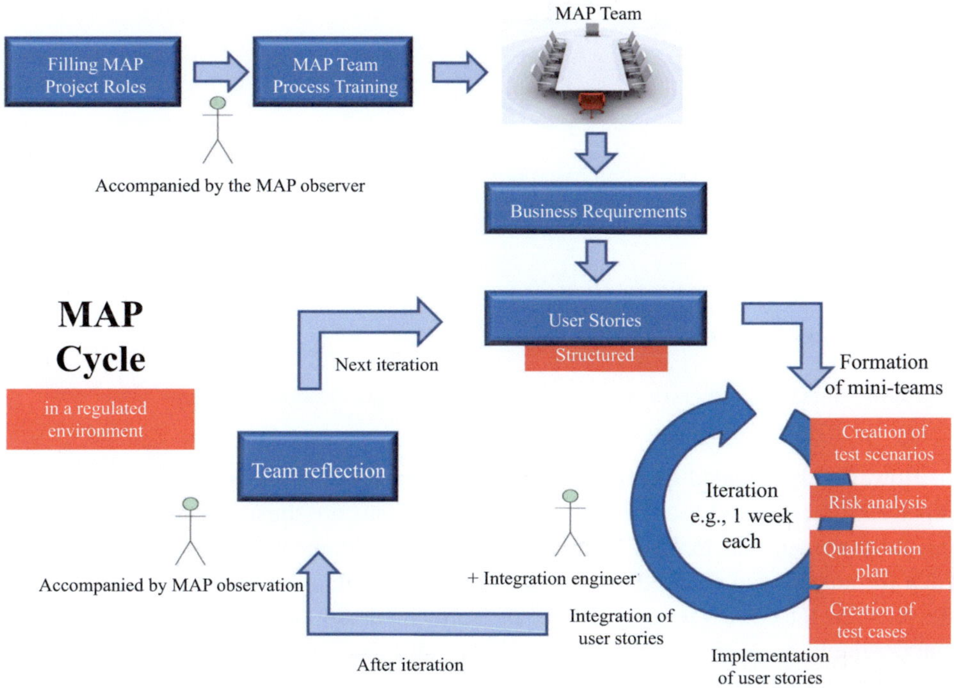

Fig. 9.17 MAP reference process in regulated environments

the first GAMP 5©-compliant agile process model is available (Zurzevic 2015, Ch. 5). The focus here is on risk analysis and risk management, which allow all requirements to be mapped to the corresponding tests.[62]

However, MAP can also be adapted to the requirements of regulated environments. For this, the *MAP Cycle*, the MAP reference process, must be extended (Fig. 9.17). Similar to Scrum4LS, the creation of

- test scenarios[63]
- a risk analysis to prioritize the tests
- a quality assurance plan (qualification plan) with quality assurance strategy
- detailed test cases

is explicitly required.

[62] This is done using a "traceability matrix".

[63] Test scenarios are rough representations of possible test procedures.

Fig. 9.18 Structured test cases "replace" comprehensive specification documents

However, the detailed specifications usually formulated in regulated environments are replaced by *structured user stories*[64]. The requirements are thus structured as usual, but not fully written out. Instead, MAP in regulated environments places the emphasis on fully formulated and detailed *test cases*, that is, a system of software test cases that can demonstrate the correct functionality of the software at any time. Ideally, automated tests can or should be used here. Since there are usually too few details known for test cases when creating the user stories (instead of specifications!), *test scenarios* are created first. Here, the general procedure of the tests to be created is defined. Using the subsequent *risk analysis* and the *quality assurance strategy*[65], the tests are prioritized[66] and their general procedure is defined.

The detailed test cases *replace* the usual comprehensive specification documents (Fig. 9.18). If the requirements for the software system change, the corresponding test cases naturally change as well. It is therefore entirely sufficient to adapt the tests. The unnecessary step of possibly adapting specification documents is eliminated! This is in line with the agile principle of not maintaining documents that are not needed for the progress of the product.

9.11 MAP Projects in the Chemical and Pharmaceutical Industry

A scientific study in the chemical industry was able to demonstrate the practical effectiveness of the agile meta-model MAP (Wolf 2008).

[64] This means that only about three clauses are formulated per requirement. The details are then identified in discussions with the customer. This is where MAP differs from Scrum4LS.

[65] The quality assurance strategy is part of the quality assurance plan (qualification plan).

[66] How many tests need to be performed?

The aim of the study was to develop a web-based training management software within an agile software development team of seven employees for the Rheinfelden plant of the chemical corporation. MAP's assertion that the process develops autonomously within a suitable team was confirmed. XP, as the initial process, merely served as the "method toolbox" from which a custom software development process was formed. The deviations from "pure" XP were documented in the study.[67] The author describes the formation of the software development process as follows:

> "It is difficult to define a new perfect process[68], and this is often the wrong approach. Rather, a successful process should develop autonomously within the project. Often, only a few initial rules are needed, as the author[69] describes with his defined approach of the 'Meta Agile Process Model.' Accordingly, the development of the new software development process in the IT department proceeded in this way. XP served here as a 'toolbox' from which suitable methods were selected and applied in the project."

The newly developed process defined and filled the following roles:

- Customer
- Project Manager
- Quality Manager
- Developer
- Tester
- Integrator

In particular, the existence of the *MAP Integration Engineer* was thus considered indispensable for the success of the project. Since customer acceptance of the previous training management software was not very high, great importance was also attached to the comprehensive involvement of the customer in the project. MAP was therefore validated in this industrial project.

Another scientific study (Bockstaller 2022) addressed the question of whether MAP is suitable for use in the pharmaceutical industry while complying with the regulated requirements of the European Union and the USA for computer validation.

To answer this question, a case study was conducted with three successful pharmaceutical production teams. These teams, which had already been working together for some time, underwent the self- and external assessment presented in Sect. 9.5.4, which showed that the MAP types required for successful teams were present in first or second place among the members of all three teams (Bockstaller 2022, Sect. 9.6.4). Furthermore, the MAP reference process (Sect. 9.6) was extended to include regulatory

[67] For example, the team quickly abandoned pair programming (see also Sect. 8.5.3).

[68] Within the framework of MAP.

[69] This refers to the author's article in (Hanser 2008).

minimum requirements of the CSV process, such as the creation of the validation plan and risk analysis or the preparation of the validation report. The flexibility of MAP enables the process to be adapted to the requirements of the regulated pharmaceutical industry without losing agility. The MAP Cycle remains fully intact and is merely supplemented by additional activities and documents (Bockstaller 2022, Fig. 10).

The encouraging results of the aforementioned industrial projects demonstrate the flexibility and adaptability of the Meta Agile Process Model (MAP). Further results, especially regarding team self-assessment on the MAP-Model online platform (Hanser et al. 2024), are eagerly awaited.

References

Baldegger R (2004) Erfolgreich im Team. Baldegger Verlag

Baldegger R, Gotsmann L (2001) Ganzheitliches Projektmanagement. Baldegger Verlag

Beck K (2000) Extreme Programming. Addison Wesley

Beer S (1979) The Heart of Enterprise. Wiley

Beer S (1981) Brain of the Firm (2nd ed). Wiley

Belbin R M (1981, 2004) Management Teams. Elsevier

Belbin R M (1993, 2007) Team Roles at Work. Elsevier

Bockstaller R (2022) MAP—Meta Agile Process im Kontext der Pharmaindustrie. Masterarbeit, DHBW Center for Advanced Studies & F. Hoffmann-La Roche AG

Cockburn A (2005) Crystal Clear: A human powered Methodology for small Teams. Pearson. Dt. Übersetzung: Crystal Clear: Agile Software-Entwicklung für kleine Teams. mitp-Verlag

DWDS (2023) https://www.dwds.de/wb/sozietär%C3%A4r. Zugriff August 2023

Hanser E (2008) Agile Software-Entwicklung: Das „Projektmanagement-Labor" der BA Lörrach. In Dorn K.-H. et al (Ed) Innovationen durch Projektmanagement—oder?! Beiträge zur Konferenz „interPM". dpunkt Verlag

Hanser E (2009) https://gpm-hochschulen.de/methoden/methodenwuerfel/map/. Zugriff August 2023

Hanser E, Wehinger J. (2012) Integration MAP in VSM. Private Notizen

Hanser E (2013) Private Notizen

Hanser E (2014) Kompetenzzentrum für agile IT Prozesse (KAP), https://dhbw-loerrach.de/kompetenzzentrumagileprozesse. Zugriff Dezember 2024

Hanser E (2015) Erfolgreiche Teams mit dem Meta Agile Process Model (MAP). In „Agiles Management—Innovative Methoden und Best Practices". Symposion

Hanser E, Heizmann J, Vavra C (2024) https://map-model.de/. Zugriff September 2024

ISPE (2022) https://ispe.org/sites/default/files/publications/guidance-documents/2022-TOC/ISPE-GAMP5-Ed2_TOC.pdf Zugriff Juni 2024

Kneuper R (2005) CMMI—Verbesserung von Softwareprozessen mit Capability Maturity Model Integration. dpunkt Verlag

Kuhrmann M, Hanser E et al. (2017) Hybrid Software and System Development in Practice: Waterfall, Scrum, and Beyond. ICSSP'17, ACM

Pichler R (2008) Scrum—Agiles Projektmanagement erfolgreich einsetzen. dpunkt Verlag

Schwaninger M. (2000) Das Modell Lebensfähiger Systeme—Ein Strukturmodell für organisationale Intelligenz, Lebensfähigkeit und Entwicklung. Universität St. Gallen

Schwaber K. (2004) Agile Project Management with Scrum. Microsoft Press

Walker J. (2020) The VSM Guide, www.esrad.org.uk/resources/vsmg_3/screen.php?page=preface, Zugriff August 2023

WEIT Verein zur Weiterentwicklung des V-Modells XT (2019) V-Modell XT—Release 2.3 https://ftp.tu-clausthal.de/pub/institute/informatik/v-modell-xt/Releases/2.3/V-Modell-XT-Gesamt.pdf, Zugriff Juni 2024

Wehinger J. (2013) Jenseits der Vorgehensmodelle—Projektteams wirksam in Organisationen verankern, das Viable System Model und MAP. In „Vorgehensmodelle—Anspruch und Wirklichkeit", Lecture Notes in Informatics

Wells D. (2009) www.extremeprogramming.org. Zugriff August 2023

Wirdemann R (2009) Scrum mit User Stories. Hanser

Wolf O (2008) Entwicklung eines Schulungsverwaltungssystems unter Anwendung der Methoden des Extreme Programmings. Diplomarbeit, Berufsakademie Lörrach & Evonik Degussa GmbH

Zurzevic D (2015) Identifizierung der gesetzlichen Voraussetzungen und der prozeduralen Rahmenbedingungen für Vorgehensmodelle zur Softwareentwicklung im pharmazeutischen Umfeld. Masterarbeit, DHBW Stuttgart

MIX
Papier aus verantwortungsvollen Quellen
Paper from responsible sources
FSC® C105338

If you have any concerns about our products,
you can contact us on
ProductSafety@springernature.com

In case Publisher is established outside the EU,
the EU authorized representative is:
Springer Nature Customer Service Center GmbH
Europaplatz 3, 69115 Heidelberg, Germany

Printed by Libri Plureos GmbH
in Hamburg, Germany